Discoveries
in
Bible
PROPHECY

Michael D. Fortner

Trumpet Press, Lawton, OK

Version 1.5.4, 2014 (additional info added, & corrections)

Abbreviations & Volumes Used:

ESV – English Standard Version
GNB — Good News Bible
KJV – King James Version
LIT – Green's Literal Translation, or The Literal Translation
NKJV – New King James Version
NAS – New American Standard
NEB – New English Bible
YLT - Young's Literal Translation
CWD – Complete Word Study Dictionary: New Testament,
LXXE – Septuagint, English Translation of the Greek translation of the Old Testament
Strong's numbering is in parentheses ( ).

Library of Congress Catalog-in-Publication Data: 2013930119

Author: Fortner, Michael D.
Title: Discoveries in Bible Prophecy
1. Eschatology 2. Bible Prophecy 3. Book of Revelation 4. Book of Daniel 5. Great Tribulation 6. Abomination of Desolation 7. Rapture

ISBN: 978-0615863979

Learn about future books by the author at
www.usbibleprophecy.com

Trumpet Press is a member of the Christian Small Publishers Association (CSPA).

Table of Contents

Introduction..7

Chapter 1: Keys to Understanding Bible Prophecy
(1) Interpreting Apocalyptic Symbolism 13
(2) 100% Literal Interpretation? 16
(3) No Private Interpretation..23
(4) The Doctrine of Imminent Return Exposed 22
(5) The Rapture and the Feasts of Israel 27
(6) Correct Spelling and Usage..28
(7) Judgment Day & The Day of The Lord 28

Chapter 2: Five Seals of History
(1) Revelation 4: The Scene in Heaven 31
(2) Revelation 5: Victory of Christ..32
(3) First Seal: White Horse: Going Forth of the Holy Spirit....................35
(4) Second Seal: Red Horse: Persecution 39
(5) Third Seal: Black Horse: Diaspora..40
(6) Fourth Seal: Green Horse: Islam..42
(7) Fifth Seal: Souls of Martyrs 46
(8) Conclusion 47

Chapter 3: The Sixth Seal: Signs of The End and Birth Pains
(1) The Signs Begin 48
(2) The Watch Has Begun 55
(3) A Command to Keep Watch 57
(4) When You Do Not Expect Him 59
(5) Four Blood Moons 60
(6) Birth Pains of the Earth 64

Chapter 4: The Chosen
(1) Who Are The 144,000? 75
(2) The Bride of Christ..78
(3) Symbolic Number 80
(4) FirstFruits..81
(5) The Last Great Awakening 83
(6) Conclusion 85
(7) Additional Evidence..86

Chapter 5: Daniel's 70 Weeks

(1) Daniel 9:25-26 88
(2) Daniel 9:27 90
(3) The 1,290 Days 97
(4) Conclusion 99

Chapter 6: The Great Tribulation

(1) What is The Great Tribulation 101
(2) Time of Testing 102
(3) Seventh Seal: Seven Trumpets 107
(4) First Trumpet: Natural Disasters 107
(5) Second Trumpet: Volcanic Landslide 109
(6) The Affect Upon the United States 112
(7) Third Trumpet: Asteroid Impact 119
(8) Fourth Trumpet: Darkness 122
(9) Three Woes 123
(10) Other Prophecies of Great Tribulation 124

Chapter 7: The Statue of Liberty

(1) The Woman in a Basket 132
(2) The Future Destruction of the Statue of Liberty 138

Chapter 8: World War III Begins

(1) Fifth Trumpet: The Abyss is Opened 140
(2) The Destroyer 144
(3) The Abyss in Arabia 145
(4) The Dogs of War 146
(5) Sixth Trumpet: Missiles and Rockets 148
(6) The Prophet Joel 151
(7) Ramifications 155

Chapter 9: Daniel's Ten Toes

(1) Ten Toes of the Statue 156
(2) Arabs and the Ten Toes 162
(3) Double Fulfillment 163

Chapter 10: Daniel's Four Beasts

(1) Four Great Nations Today 165
(2) Lion and Eagle: British Empire & United States 167
(3) Bear: Russia 168
(4) Leopard: Saudi Arabia 168

(5) Beast With Ten Horns: Commonwealth of Independent States.......... 170
(6) The Little Horn 174
(7) Day of Judgment.. 176

Chapter 11: The End Arrives
(1) Mystery Accomplished 178
(2) Measuring the Temple 180
(3) The Two Witnesses.. 183
(4) The Great Festival... 185
(5) Other Prophecies 188
(6) Second Woe 190
(7) Seventh Trumpet: God's Wrath and Kingdom 191

Chapter 12: 2 Thessalonians
(1) Apostasy and Antichrist Must Come First...................................... 193
(2) Will Exalt Himself... 196
(3) Important Word Meanings.. 197
(4) Only One Coming of Christ... 201

Chapter 13: The Abomination of Desolation
(1) No Tribulation Temple 204
(2) Abomination of Desolation... 206
(3) The End of The Gospel Age 210
(4) Daniel 12: Time of the End.. 212
(5) Catholic Prophecies 215

Chapter 14: Matthew 24
(1) Events of the Gospel Age 217
(2) Events of the Great Tribulation.. 218
(3) The End of the Age.. 219
(4) The Wrath of God 221
(5) The Sign of the Son of Man.. 222
(6) One Will Be Taken, and The Other Left.. 224

Chapter 15: A Brief History of Christianity
(1) Christianity Begins... 226
(2) The Defeat of Paganism... 230
(3) The Woman Flees Again... 232

Chapter 16: Final Thoughts.. 237
Scripture Index 241
Selected Bibliography.. 245

(The present version of this book 1.5.4, has a mistake corrected. Previous version 1.5.2 said, "So 9/13/15 is the day to watch." It should have said, "So 9/28/15 is the day to watch." On page 64.)

Introduction

This is a new interpretation of Bible prophecy, that is 98% new. How could there be a viable new interpretation you ask? The Bible says that the correct interpretation will not be understood until we actually reach the end, *"the words are <u>closed up</u> and <u>sealed</u> until the end time"* (Daniel 12:9), yet the dominate views today are more than 100 years old. But we have finally reached the end, and we can now understand Bible prophecy. I may not have every detail exactly right, but I believe this interpretation comes closer than any other interpretation.

In order to arrive at the correct interpretation you must have certain foundational pieces in place or it throws off the entire project; much like making a mistake in your checkbook results in all numbers being off from that point onward, but you are not aware of the mistake. Then you get a statement from your bank that shows a different balance and you have to go through an entire month's worth of figures to find the mistakes. This book is that statement for Bible prophecy, it also shows the mistakes.

What does the puzzle look like once you put all the pieces together? It will come as a shock to most people, but the infamous Four Horsemen of the Apocalypse have already ridden during the past 2,000 years of wars and famines and persecution. But I don't just make that assumption, I found evidence in the text that proves it.

We are now in the period of the global birth pains of the earth. Unlike the false warning put out several decades ago, we can now see the birth pains happening all around the world, with earthquakes, droughts, floods, and record heat or record cold, and record storms and fires.

Next will be the Trumpet judgments. There will be a giant tsunami that will wipe out the east coasts of North and South America, and to a lesser degree West Africa and Europe. The tsunami of the 2nd Trumpet will greatly injure the United States, coupled with the asteroid impact of the 3rd Trumpet, will allow the final head of the beast to rise from the Abyss as seen after the 5th Trumpet, followed by the start of World War 3, which is the 6th.

The beast of Revelation will not come out of Europe, but the Islamic nations of the Middle East and Turkey. It clearly says in Rev. 9 that the angels bound at the Euphrates River will cause WW3. The Euphrates starts in Turkey and flows through Syria and then Iraq. Will the war in Syria escalate into WW3?

What about world government? There is no such thing; I prove it is false in this book, many times over. Rev. 13 says twice that the beast will *"make war."* The passages that are used to support world government are *correctly* explained in detail. Nowhere in the Bible does it say anything about a 7-year peace treaty. The passage in Daniel 9:27 that is supposed to refer to a 7-year treaty with Israel is being grossly misinterpreted. The original Protestant view of that verse is the correct view.

Daniel's vision of the four beasts and the statue with ten toes both show that there will never be a world government. Those passages are not being correctly interpreted. The Bible text never says that the ten horns will rule the world, but only the fourth beast from which the horns come. Likewise, it never says the ten toes will rule the world, but actually says they will break apart.

And contrary to popular teaching, America is in fact found in Bible prophecy, and is a major player, as you would expect. Even the Statue of Liberty is described as a woman lifted up between heaven and earth and put on a pedestal. Yes, it is really in the Bible!

The Great Tribulation will probably last about 4 years, though it is more if you count the birth pains. The 3.5 years found in Revelation refers to the last 3.5 years of the Gospel Age. And the Rapture takes place just before the 7th Trumpet, which makes the Rapture prewrath, but not 3-6 months before the end of the Great Tribulation (GT) which is what the prewrath position currently teaches. The Rapture is at the end of the GT, just before a short period of God's total Wrath upon the world. So it is really a mixture of prewrath and posttrib.

The correct interpretation of Bible prophecy proves the pretribulation Rapture theory is false, which is seen repeatedly throughout this book. I even found the smoking gun that kills the pretrib Rapture!

Those who will be in the Bride of Christ will be chosen by God before the start of the GT; during the GT many millions of people will turn to God around the world, especially in the U.S. Therefore, the entire Church will not go in the Rapture, but only those chosen to be in Bride before the GT begins. The Bride is not the Church, but a chosen righteous remnant who are worthy to rule and reign with Christ. It is those saved during the GT who will survive God's Wrath to continue the human race.

The book also proves that the Jews must convert before Christ will return. Yes, it is plainly stated in the Bible several times! Which makes one wonder how the opposite view could become a popular doctrine.

There can be a lot more information gleaned from the Bible's prophecies discussed in this book than what is written here, because my main focus is on what will actually take place in the future which we need to know and fully understand to survive the GT, and Wrath of God (for those who do not go in the Rapture). That is why this interpretation is practical, not theological. Though my interpretation greatly bears on doctrines, the information here is not presented or argued from a theological point of view. That is, I am not trying to support a particular theological position, but I have merely studied the Scriptures to find out what they mean and have changed my views to match what I found in the Bible.

Most of the existing belief systems for the last days have elements that are correct, but the complete picture they present is not the right picture. I began my study believing in the pretribulation Rapture, but was forced to change my view after years of study.

There is a reason that Jesus did not have a religious education before becoming Israel's Teacher. And there is a reason his original Apostles did not have religious educations. The one Apostle who did have religious training, killed and persecuted Christians before he was struck down on the road to Damascus. When you follow a particular belief system, called a theological construct, it typically blinds you to what does not agree with that belief system. That is just how the human mind works. Though there is a place for theological and eschatological (the study of last things) degrees, having such degrees can be a hindrance to understanding the truth. As such, I do not have any theological degrees.

You may be wondering, then, who am I to write this book? Isaac Newton was extremely intelligent; he discovered gravity and was the principle inventor of calculus and physics. In 2005, the British Royal Society voted Newton to have made a greater contribution to science than any man in history, even Einstein. Even though Newton was one of the smartest men who ever lived, and spent a lot of time studying Bible prophecy and even wrote a book on Daniel and Revelation, he was not able to see a description of missiles and rockets in the Bible (see chapter 8). You cannot see or understand what you have no knowledge or concept of. He also did not live in the last days, so there is no possible way he could have correctly interpreted Bible prophecy.

So I do not claim to be smarter than everyone else who studies Bible prophecy. But I am called of God to interpret Bible prophecy, with a God-given ability to figure things out, to think outside the box, and with the ability to argue from different points of view. I am also a trained journalist and historian (a B.A. degree in communications with a minor in history), so I am skilled at analyzing written information. But even with all my skills and calling, it has taken me 30 years to put the pieces together like a giant jigsaw puzzle.

My calling to research and understand Bible prophecy came at a very young age. I remember when I was 8 or 9 years old, I was sitting on the side of my bed reading Rev. 6:1 about the white horse and wondering what it meant, when God spoke to me for the very first time. He said, *"Would you like to interpret that?"* I said, *"Wow, yea, that would be great, but there is not enough infor-*

mation in the text to be able to figure it out." It did not even occur to me that God had just spoken to me, and I forgot all about it until about two years after I had begun researching and writing a book on Bible prophecy.

I have often wondered why God called me to this project rather than an eloquent, well-known minister with a national platform to get the message out to the world. I am sure God has his reasons.

For example, if a major preacher had been teaching these discoveries in a large church over the last 30 years, he would've been correcting himself every few years. As his knowledge and understanding increased, his interpretation of this passage or that verse would naturally have changed. So he would not have looked like a sound Bible teacher as his views continually changed. Perhaps this is why God called me to preach when I was 20 years old but did not give me the inward urge to preach. I had no desire to preach, but I did have a great desire for in-depth Bible study. Fortunately, the puzzle is finally complete, nevertheless, I don't claim to be infallible, I may be wrong on some point.

With all the crying wolf that has taken place in the last 40 years, the Church now faces a lack of interest in Bible prophecy. I knew that those false warnings would cause some people to reject the genuine warning once it finally arrived, and that has happened. Interest in Bible prophecy has declined with every false cry of "RAPTURE! RAPTURE!" Now it is happening again! With the 4 Blood Moons that will take place on Jewish feast days in 2014 and 2015. The meaning of the 4 Blood Moons are discussed in chapter 3, but they do not signal or herald the Rapture.

Because of declining interest, and because I am not a well-known minister, I do not expect this book to become a best-seller until the tsunami of the 2nd Trumpet hits, then it will become a best-seller.

I cite references and tell you where I get information and interpretation, otherwise, you can assume that the interpretation is my own; about 98% of this book is my own interpretation. Even when I quote others, I often will make observations related to the quote which are not found in the original quote.

Even though I use the NIV as the main translation in this book, I frequently give a verse in the KJV or Green's Literal Translation or some other version because a particular verse may be much more clear in meaning in another translation. Sometimes it takes reading a verse in several translations to see clearly what it actually says in the original Greek.

You will notice that in this book there are no "end notes" at the end of the chapter or the end of the book. With end notes, if readers want to know where a quote is from they must mark the location of the end notes and continually look back to see what it says, but it may only say "Ibid" or some other information that is not important. So after reading almost 500 books, I have come to hate end notes. Therefore, in this book I have done something truly shocking and revolutionary, I actually tell you where the quote is from, either within the text or after each quote so you do not have to stop reading and look it up! And I don't use footnotes because I want the printed book to look just like the e-book. Since there are no pages in e-books it is very hard to have footnotes or end notes.

Also, all underlining in this book is my own, and is never found in the original quotes.

Now a word about quotes. Because of the misuse of source material in other books, from science to religion, some people will suspect that I have taken passages out of context or that I have misrepresented what the prophecy actually says, so I include the actual quotes so you can read them for yourself, at least most of the time. And it is important that you read the quotes to get the most out of this book; I assume that you will read the Scripture passages.

Also, I believe the reader will get the most out of this book by reading it slowly and underling many sentences, because it is very easy to misread critically important statements. I even do some underlining for you.

Disclaimer: I include a few extra-biblical prophecies because I believe them to be genuine, but that does not mean I agree with every teaching or action taken by the ministers who gave the prophecies.

Chapter 1
Keys To Understanding Bible Prophecy

In order to understand Bible prophecy it is important to know some key facts about Bible interpretation. Most dreams and visions contain symbolism, and the Bible actually tells us how to interpret symbolism literally. Another important point is that even though we should interpret the Bible literally, often it is not 100% literal. I will prove that many statements in the Bible, not just Bible prophecy, are literal, yet are not 100% literal. Problems arise when we take many statements as being 100% literal.

(1) Interpreting Apocalyptic Symbolism
God speaks through dreams and visions which we find many times throughout the Bible. In Genesis, Jacob had a prophetic dream of speckled and spotted goats that foretold his future income. Joseph had two dreams, one of sheaves of wheat bowing to him, and one of the sun and moon and eleven stars bowing to him. Then later when in prison, the Pharaoh's wine steward and chief baker each had a dream which Joseph interpreted, which was followed by Pharaoh having a dream which Joseph interpreted. Later the king of Babylon had a dream which Daniel interpreted, and Daniel himself also had prophetic dreams and visions.

All of those dreams and visions had literal meaning; for example, in Pharaoh's dream the lean cows eating the fat cows meant that there would be seven years of plenty and seven years of famine. During the seven years of famine the people were to eat grain which they stored up during the seven years of plenty. Clearly, the images were symbolic, but had literal meaning.

In the New Testament, after Jesus was born, Joseph had a dream where an angel told him to take Mary and Jesus into Egypt because the king was trying to kill Jesus. But that dream was not symbolic, it was plain. Then Paul had a dream of someone beckoning him to come to Macedonia, so it was another plain dream. But the visions of Apostle John in Revelation are 99% symbolic.

Visions are like dreams; most people understand that even simple, normal everyday objects or events in dreams almost always have meaning beyond the normal. The stalks of wheat that bowed down to Joseph symbolized his family bowing to him. But a big problem with Bible prophecy interpretation today, is that much of it is seen as being literal, therefore it is taken at 100% face-value, when it should not.

A symbol is an object standing for or representing something else; an emblem, a letter, figure, or character, such as a flag that is the emblem of a nation and represents certain things that the nation stands for or believes. *Funk and Wagnell's Ency.* says:

> The bases of symbolism is a physical connection, an association, or a chance resemblance between the symbol and the thing symbolized . . . the olive branch has denoted peace; the palm, triumph; and the anchor, faith or hope. (Vol. 22, p. 385)

In Revelation we are actually shown how its symbols are supposed to be interpreted. In the first chapter, John saw seven golden lampstands and seven stars in Christ's hand; then Jesus explained it, *"The seven stars are the angels of the seven churches, and the seven lampstands are the seven churches"* (1:20). This shows us that the symbols of the Revelation, and all other Bible prophecies, have a definite literal meaning. So the book of Revelation is not just allegory with an unknowable meaning, but contains literal, factual information that is encoded with symbols and metaphorical language.

We also know from the above verse that God expects us to figure out the meanings of the symbols in Revelation, because he gave us this example of interpreting its symbols. The beast has a definite meaning, and the seven heads have a definite meaning that we can learn; likewise the second beast, the image of the beast, and mark of the beast.

Therefore, regardless of what you have been told, God is not going to turn the oceans into blood; that is symbolism that must be interpreted. And when Christ returns, he will not have a literal sword sticking out of his mouth! The sword represents words of judgment that will bring death to the wicked.

Rev. 9:14-15 clearly says that four angels bound at the Euphrates River will be released to kill one-third of mankind, so I guess we don't need to worry about nuclear war destroying the world, because these angels are going to do the killing, right? No! It means that World War 3 will begin in that region, or by the people that live in that region, which is dominated by Islam.

In order to kill 2.4 billion people in warfare, the beast must be engaged in a massive war with many nations; which means it cannot at the same time be ruler of the whole planet. Will it be a global civil war? Nonsense! The passage also tells us WW3 will be caused by Muslims; not a revived Roman Empire. Revelation 13 twice says the beast will *make war*. The beast will attempt to conquer as much of the world as it can reach. It will come out of the Abyss for one reason, to wage jihad. The result will be WW3.

However, we should not take symbolism too far. For example, the anchor represents faith and hope, but an anchor is also big and heavy and could drop on your foot and crush it. Does that mean that we should not have a lot of faith? No, it means the relationship between the symbolism and what is symbolized is only partial, not total. The symbolism of an object does not have to be exact, it only needs to be close.

So, just like the dreams and visions of the Old Testament, we can expect the symbols of Revelation to have literal meaning which God wants us to learn. The symbols are not merely allegorical, such as referring to the general spread of evil in the world. No, specific images have specific meaning.

Theology does not have the answer to the meaning of Bible prophecy, because it is a practical, actual interpretation of symbolism. Take for example the 200 million fire breathing horses. It has a literal *interpretation*, which Bible commentaries have a difficult time with. Some commentaries actually say that there will be 200 million fire-breathing horses (Rev. 9), but it is symbolism that must be interpreted. And John was not trying to describe a modern weapon, he actually saw a horse with the head of a lion breathing fire. However, once it is correctly interpreted, it turns out to be a modern weapon that we will learn about in chapter 8.

(2) 100% Literal Interpretation?

Another key to understanding Bible prophecy is that many passages are not meant to be taken 100% literally. I use the literal method of interpreting Scripture, which is the only sound method to use when a passage is not figurative or symbolic, but what Bible scholars do not understand, is that even when a passage is to be interpreted literally, that does not mean that every word in the passage is 100% literal. Here is an example that also fits in with the last section:

> 14 The great day of the Lord is near. . . 15 That day will be a day of wrath, a day of distress and anguish, . . . a day of <u>clouds and blackness</u>, 16 a day of trumpet and battle cry . . . 18 . . . In the <u>fire of his jealousy the whole world will be consumed</u>, for he will make a sudden end of <u>all who live in the earth</u>. (Zephaniah 1:14-16, 18)

Will the entire world be literally consumed, that is burned up with fire, to such and extent that planet Earth no longer exists? No, that will not happen, it merely means the entire surface of the world will be burned. Notice the statement, *"he will make a sudden end of all who live in the earth"*; we know that this is not 100% literal because there are many passages that speak of this same Day of Judgment and say mankind will survive. Therefore, God will not kill everyone on Earth. So even though the statements in the above passage are not metaphorical, or symbolic, and must be understood literally, they are not 100% literal.

However, this point of view raises some problems because there are statements that seem to suggest that they must be taken at literal face value, yet they should not. The most well-known of these is where Jesus said that he would be in the grave for three days and three nights (Matt. 12:39-40):

> For as Jonah was three days and three nights in the belly of a huge fish, so the Son of Man will be three days and three nights in the heart of the earth. (v40)

Was Jesus actually in the grave for three days and nights? He was not even in the grave for 48 hours, which is two days and nights. He was put in the grave on Friday afternoon and rose Sunday morning, so it covered parts of three days and two full nights. (Some people believe Jesus actually died on Wednesday, but the text of Scripture itself says he rose on Sunday, not Saturday; Mark 16:9, Luke 24:1,7,21,46, http://biblelight.net/pasover.htm.)

When it comes to interpreting the Bible, it is very tempting to take everything at 100% literal face value, but sometimes even when it is to be understood literally, it is not meant to be 100% literal. It is hard to interpret the Bible correctly if we do not interpret it literally, but you run into trouble if you insist on applying a 100% literal face value to every passage. As the above passage illustrates, some passages that appear to be 100% literal are not.

Some people may say, *oh, but that is just how the Bible or the Jews use "days."* Perhaps, but it also shows that the Bible is literal but not 100% literal, because there are many examples throughout the Bible. For example, many times the Bible uses the terms "*all the earth*" and "*the whole world;*" but does not refer to the entire globe, as many people wrongly believe. Here are just a few such passages:

> . . . all the earth came to Egypt to Joseph to buy grain, because the famine was severe over all the earth. (Gen. 41:57) ESV

> The whole world sought audience with Solomon to hear the wisdom God had put in his heart. (1 Kings 10:24)

All nations on planet Earth did not go to Egypt to buy grain, neither did all nations seek an audience with Solomon. Nor does it refer to the known world. Here are more examples:

> In those days a decree went out from Caesar Augustus that all the world should be registered. (Luke 2:1) ESV

> "Look, the world has gone after him." (John 12:19) ESV

The whole planet was not taxed by the Romans, neither did the whole planet follow Jesus while he was on Earth. Nor did it mean the known world because all the Roman Empire did not follow Christ; not even all of the Jews followed Christ, so it proves that the statement cannot be taken at 100% literal face-value.

Even though Rome claimed to rule the world, and they proclaimed that *"all roads lead to Rome,"* they knew that the world was much bigger than the empire because they traded with far away places like India. So to say that Rome ruled the world was merely a way of saying that it ruled all the area within a reasonable distance of Rome, that Rome ruled its area of the world.

This shows that the Bible often speaks of the whole world or the whole Earth, but it really means a large number of people, or most of the nations surrounding Israel, or that were within reasonable travel distance of Israel.

Another example is found in Daniel 8, about the goat and the ram, which was about Alexander the Great defeating Media/ Persia. The goat was seen *"crossing the whole earth,"* which it clearly did not do:

> As I was thinking about this, suddenly a goat with a prominent horn between his eyes came from the west, crossing the whole earth without touching the ground. (Daniel 8:5)

It did not even cross the entire known world to arrive in Persia. Neither did it travel by not touching the ground, it merely means that it traveled very fast without facing any major obstacles.

So when the book of Revelation says the whole world will worship the beast, it *does not* refer to the entire planet or the known world. Here is even more evidence to support the point of this section:

> 2 "I am going to make Jerusalem a cup that sends <u>all the surrounding peoples</u> reeling. Judah will be besieged as well as Jerusalem. 3 On that day, when <u>all the nations</u> of the earth are gathered against her, I will make Jerusalem an immovable rock . . ." (Zechariah 12:2-3)

This passage first states that it refers to all the nations that <u>surround Israel</u>, and then it states that all nations on the planet will attack Jerusalem, but if we are going to take that statement at 100% literal face value, then it would have to include nations that do not even have armies or navies, and there are over 20 of them!

If you insist on taking that statement at 100% literal face value, then we must also take all statements in the Bible at 100% literal face value, which means the land of Canaan had streams and rivers flowing with milk and honey! No less than 20 verses state that the land was *"flowing with milk and honey,"* (Ex. 3:8). But those statements are exaggeration, hyperbole; it was just a way of saying that it was a very fertile and fruitful land.

Likewise, when it says all nations will attack Jerusalem, it does not literally mean that every single nation on the planet will attack Jerusalem, it is an exaggeration. Not convinced yet? Watch for a column of smoke:

> Edom's streams will be turned into pitch, her dust into burning sulfur; her land will become blazing pitch! 10 <u>It will not be quenched night and day; its smoke will rise forever</u>. From generation to generation it will lie desolate; no one will ever pass through it again. (Isaiah 34:9-10)

Seriously, do you really believe that the smoke of Edom's burning will rise *forever*? Ten billion years into the future the smoke of Edom will still be rising? No, it will not! In Rev. it says, *"that ancient serpent called the devil, or Satan, who leads the whole world astray"* (12:9). There you have it, Satan is going to deceive every person on the face of the whole earth, right? There won't be one person alive who doesn't worship Satan, right? Wrong.

Yet, there is a verse that seems to indicate the whole planet: *"And he was given authority over every tribe, people, language and nation"* (Rev.13:7). But it refers to the Middle Eastern / Mediterranean world where all previous heads of the beast have ruled.

The previous heads of the beast made literal warfare against God's people throughout the Middle East, North Africa, and southern Europe. The final head of the beast will also wage war against Christians and Jews. The next head of the beast will invade nations that are not in the Mediterranean area, but it will not be able to invade the whole planet. Nevertheless, Muslims in Europe and other places will wage civil war against their host nations and bring much death and destruction.

But even more than this argument about the whole world, the prophecies in the Old Testament, when correctly interpreted, also reveal that there will NOT be a one-world government that has control over all nations on Earth. This will be shown many times over throughout this book.

The purpose of the final head of the beast is to wage war upon the world, especially God's people. This war will kill 1/3rd of the global population. Yet we are expected to believe that the beast is going to come to power by bringing world peace, and rule the entire planet; that is total fiction, and proven in chapter 5.

There is yet more. In Daniel 4:22, it says the king's dominion has reached *"to the ends of the earth."* Really? How about that, King Nebuchadnezzar ruled China! No, he did not. Only a few decades later, Babylon was conquered by the Media-Persian Empire, that was right next door. So Babylon did *not* even rule the known world. Many people agree with this, but still will insist that some other similar passage about the future Antichrist should be taken 100% literally.

We even use this same type of terminology today. Did you know we have never had a world war? Yes, it is true. We have had two wars that we call world wars, but the whole world was not at war, just many nations and much of the world's surface, but not literally every nation.

One lady emailed me with the claim that the ten horns of Revelation will only rule for one hour with the beast, a literal 60 minutes, because that is what it says in Rev. 17:12:

> And the ten horns you saw are ten kings . . . will receive authority as kings one hour with the beast. (LIT)

This verse means that there is a set time for these events to be completed, and it will not last for centuries or decades. In Rev. 3:10 Jesus called the Great Tribulation, *"the hour of trial"* so I guess we don't have to worry about the Great Tribulation (GT), because it will only last for one hour! What? You don't believe it will only last for one hour?

I hope you can see what kind of mess you get into by taking every word 100% literally. In addition to this direct evidence, the correct interpretation of Bible prophecy provides even more evidence, which you will see several times in this book.

(3) No Private Interpretation

How can an individual understand Bible prophecy, doesn't the Bible say that no one person can interpret Scripture? No, it does not! This is an example of inaccurate interpretation. Often, when someone offers new insights on Bible prophecy, someone else will jump in and say, *"there is no private interpretation"* (2 Peter 1:20). But that passage is not being accurately understood. It is taken out of context, and is often not translated correctly because the Greek is difficult to understand. Here is the NIV in context:

> Above all, you must understand that no prophecy of Scripture came about by the prophet's own interpretation. 21 For prophecy never had its origin in the will of man, but men spoke from God as they were carried along by the Holy Spirit. (2 Peter 1:20-21)

This means that no prophecy in the Bible ever originated within the mind of a prophet; the prophet did not think up or invent his prophecies. It does not mean that no individual can understand prophecy. This passage is often used in an attempt to discredit new insights into Bible prophecy, but wrongly so. No place in Scripture does it say that only committees can hear from God or be led by God, or are called by God. Most likely, the opposite is true.

The above verse is just being used in an effort to silence people who teach something other than what the critic agrees with. God has not given the correct interpretation to a committee, or to many different people at the same time, because Bible prophecy "experts" are not in agreement.

(4) The Doctrine of Imminent Return Exposed

If we listen to most prophecy teachers, Jesus was soon to come for the past 2000 years, but that is not true. The pretribulation Rapture theory includes the doctrine of the imminent return of Christ that says the Rapture can happen at any moment, followed by the Great Tribulation, and that it could have happened at any time since Christ returned to heaven. These two doctrines are welded together like steel, and therefore cannot be separated. Just because we do not know when the end will come does not mean it is imminent. There are in fact many verses of Scripture that prove that Jesus would stay away a long time. Here is an example from Matthew 24. Jesus said:

> "6 You will hear of wars and rumors of wars, but see to it that you are not alarmed. Such things must happen, but **the end is still to come**. 7 Nation will rise against nation, and kingdom against kingdom. There will be famines and earthquakes ..." (Mat. 24:6-7)

These verses describe many years of history, "*Nation will rise against nation.*" This means many wars will take place before Christ returns. This statement alone destroys the imminent Rapture/return theory, because it shows that there is a specific end to the Gospel Age, and that it is in the distant future from the time of Christ and even after many years of history, "*the end is still to come.*" But we are finally nearing that end.

In Matthew 25, in the parable of the ten virgins, it says, "*While the bridegroom tarried, they all slumbered and slept"* (v.5). That word, "tarried" means "delayed." This is another passage that says he will not come soon after he left. In another passage about a servant who beats the other servants, Jesus said:

> But suppose that servant is wicked and says to himself, 'My master is staying away a long time,' 49 and he then begins to beat his fellow servants . . . (Matthew 24:48-49)

The KJV says, *"My Lord delayeth his coming."* Even though it is the servant who thinks to himself that his master is staying away a long time, the meaning is that the master is staying away a long time, which is why the servant had those thoughts. Clearly, Jesus told us he would stay away a long time.

Paul actually taught against the imminent Rapture theory. Yes, Paul spoke out in Scripture against the belief in an imminent return of Christ:

> That ye be not soon shaken in mind, or be troubled, neither by spirit, nor by word, nor by letter as from us, as that the day of Christ is at hand. (2 Thess. 2:2) (KJV)

About half the translations say the same as the KJV, that the Day of the Lord *"is at hand,"* which means about to happen right away. Other translations say, *"is come"* or *"is present."* According to *Robert's Word Pictures*, the passage should read, *"is imminent."* Robert's Word Pictures says:

> As that the day of the Lord is now present . . . Perfect active indicative . . . intransitive in this tense to stand in or at or near. So "is imminent" (Lightfoot). . . . Certainly it flatly denies that by conversation or by letter he had stated that the second coming was immediately at hand. . . . It is enough to give one pause to note Paul's indignation over this use of his name by one of the over-zealous advocates of the view that Christ was coming at once. . . . Moreover, Paul's words should make us hesitate to affirm that Paul definitely proclaimed the early return of Jesus. He hoped for it undoubtedly, but he did not specifically proclaim it as so many today

assert and accuse him of misleading the early Christians with a false presentation.

The *Complete Word Study Dictionary* says, "*To be present, instant, or at hand . . . Impending.*" It is translated "present" in 1 Cor. 3:22 and Gal. 1:4. There you have it, not only did Christ speak against the imminent Rapture / return in the parables, but Paul spoke against it as well. On this point both Roberts and Lightfoot are in agreement.

What about the passages where we are told to be watchful? There are two ways of looking at those passages, one is that they mainly apply to the generation that will in fact see the return of Christ, and another is best illustrated with this story:

Suppose you were told to take a certain road and when you come to a large statue of a horse carved in the rock, then you should turn right at the road next to it. You don't know where that rock is located, so you must watch for it right from the start of your journey. You don't know that the rock is located 2,000 miles away. The rock is not hovering up in the sky waiting to slam down to earth whenever a command is given. It may seem to be imminent because you must watch for it from the start of the trip, but it actually is not. It is firmly planted in the ground 2,000 miles away; you just don't know where it is located.

If the rock were imminent, it could appear at any time, it cannot appear at any time because it is firmly planted in the ground 2,000 miles away. If we could see 2,000 miles away we could see the rock there. But we cannot see that far ahead, so we must keep looking for it. I hope you can see how this is not imminence.

If the doctrine of imminence has a smoking gun, it is the statement by Peter that Christ must stay in heaven until the time when all things will be restored: "*Repent, then, and turn to God . . . even Jesus. Heaven must receive him until the time comes for God to restore everything*" (Acts 3:19-21). This passage says that Jesus will stay in heaven *until* some future time when God will restore the whole earth, including plants and animals. (The smoking gun that kills the pretrib theory is in a later chapter.)

Peter certainly did not look for a soon return, because he knew that the prophecy Jesus made must be fulfilled: *"when you are old, you will stretch out your hands, and another will dress you and carry you where you do not want to go"* (John 21:18). So Peter knew he was going to live to be an old man, therefore, he knew Jesus was not going to return in his lifetime.

As you can see, the correct interpretation of Bible prophecy provides great evidence against the pretribulation Rapture theory, as we will see throughout this book, including the next section.

(5) The Rapture and the Feasts of Israel

Another thing that proves the imminent return theory is false is the truth about the Fall Feasts of Israel as they relate to the return of Christ.

Most Protestant Christians believe in what we call the Rapture, which is the catching away of Christians to heaven at the end of this age. Some believe it will happen at the start of a seven-year tribulation, others in the middle, some others at the end, and others about three-quarters of the way in, known as the prewrath theory. Belief in the Rapture is based on the words of Paul in 1 Cor.:

> Listen, I tell you a mystery: We will not all sleep, but we will all be changed— 52 in a flash, in the twinkling of an eye, <u>at the last trumpet</u>. For the trumpet will sound, the dead will be raised imperishable, and we will be changed. (1 Corinthians 15:51-52)

Christ will return in the sky at the last trumpet, and those who have died will be resurrected with immortal bodies so they can live forever. The living will be instantly changed to also become immortal, and all will join Christ in the clouds where we will return to heaven and have the marriage supper of the Lamb as described in Rev. 19.

Notice that Paul said, *"at the last trumpet."* He is referring to the Feast of Trumpets (Rosh Hashanah). Jesus fulfilled all the Spring feasts such as Passover and Pentecost; he was our Passover sacrifice for sin, and he sent the Holy Spirit at Pentecost. Likewise, he must, and will, also fulfill all the Fall feasts. This fact alone destroys the teaching that the Rapture could take place at any time. Because it can only happen in conjunction with the Fall Feasts.

Kevin Howard explains the Feast of Trumpets:

> In most basic terms, the Feast of Trumpets — the first of the three fall feasts — depicts the coming of the Messiah to rapture the Church and judge the wicked. (*The Feasts of the Lord,* page 26)

At the Feast of Trumpets, the shofar ram's horn was blown 100 times, this is what Paul was referring to. The Rapture takes place at the *last trumpet* of the Feast of Trumpets.

The Day of Atonement, also called the Day of Judgment, is 10 days after the Feast of Trumpets. Yet, it is believed that the books of judgment are opened at the Feast of Trumpets, for those who do not go in the Rapture. One book is for those who will be given life, one for those who will be given death, and one for those who's final account has not yet been determined; so if they repent between now and the Day of Atonement, then they also will be given life. The Jews believe that most people are in the book that requires repentance.

When the Jews would meet another Jew he would say, *"May you be inscribed and sealed in the book of life for a good year."*

Since Christ will judge the world at his return, this is when the books are opened and the judging begins, but the sentence is not carried out until the Day of Atonement 10 days later. This entire period, beginning with the Feast of Trumpets, must be what the Bible refers to as the Day of the Lord, not just the final day, and certainly not a 7-year Great Tribulation (GT). During the 10 days between the start of the Feast of Trumpets and the Day of Atonement, we are supposed to engage in prayer, introspection, repentance, and seeking forgiveness from people we have wronged, which is similar to the New Testament admonition, *"But if we judged ourselves, we would not come under judgment"* (1 Cor. 11:31).

Bruce R. Booker, in his book, *The Feasts of the Lord,* tells us that there is not much information in Scripture about this feast, so most of the information we have comes from Jewish tradition. Upon hearing the shofar blown in the Temple 100 times,

> . . . the Rabbis say that one is to remember that Yom Kippur the 'Day of Atonement' is just 9 days away . . . the sound of the shofar warns us that we need to examine our lives and make amends with all those we have wronged in the previous year, and to ask forgiveness for any vows we may have broken. It is seen as a time to get right with one's friends and neighbors, and prepare to stand before God on a Judgment Day, the Day of Atonement. (page 209)

During modern Jewish observance, they read three liturgies around the themes of Malkhiyot (Kingship), Zilhronot (Remembrances), and Shofarot (Rams' horns). Howard says:

> The *Malhiyot* emphasizes *God's majesty* and His lofty position as Sovereign King of the universe as it proclaims: "May all the inhabitants of the world realize and know that to thee every knee must bend, every tongue must vow allegiance . . . . The Lord shall be King forever and ever." (*The Feasts of the Lord*, page 111)

There are similar passages in the Bible, such as, "*at the name of Jesus every knee should bow, in heaven and on earth and under the earth, and every tongue confess that Jesus Christ is Lord*" (Phil. 2:10) (ESV).

The Feast of Trumpets is the first of the Fall Feasts and took place at the end of the harvest season. Likewise, the Rapture takes place at the end of the Gospel Age, the time of harvest of souls to God.

A significant tradition related to the Feast of Trumpets says the resurrection of the dead will take place at this feast, which is why many Jewish gravestones are "*often engraved with a shofar*" (Ibid, page 114).

This is the only feast that the day and hour was unknown because it started on the 1st of the month, which was only known by the sighting of the new moon. Therefore, watchmen had to stand watch during the night until they see the new moon. Only then did they know it was the day to begin the Feast of Trumpets. Many people, such as Mark Biltz, believe the statement Jesus made about us not knowing the day or the hour of his return refers to this feast. And we are commanded to "watch" for signs of Christ's return in the same way that the watchmen had to look for the new moon.

We will see the Rapture followed by the Days of Awe and Day of Atonement (Judgment) elsewhere in this book.

(6) Correct Spelling and Usage

Because many books and 80% of all websites improperly use the words "prophecy" and "prophesy" I will explain the differences. "Prophecy" is a noun and "prophesy" is a verb. "Prophecy" is pronounced "pro-phe-see," and "prophesy" is pronounced "pro-phe-sigh." To prophesy is to speak forth a prophecy. A prophecy is a prediction that a prophet makes when he prophesies. Some examples of proper use are: "The prophet Isaiah wrote down many prophecies." "Isaiah prophesied about the Great Tribulation."

(7) Judgment Day & the Day of the Lord

It is surprising how many Christians do not know that when Christ returns it will be the Day of Judgment. Jesus told us about it in the parable of the sheep and goats (Matthew 25:31-46). Jesus gave a parable about how he will judge the world at his return:

> "When the Son of Man comes in his glory . . . All the nations will be gathered before him, and he will separate the people one from another as a shepherd separates the sheep from the goats." (25:31-32)

The entire population of the planet will not literally be brought to one place to be judged, this is a parable. A parable is like a dream or vision, it contains truth and must be interpreted. If God were to gather the whole world before Christ to be judged, and each judgment only lasts 30 seconds, it would take 6,659 years to judge 7 billion people, going continuously 24 hours a day, 7 days a week. This parable means that when Jesus splits the sky at the Rapture he will instantly judge every person on Earth, except those who will go in the Rapture; they will have been judged already, which is explained in another chapter.

Those who are goats will die in the fire of his Wrath, and those who are sheep will be allowed to live and enter the Millennial Kingdom; or go to heaven if they happen to die in the earthquakes or other natural disasters. This is the judgment that will bring the Wrath of God upon the world and kill billions of people.

The Bible refers to this period as, *"the day of the Lord," "the hour of his judgment," "the day of judgment," "the day of God," "that day," "the day,"* and *"the day of vengeance"* and *"the Day of Christ."* These references do not refer to the end of the universe or the end of the planet, or even the end of human civilization on Earth, but merely the end of the world as we know it today. God has a set time appointed to bring judgment upon the whole world for its sins. Earth will be cleansed of evil, and life on Earth will continue for thousands of years.

About the coming Day, the Bible says:

> The day of the Lord is near for all nations. As you have done, it will be done to you; your deeds will return upon your own heads. (Obadiah 1:15)

The Day of Judgment will be a day when the wicked are separated from the righteous as wheat is separated from the chaff, or when ore is refined in a furnace separating the gold from the impurities (Malachi 3:2-3). The prophet Malachi called it the *"Great and terrible day of the Lord"* (Mal. 4:5). *Baker's Evangelical Dict. of Biblical Theology* says:

> In the prophetic books the day of the Lord signifies the time when God intervenes in the affairs of nations to judge the wicked and rescue the righteous. In Malachi the judgmental aspect is emphasized, in that the day of the Lord is a "dreadful day" in which evil-doers will be set on fire (4:1, 5). Much of the judgment connected with the Messiah will take place at Christ's second coming . . .

The prophet Isaiah spoke of this time of God's wrath:

> See, the day of the LORD is coming --a cruel day, with wrath and fierce anger-- to make the land desolate and destroy the sinners within it. 10 The stars of heaven and their constellations will <u>not show their light</u>. The rising <u>sun will be darkened</u> and the <u>moon will not give its light</u>. 11 I will punish the world for its evil, the wicked for their sins. I will put an end to the arrogance of the haughty and will humble the pride of the ruthless. 12 I will <u>make man scarcer than pure gold</u>, more rare than the gold of Ophir. (Isaiah 13:9-12)

In verse 12 it says mankind will become more scarce than pure gold, which means that few people will be left alive after the Wrath of God. They will probably number in the hundreds of millions. Ezekiel said:

> "For the day is near, the day of the Lord is near-- <u>a day of clouds</u>, a time of doom for the nations." (Ezekiel 30:3)

Notice the references to clouds and darkness. The whole world will be covered with black clouds from asteroid impacts, nuclear war, and burning cities.

There is no way that the Day of the Lord is 7 years long, like the pretrib theory teaches. Why would 3.5 years pass without any Wrath from God, once the Day of the Lord begins? So the Day of the Lord cannot begin at the start of the GT. It does not make good sense.

Chapter 2
Five Seals of History

When the apostle John saw the visions of the Revelation, which is "Apocalypse" in Greek, he faithfully wrote down everything he saw and heard. He did not draw upon the prophecies of Daniel or any other prophecy because he did not write it from his own intellect. It is not a work of fiction or imagination, he merely wrote down what he saw and heard.

(1) Revelation 4: The Scene in Heaven

Revelation 4 is a brief description of the throne room in heaven. The most important thing to notice is that Jesus is <u>nowhere</u> described or even mentioned:

> 1 After this I looked, and there before me was a door standing open in heaven. And the voice I had first heard speaking to me like a trumpet said, "Come up here, and I will show you what must take place after this." 2 At once I was in the Spirit, and there before me was a throne in heaven with someone sitting on it. 3 And the one who sat there had the appearance of jasper and ruby. A rainbow that shone like an emerald encircled the throne. 4 Surrounding the throne were twenty-four other thrones, and seated on them were twenty-four elders. They were dressed in white and had crowns of gold on their heads. 5 From the throne came flashes of lightning, rumblings and peals of thunder. Before the throne, seven lamps were blazing. These are the seven spirits of God. 6 Also before the throne there was what looked like a sea of glass, clear as crystal.
>
> In the center, around the throne, were four living creatures, and they were covered with eyes, in front and in back. 7 The first living

creature was like a lion, the second was like an ox, the third had a face like a man, the fourth was like a flying eagle. 8 Each of the four living creatures had six wings and was covered with eyes all around, even under its wings. Day and night they never stop saying: "'Holy, holy, holy is the Lord God Almighty,' who was, and is, and is to come."

9 Whenever the living creatures give glory, honor and thanks to him who sits on the throne and who lives for ever and ever, 10 the twenty-four elders fall down before him who sits on the throne and worship him who lives for ever and ever. They lay their crowns before the throne and say: 11 "You are worthy, our Lord and God, to receive glory and honor and power, for you created all things, and by your will they were created and have their being." (4:1-11)

Many commentators place the Rapture at the start of Rev. 4 because it says, *"Come up here."* But there is no mention of a great celebration in heaven, or any mention of the coming of the Kingdom of God, only a mention of the 24 elders and four living creatures. However, in Rev. 11 a loud voice from heaven says, *"Come up here,"* and two dead people come to life and ascend into heaven. This is followed by the coming of the Kingdom of God, rewards for the prophets, and total judgment on the Earth. Which is more likely to be the Rapture? There is no evidence to believe the 24 elders are Raptured saints, but there is plenty of evidence that the Rapture has not taken place in Rev. 4, as we shall see.

(2) Revelation 5: Victory of Christ

In Rev. 4, Jesus was neither seen nor heard; now in Rev. 5, take <u>careful notice</u> that a search is made for someone worthy to open the book:

1 Then I saw in the right hand of him who sat on the throne a scroll with writing on both sides and sealed with seven seals. 2 And I saw a mighty angel proclaiming in a loud voice, "Who is worthy to break the seals and open the scroll?" 3 But <u>no one in heaven</u> or on earth or under the earth could open the scroll or even look inside it. 4 I wept and wept because no one was found who was worthy to open the scroll or look inside. (5:1-4)

No one <u>in all of heaven</u> or on Earth is found worthy to open the scroll, absolutely no one! It does NOT say, that no one but Jesus Christ was found worthy; it says NO ONE was found. After the search was made in all of heaven and Earth, John wept because *no one was found.* But he does not just weep, he *"wept and wept."* If Jesus had been found worthy, then why did John weep? He wept because no one was found.

Why wasn't Jesus found worthy? Because this is a vision of the entire Gospel Age, beginning at the beginning. Like dreams, visions are not bound by time or space. Though Jesus actually died and rose from the grave many years before this vision was given, his death and resurrection has not yet taken place in this vision. That is why Jesus was not seen in heaven in Rev. 4, and why he was not found worthy to open the book. Only the crucified, resurrected Christ is worthy to open the seven-sealed book.

The KJV says *"no man"* was found worthy, but because Jesus is divine he can open the book, right? The original Greek says *"no one,"* not *"no man."* No one was found, and that includes Jesus. The next verses describe Christ entering heaven for the first time after his death, burial, and resurrection, after he became worthy:

> 5 Then one of the elders said to me, "Do not weep! See, the Lion of the tribe of Judah, the Root of David, <u>has triumphed</u>. <u>He is able to open the scroll</u> and its seven seals." 6 Then I saw a Lamb, looking as if it had been slain, standing in the center of the throne, encircled by the four living creatures and the elders. He had seven horns and seven eyes, which are the seven spirits of God sent out into all the earth. 7 He went and took the scroll from the right hand of him who sat on the throne.
>
> 8 And when he had taken it, the four living creatures and the twenty-four elders fell down before the Lamb. Each one had a harp and they were holding golden bowls full of incense, which are the prayers of God's people. 9 And they sang a new song, saying: "You are worthy to take the scroll and to open its seals, because you were slain, and with your blood you purchased for God members of every tribe and language and people and nation. 10 You have made them to be a kingdom and priests to serve our God, and they will reign on the earth." (5:5-10)

Jesus has "triumphed," or literally, *overcome*. Other translations of 5:5 say, *"has overcome"* (NAS); *"has won a victory"* (Beck); "has prevailed" (KJV). He is seen symbolically as a lamb slain as a sacrifice for our sins: *"Look, the Lamb of God, who takes away the sin of the world"* (John 1:29). But the Lamb is seen standing, for he has risen from the grave and has taken his rightful place in Heaven. (Lambs were sacrificed for sin during the pre-Christian era. Jesus is the lamb-like sacrifice for the entire world; all those who believe in him have their sins forgiven.)

The wording of the passage suggests that it has just happened. Notice how verse 9 is worded, *"you were slain, and with your blood you purchased men for God"* (NIV). Why would that statement be made 2,000 years after it actually happened? Why would it be placed here if the Rapture has already taken place? No, the statement occurs here because Christ has just now died on the cross and purchased people for God in this vision. Why would that statement be made just before Christ allows the Antichrist to come upon the world? It would not fit.

And the word is "men" not "us" as the KJV says. If it were "us" then those in Heaven would have been purchased, so the Rapture could have taken place, but that is not what the original Greek says. Since Christ just now enters Heaven in this vision, great celebration naturally follows:

> 11 Then I looked and heard the voice of many angels, numbering thousands upon thousands, and ten thousand times ten thousand. They encircled the throne and the living creatures and the elders. 12 In a loud voice they were saying: "Worthy is the Lamb, who was slain, to receive power and wealth and wisdom and strength and honor and glory and praise!" 13 Then I heard every creature in heaven and on earth and under the earth and on the sea, and all that is in them, saying: "To him who sits on the throne and to the Lamb be praise and honor and glory and power, for ever and ever!" 14 The four living creatures said, "Amen," and the elders fell down and worshiped. (Rev. 5:11-14)

Christ has received the little book and is about to open it. If the

Great Tribulation has already started, then why are they celebrating, are they happy that the Antichrist is about to come upon the world? Nonsense! Not one word is said about the coming of the Wrath of God upon the world, but there is another passage later in Revelation where it says the Wrath of God has come upon the world, accompanied by thunder and lightning (Rev. 11:15-19).

Notice the statement, *"Worthy is the Lamb, who was slain, to receive power and wealth and wisdom and strength and honor and glory and praise!"* The inference is that Christ is just now receiving these things, that is, immediately after his entrance into heaven, not 2,000 years later!

In Rev. 4, the seven spirits of God were seen in the form of lamps. These spirits are represented symbolically on Earth by the golden menorah of the Jewish Temple. But because of the victory of Christ, God's spirits are now seen as the eyes of Christ, *"sent out into all the earth."* Salvation is no longer just for the Jews, but for all mankind.

Rev. 4 says there was only *"someone sitting"* on the throne. In Rev. 4, praise is given only to God; in Rev. 5 praise is given to *"him who sits on the throne and to the Lamb."* Immediately following the praise and celebration, Christ opens the first Seal.

(3) First Seal: White Horse

The typical interpretation of this white horse is that it represents the Antichrist, but it is not the Antichrist!

> I watched as the Lamb opened the first of the seven seals. Then I heard one of the four living creatures say in a voice like thunder, "Come!" 2 I looked, and there before me was a white horse! Its rider held a bow, and he was given a crown, and he rode out as a conqueror bent on conquest. (Revelation 6:1-2)

The NKJV translation says, *"a crown was given to him, and he went out conquering and to conquer."* There are three different interpretations of this rider. *The International Bible Commentary*, edited by F.F. Bruce, says:

One long-established interpretation understands this of the victorious progress of the gospel, the rider on the white horse being Christ, as in 19:11. (p. 1607)

The Zondervan NIV Bible Commentary puts forth the dominate evangelical view today, that it is the Antichrist. The commentator admits that the symbolism of the white horse is always *"associated with righteousness and Christ,"* but rejects it because the other three horses clearly represent war and judgments. He goes on to say:

> The references in 19:11-16 to the rider on the white horse as "Faithful and True" and as one who judges and makes war with justice stands in contrast to the rider in 6:2, who is <u>not faithful or true and who wages war for unjust conquest</u>. Moreover, <u>the Lamb opens the seals and would not be one of the riders</u>, nor would it be proper to have an angelic being call forth Christ. Again, a "bow" would most naturally be connected with the enemy of God's people (Eze 39:3). . . . The evidence, however, seems to favor . . . the Antichrist and his forces that seek to conquer . . . (Vol. 2, p. 1160-1161)

The Wycliffe Bible Commentary by Moody Press, first published in 1962, also says it cannot be Christ because of the other three horses and quotes another commentator saying:

> Can there be any doubt that this is the vision of antiChrist? It so resembles the real Christ that it deceives people, even many a reader of this passage! (Thomas F. Torrance, *The Apocalypse Today*, p. 44)

The above opinions use enormous quantities of faulty reasoning. There is no justification for associating the 1st Seal with the Antichrist just because of the other three Seals. The Bible contains many passages with references to many different things all mixed together. This is why we are told to rightly divide the Scriptures. The context of the surrounding verses is very important, but the other three horses do not ride out of the 1st Seal; they are clearly separated by being placed into four separate Seals. In taking the other Seals into account, the commentators are ignoring the symbolism of the 1st Seal, the white horse. The book of Revelation is a symbolic book, to discount the symbolism in favor of anything else is departing from any chance of understanding the passage. At no point does it say that the rider on the white horse is not faithful or true or that he wages war unjustly, NOWHERE!

Many commentators, as illustrated above, believe that the rider of the white horse is the Antichrist and that he is on a white horse because he comes with deception and claims to be Christ. READ THIS CAREFULLY. The WORD of God NEVER attempts to deceive us in any way. Satan may portray himself as an angel of light, but the Bible calls him a serpent, a red dragon, and the father of lies. **THE SCRIPTURES DO NOT PORTRAY SATAN AS AN ANGEL OF LIGHT, AND THEY DO NOT PORTRAY THE ANTICHRIST RIDING A WHITE HORSE! THE FIRST SEAL IS NOT DESIGNED TO DECEIVE US!**

After reading the above information, one person sent me an email with a Scripture reference that says Satan portrays himself as an angel of light. Yes, indeed he does, outside of the Bible! Satan can appear as a righteous angel, but the Bible does not portray Satan as a righteous angel!

It violates every rule of Scriptural interpretation and good sense to suggest that the Bible presents information designed to trick us, or that the Bible does not mean "white" when it says "white." White is and always will be a symbol of purity and righteousness throughout the Bible, and in most cultures in history. Jesus said of the righteous:

> "They will walk with me, dressed in white, for they are worthy. He who overcomes will, like them, be dressed in white." (Rev. 3:4)

But the commentators are right when they say the rider on the white horse is not Christ, because the rider is the Holy Spirit! The first thing to happen after Christ ascended into heaven was the sending of the Holy Spirit. Peter said, *"Exalted to the right hand of*

God, he has received from the Father the promised Holy Spirit and has poured out what you now see and hear" (Acts 2:33).

The Greek for "conquer" in 6:2 is *nikao* (3528 Strong's number) and means *"to overcome"* (VED). Strong's says, "to *subdue . . . conquer, overcome, prevail, get the victory."* The Greek for the triumph of Christ in Rev. 5:5 is the same word used for "conquer" in Rev. 6:2.

The literal translation of 6:2 reads, *"and he went out overcoming, and that he might overcome"* (LIT). The BBE translation says, *"he went out with power to overcome."* Christ has sent the Holy Spirit, in order that we might overcome. All Christians will either overcome Satan and the world or be overcome by them, which is a far cry from *"unjust conquest"*! The NLT says the rider *"rode out to win many battles and gain the victory."*

The four cherubim represent the unfolding plan of God for his people, as in Ezekiel. Therefore, it is no surprise that *"one of the four living creatures"* calls forth this horse, because the four horses of the 1st four Seals represent stages in God's plan for Christians and Jews and the world. In the next Seal, the second living creature says "Come!" then the third, then the fourth. Therefore, it is the first living creature that calls the white horse. The first living creature is *"like a lion."* In Rev. 5 Jesus is called *"the Lion of the tribe of Judah."* The connection is unmistakable.

What's more, the crown the rider wears is not that of an earthly kingdom. The Greek is *stephanos* (4735) and denotes *"the victor's crown, the symbol of triumph in the games ... a token of public honor for distinguished service"* (VED). It is the same word used for the crown of thorns that Jesus wore. This crown is for the victory of Christ described in Rev. 5. The same Greek word appears in Rev. 2:10, where Jesus said, *"Be faithful, even to the point of death and I will give you the crown of life."* The ten kings of the ten-horned beast in Rev. 13 do not wear victors' crowns but diadems, which are earthly crowns.

Therefore, the rider on the white horse is the Holy Spirit who empowers us to overcome. What is more, nothing is said in the 1st Seal about taking peace from the Earth; nothing is said about men slaying each other; nothing is said about war. It is not in the text! The rider does not engage in physical battles, but spiritual battles.

(4) Second Seal: Red Horse

> 3 When the Lamb opened the second seal, I heard the second living creature say, "Come!" 4 Then another horse came out, a fiery red one. Its rider was given power to take peace from the earth and to make men slay each other. To him was given a large sword. (Rev. 6:3-4)

In the Greek this particular sword is *machaira* (3162), which is *"a short sword or dagger"* (VED). It is used for close personal violence, but not war. The *Complete Word Study Dictionary* says, *"A knife, slaughter-knife, a sword for cutting."* Homer Hailey's commentary on Revelation says machaira is *"the word translated 'knife' at the offering of Isaac by Abraham"* (p. 190) in the Septuagint (the Greek version of the OT). In the NT it is found in Matthew where Jesus said:

> "Do not suppose that I have come to bring peace to the earth. I did not come to bring peace, but a <u>sword</u>. . . . 36 a man's enemies will be the members of his own household." (Mat. 10:34, 36)

If *machaira* means a small sword, why does Rev. describe it as large? Since the word for sword specifically tells us that it is a small sword or dagger, the "large" cannot describe the size of the sword, but rather the size, amount, or intensity of the conflict.

The second living creature that announced this Seal was *"like an ox."* Some translations say "calf." In the Greek *moschios* (3448), *"primarily denotes anything young"* (VED). Calves were frequently used in sacrifices. Christianity at this time was very young, and many thousands of people sacrificed their lives and property for the sake of the Gospel.

This Seal represents all conflict and persecution that resulted from the spread of Christianity throughout history. It began with the death of Stephen, the first martyr, and continues today. According to Ayaan Hirsi Ali, writing in *Newsweek* magazine, a

Christian is martyred every five minutes in the Middle East (http://www.thedailybeast.com/newsweek/2012/02/05/), and that was before the Arab Spring began. It is far worse now.

(5) Third Seal: Black Horse

> 5 When the Lamb opened the third seal, I heard the third living creature say, "Come!" I looked, and there before me was a black horse! Its rider was holding a pair of scales in his hand. 6 Then I heard what sounded like a voice among the four living creatures, saying, "Two pounds of wheat <u>for a day's wages</u>, and three pounds of barley for a day's wages, and do not damage the oil and the wine!" (Rev.6:5-6)

In the original Greek, it says "*a denarius*," not "*a day's wages*." Modern translations use "*a day's wages*" because a denarius was a day's wages at that time. It was not an accident or coincidence that the voice said "denarius" when it would have been just as easy to say *a day's wages*. The denarius was a Roman coin. The specific mention of the denarius puts the event of this Seal during the time of the Roman Empire. No nation on Earth will be using Roman money during the Great Tribulation. Italy does not even use the denarius today.

This Seal describes the destruction of Jerusalem in 70 A.D. by the Romans, which brought an end to the Jewish revolt of 66-70 and resulted in the scattering of the Jews. The prophet Daniel said, "the *Most High is sovereign over the kingdoms of men and gives them to anyone he wishes*" (Daniel 4:17). It was God's will for Rome to rule over the nations, so when the Jews rebelled, they reaped the natural consequences. Paul said those who rebel against the governing authorities "*will bring judgment upon themselves*" (Romans 13:1-2). I believe Paul was referring directly to the Zealots, and actually predicted their destruction.

When the Jews were not revolting, they were desiring and planning to revolt. This is one of the reasons the Jewish leaders plotted to crucify Christ; they were afraid he would lead a revolt. During the Jewish revolt, the Roman Empire changed emperors several times in only one year, so if the Jews were ever to gain their freedom from Rome it would have been during that time. But revolting against Rome was futile. Nero died in 68, was succeeded by Galba (68-69), then Otho (69), then Vitelius (69). General Vespasian was retaking Palestine from the rebels when he became emperor (69-79).

Even though Vespasian was favored by most of the army and the people, he still had to defeat Vitelius in battle to become emperor. But the Jews still could not gain a victory because Vespasian's son, Titus, continued putting down the Jewish revolt while Vespasian was away. A detailed account of what took place was recorded by Joseph ben Mattias (Josephus), a Jewish rebel who was captured early in the rebellion. He was present with Titus during the siege of Jerusalem. Afterwards, he was commissioned by Vespasian to write a history of the Jewish people.

The Romans surrounded Jerusalem and built a wall around it; thereby causing a famine in which many thousands perished. The famine was in grain. Notice the statement, *"and do not damage the oil and the wine!"* The *"wine and oil"* refers to the sacred wine and oil used by the Jewish priests in the Temple. It was as if God gave orders to the Romans not to harm the sacred wine and oil.

Though the Romans destroyed the city and the Temple, they are not the ones who hurt the wine and oil. It was the Jews themselves who hurt the wine and oil, for the Zealots committed gross sacrilege within the sanctuary, such as murdering the priests and worshipers, stealing the golden utensils, drinking the holy wine and using the oil, before the Romans ever entered the city. Josephus writes in *Wars of the Jews*:

> But John made use of this festival as a cloak for his treacherous designs and armed the most inconsiderable of his party, . . . with weapons concealed under their garments and sent them with great zeal into the temple, in order to seize upon it; . . . while the people that stood trembling at the altar, and about the holy house, were rolled on heaps together, and trampled upon, and were beaten both with wooden and with iron weapons without mercy . . . and all those that had formerly offended any of these plotters, were now known, and were led away to the slaughter. (Book 5, Chapter 3, section 1)

But as for John, when he could no longer plunder the people, he betook himself to sacrilege, and melted down many of the sacred utensils . . . on which account he emptied the vessels of that *sacred wine and oil* which the priests kept to be poured on the burnt-offerings, and which lay in the inner court of the temple, and distributed it among the multitude, who, in their anointing themselves and drinking, used (each of them) above an hin of them . . . (*Wars*, Book 5, Chap. 13, sect. 6-7)

The third living creature "*had a face like a man.*" This terrible famine and its results were not caused by a drought or plague of locusts but was totally man-made. Titus actually gave orders not to harm the Temple, but because the Zealots were using the Temple as a fortress, fighting naturally occurred in and around the Temple which led to its timbers catching fire, so the Romans finished the destruction by completely destroying it stone by stone.

(6) Fourth Seal: Green Horse

7 When the Lamb opened the fourth seal, I heard the voice of the fourth living creature say, "Come!" 8 I looked, and there before me was a pale [green] horse! Its rider was named Death, and Hades was following close behind him. They were given power over a fourth of the earth to kill by sword, famine and plague, and by the wild beasts of the earth. (Rev. 6:7-8)

The original Greek for "sword" here is *rhomphaia* (4501), and is a "*sabre, ... a long and broad cutlass (any weapon of the kind, literally or figuratively)*" (Strong's). This is a large weapon representing literal warfare.

Thus far we have three major world events: the spreading of Christianity, the martyrdom of Christians, and the scattering of the Jews. The 4th Seal is also an event of equal importance. The next major event to occur that could fit this Seal is the rise of Islam that spread from Arabia into Christian nations by force of arms.

In the Greek, the word for "pale" is most often translated "green," but is translated "pale" here because the translators are interjecting what they suppose the proper word should be. After all, who has ever heard of a green horse?! *Barnes Notes on The NT* says, *"The colour of the horse was pale--χλωρος. This word properly means pale-green, yellowish-green, like the colour of the first shoots of grass and herbage."* CWD says, *"Green, as the grass or plants."* It is the same word used for "green" in Rev. 9:4 where it says, *"They were told not to harm the grass of the earth or any <u>green</u> plant or any tree"* (ESV).

The color of Islam is Green, much like the color of grass. You can see the color in many national flags, such as Saudi Arabia. Just Google the flag of Saudi Arabia or look in an encyclopedia.

Therefore, this green horse represents the death and suffering that followed the spread of Islam. The reason hell follows this horse is because it is not just warfare, but includes forcing people to convert to Islam, which will send the converts to hell.

Notice the verse does not say they were given power to kill a fourth of the world population, but merely *"power over"* a fourth; indicating this horse will ride over a fourth of the planet, or will grow to become a fourth of the world population; both are true of Islam. The rule of Islam spread until it ran from the western edge

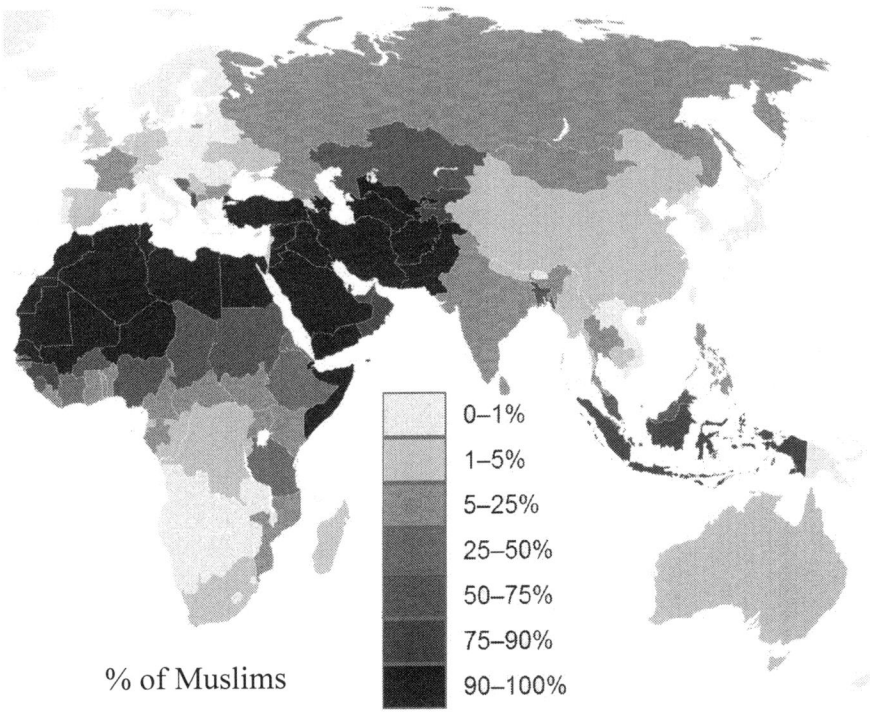

% of Muslims

0–1%
1–5%
5–25%
25–50%
50–75%
75–90%
90–100%

of Africa to the borders of China, creating an empire larger than Rome. But it has extended beyond the nations of its empire, into Indonesia, Nigeria, and now even has a significant population in Europe, Canada, and other countries. Even though India does not have a high percentage of Muslims, it has a high population, about 200 million.

Islam currently has about 20-25% of the global population and will soon be the world's dominate religion. Europe's Muslim population is growing so fast that by 2050 Muslims will be the majority in several nations and near the majority in several others.

The prophet Ezra predicted the coming of Islam in his book 2 Ezra which is part of the Apocrypha (which means "hidden" not "false" as some people claim):

> What a terrifying sight, appearing from the east! The nations of the dragons of Arabia shall come out with many chariots, and from the day that they set out, their hissing shall spread over the earth, so that all who hear them will fear and tremble. (2 Ezra 15:28-29) (NRSV)

(2 Ezra is called 4 Esdras in the Vulgate, and 3 Esdras in Russian Bibles, and 2 Esdras in the King James version. You can find it online in several translations. The Apocrypha was part of the Septuagint, the Latin Vulgate, and the original KJV Bible. It is still included in some Bibles, especially in the Eastern Church.)

The fourth living creature was *"like a flying eagle." Unger's Bible Dictionary* says the eagle figuratively means, *"great and powerful kings... also of rapidity of the movement of armies"* (p. 58, 282). This exactly describes the Islamic invasions that were very quick. The Islamic armies were like the German Blitzkrieg of World War 2.

Many people are looking for the rise of a one-world government from Europe ruled by the Antichrist, as though there were some super-secret groups who are plotting to take over the world. Well, I have news for you, there is a group that openly declares their goal of world domination, and literally millions of Christians have already suffered and died under its armies of conquest. It is

Islam, which began in the 7th century in Arabia. Muhammad died in 632 A.D., and within 50 years, Islam had conquered modern Syria, Iraq, Lebanon, Israel, Egypt, and Iran (ancient Persia).

The Arabs, also called Saracens and Ishmaelites, continued invading country after country until they had conquered present-day Libya, Algeria, Tunisia, Morocco, Spain, Afghanistan, Pakistan, Armenia, Cyprus, Turkey, Bosnia, parts of India, and more. They even established a foothold in Italy for a short time as they attempted to conquer Europe. Muslims ruled the second largest empire in history, after the Mongols; it stretched from the Atlantic Ocean to the borders of China. For almost a thousand years the sword of Islam never stopped dripping new blood and enslaving millions of survivors.

Murder and slavery became an integral part of Islam when Muhammad slaughtered the male members of an opposing tribe and sold the women and children into slavery. This continued throughout the Muslim invasions. The spread of Islam has left a trail of blood, suffering and destruction like no other ideology in world history. *Politicalislam.com* estimates that 270 million people have been killed in 1400 years of jihad. I think that figure is conservative. Islam teaches hatred for non-Muslims, especially Jews, and approves of lying and deceit to further the cause of Islam.

Imams throughout the Islamic world preach that America, Britain, and Israel must be destroyed, and fill their followers with lies about us, saying that all the world's wars and problems are caused by America, Britain, Israel, and democracy. They pray over loud speakers for Allah to destroy us, calling the people to rise up against us. It is beyond any doubt that the 4th Seal points directly to Islam as the green horse that is still spreading, and will wage wars of conquest once again in the near future.

In 2006, a Dutch cartoonist drew a cartoon of Muhammad wearing a turban-bomb to make a political statement against suicide bombers, the reaction was global. Muslims were screaming in the streets. They yelled threats of death and held signs that said: *"Exterminate those who slander Islam," "Islam will dominate the world," "Behead those who insult Islam," "Butcher those who mock Islam," "Freedom go to HELL," "Europe you will pay. Your 9/11 is on its way," "Europe is the cancer, Islam is the answer,"* and *"Be prepared for the real Holocaust!"* People were killed in the demonstrations and riots, and several Christians were murdered by Muslims as retaliation for the cartoon. The demonstrators were not members of al-Qaeda, but ordinary followers of the religion of peace! The cartoonist now lives under armed guard and moves from place to place because of the threats to his life.

Do not be fooled. The plan to conquer the world and slaughter Christians and Jews is not a secret conspiracy. It is broadcast daily on TV, radio, the internet, and in print. It has existed as an established doctrine of Islam for 1400 years, but when Islam lost its empire in WWI and the Jews returned to Israel, these events fueled the embers that have become a raging fire.

For several years I thought I was the only one who saw that the beast of Revelation was based in Islam and that another Islamic empire will rise, but I have learned of a few other people who also see it. Here is a quote from *The Rise of the Islamic Empire and the Threat to the West*, by Anthony Dennis:

> In short, the coming Islamic Empire will be a world power in every sense of the word, whose people will share a vibrant religion and a common Islamic culture. Like its Muslim predecessors, the Islamic Empire of the early 21st Century will also have an appetite for territorial expansion and military conquest. A modern, worldwide jihad against non-Muslim populations and societies complete with nuclear weapons promises to bring the highest casualty rates in the history of mankind. World War III, if it does come, will probably occur between the Islamic Bloc and the Western nations. It will be the deadliest war ever fought by humanity. (Wyndham Hall Press, 2001)

A growing number of Christians are waking up to the truth that Islam is the religion of the beast and false prophet, but most of them think they are going in a pretribulation Rapture. It is time to open your eyes to the threat; open your eyes to the truth!

(7) Fifth Seal: Souls of Martyrs

9 When he opened the fifth seal, I saw under the altar the souls of those who had been slain because of the word of God and the testimony they had maintained. 10 They called out in a loud voice, "How long, Sovereign Lord, holy and true, until you judge the inhabitants of the earth and avenge our blood?" 11 Then each of them was given a white robe, and they were told to wait a little longer, until the number of their fellow servants and brothers and sisters were killed just as they had been. (Rev. 6:9-11)

These are all the martyrs for Christ from the start of Christianity through the present. They cry out for justice. They want God to pour out his Wrath upon those who murdered them. They are told there will be others who must suffer and die for Christ before judgment will come, which means the Wrath of God has not yet started. It also means the Rapture has not taken place yet.

And these people are not whole persons, but only "souls." They will return with Christ to become whole persons at the Rapture. But could these souls be people who were martyred after the Rapture? Where are those who were Rapture? Don't they want justice also? Were there not many Christians martyred before the Rapture? Where are they mentioned? They would not be described as being merely "souls."

This Seal tells us that we have not yet reached the end of the age within the book of Revelation.

(8) Conclusion

You may have guessed from the information in this chapter that the Seals and Trumpets run in succession. Revelation chapters 4-9 describe events that are in chronological order. The Trumpet events take place during the Great Tribulation.

Chapter 3
The Sixth Seal: Signs of the End and Birth Pains

(1) The Signs Begin

The 6th Seal describes earthly and cosmic events that can only be the Day of Judgment:

> 12 I watched as he opened the sixth seal. There was a great earthquake. The sun turned black like sackcloth made of goat hair, the whole moon turned blood red, 13 and the stars in the sky fell to earth, as figs drop from a fig tree when shaken by a strong wind. 14 The sky receded like a scroll, rolling up, and every mountain and island was removed from its place.
>
> 15 Then the kings of the earth, the princes, the generals, the rich, the mighty, and everyone else, both slave and free, hid in caves and among the rocks of the mountains. 16 They called to the mountains and the rocks, "Fall on us and hide us from the face of him who sits on the throne and from the wrath of the Lamb! 17 For the great day of their wrath has come, and who can withstand it?" (Rev. 6:12-17)

These verses accurately describe a time of great catastrophe that will bring an end to the world as we know it through massive earthquakes, asteroid impacts, volcanic eruptions, and tsunamis. But notice that this description of Judgment Day only takes up six verses, which is a surprisingly small amount of space for one of the most important events in the history of the planet. More space is given to saints singing a new song in heaven in Rev. 15 than to Judgment Day here. There must be a reason for this lack of information.

Notice that the events of the first five Seals were events that have continued into our present time. The events after the 4th Seal did not immediately result in 1/4th of the world being conquered for Islam; it has taken 1,400 years. Therefore, the opening of the 6th Seal is actually the beginning of the natural and cosmic events that will ultimately result in the stars falling from the sky, the mountains moving from their places, and a global earthquake. In other words, the opening of this Seal actually starts the birth pains of the coming birth of the Kingdom Age. The events described here are given in greater detail in later chapters of Rev.

This Seal also includes the signs in the heavens designed to warn us of the coming global destruction at the return of Christ to judge the world. Notice that two of the things mentioned under this Seal are an eclipse of the sun and a blood-red moon which is caused by a total eclipse of the moon. The Bible says that the planets were given to us for signs and seasons (Gen. 1:14). When Christ came the first time there were signs in the heavens which brought the wise men to worship Jesus as a future king. Likewise, there will be signs in the heavens before his return.

Prophecy teachers have been teaching for over a hundred and fifty years that the end is near, especially the past fifty years, but there have always been wars, famines, and social turmoil. Even though we must look at the world events, these things alone are not signs of the end. The most important signs that Jesus spoke about are not here on Earth but are in the heavens above. Great and momentous events will take place among the planets of our solar system (this will be discussed in detail in a future book).

In Matthew 24:29 Jesus described the events of the Day of Judgment, *"the stars will fall from the sky, and the heavenly bodies will be shaken."* These events will come upon the entire solar system, which is why the stars will fall and the planets will shake. But before the events of that Day, other less catastrophic events will take place that will serve as warning signs of the coming global destruction. In the book of Luke, chapter 21, Jesus said:

> "There will be great earthquakes, famines and pestilences in various places, and fearful events and great signs from heaven." (Luke 21:11)

The above tells us that "signs" of Christ's return will be seen in this solar system. Later in the same chapter, Jesus tells us more about the events in the heavens. Whatever these events are, they will cause many people to be in great fear about what is coming upon the world:

> "There will be signs in the sun, moon, and stars. On the earth, nations will be in anguish and perplexity at the roaring and tossing of the sea. 26 Men will faint from terror, <u>apprehensive of what is coming on the world</u>, for the heavenly bodies will be shaken." (Luke 21:25-26)

Many prophecy teachers point to upheavals in the world today as a fulfillment of these verses, but this is far from true. The reason the nations will be in anguish and perplexity are the strange and unusual things that will happen on earth and among the sun, moon, and planets. The sea does not mean people or nations being in turmoil, it refers to the oceans. The cosmic events that will affect the sun, moon, and stars also will affect our oceans, causing great swells and tides, because the moon affects the ocean tides. The verse also likely refers to more powerful hurricanes.

Cosmic events are the only *certain* signs of the coming Day of Judgment, because Judgment Day will be caused mostly by events in this solar system. People will die of heart attacks, frightened about the unusual things that will happen in this solar system, *"for the heavenly bodies will be shaken"*-- which are the planets in our solar system, including Earth.

If people will die from fear, they will also likely engage in rioting and looting because they will fear that the end of the world is coming. Scenarios from Hollywood disaster movies about the end of the world will actually happen.

Why will people believe the end is coming? Because the planets in this solar system will be shaken. But what does "shaken" mean? It cannot mean that they will have quakes, like earthquakes. No, it means they will do strange and unusual things that can be seen from Earth; which means some may speed up or slow down as they orbit the sun, or some may move out of their orbits into a closer or farther orbit. We will be able to see them do things which will cause people on Earth to wonder what will happen to Earth also. When the worst of these strange events take place, then the Wrath of God is about to destroy the world. Luke 21 continues:

> 27 "At that time they will see the Son of Man coming in a cloud with power and great glory. 28 When these things begin to take place, stand up and lift up your heads, because your redemption is drawing near." (Luke 21:27-28)

These verses tell us that we will see the start of these events before the return of Christ, probably several years before, and that they will continue right up to and including the day that Christ returns in the sky. God is not going to bring great destruction upon the world without giving us lots of warning. The events of the GT are part of that warning.

The pretribulation Rapturists try to argue that the signs could start right after the Rapture, since they claim there will be seven years between the Rapture and the bodily return of Christ. But Jesus continues on this subject and tells us that it will be more than a few years, but will be a few decades between the beginning of the signs and when he returns. Luke 21 continues:

> He told them this parable: "Look at the fig tree and all the trees. 30 When they sprout leaves, you can see for yourselves and know that summer is near. 31 Even so, when you see these things happening, you know that the kingdom of God is near. 32 I tell you the truth, this generation will certainly not pass away until all these things have happened." (Luke 21:29-32)

Jesus is not talking about the nation of Israel or any other nation in his reference to trees, he is still talking about the signs pointing to his return. When you see leaves begin to appear on a tree, then another and another, you know that Spring is here and that Summer is getting closer and closer. In the same way, when we see more and more strange and unusual things happening on Earth and in this solar system, we will know that Christ's return is getting closer and closer. This passage also tells us that it will be 20 - 30 years from the first of the signs to his return, or he would not have said that the generation who sees the first signs will live to see his return.

Neither will it be hundreds of years between the first signs and his return, but only one generation or less. This passage in Luke 21 tells us that there is no need to look for Christ's return until after we see fearful cosmic events in this solar system, *but the first signs were seen 20 years ago*!

So this information actually destroys the doctrine of Imminent Return of Christ which is the foundation of the pretribulation Rapture doctrine. This doctrine says the Rapture could have happened at any time since Christ returned to heaven. But the Rapture cannot happen until after strange and unusual events start happening in our solar system. People are going to be concerned in the near future about the turmoil in the world, but that has happened throughout recorded history; such events <u>by themselves</u> are not signs of Christ's return, only unusual or frightening events in this solar system. No riots or economic collapse point to the return of Christ; those things have always happened, except for the fact that <u>they will become much more frequent and painful, and will be accompanied by birth pains of the earth and signs in the sky</u>.

Why will the signs of Christ's return be seen in the sky in the form of fearful events? Because when Christ returns the world will receive massive destruction from the sky, that is, from space, as he told us in Luke 17:

> But the day Lot left Sodom, fire and sulfur rained down from heaven and destroyed them all. It will be just like this on the day the Son of Man is revealed. (Luke 17:29-30)

This passage, and many others, tell us that when Christ returns, fire will rain down from the sky and destroy most of the world's population. Many Christians get upset when someone says Sodom and Gomorrah were destroyed by a volcanic eruption or an asteroid impact; *"No, they were not, God destroyed them!"* Excuse me?! Does God make it rain? Did God send Noah's Flood? Did God cause an earthquake to open the earth and swallow Korah and all those with him (Num 16:32)? Yes, he did. God uses the natural world he created much of the time, so the fire that will destroy the world will not be God breathing fire out of his mouth; it will be a natural event.

The complete passage of Luke 17 referenced above also mentions Noah's Flood, therefore, some people want to say that it merely means that Christ will come with destruction. But there are many other places that mention fire at the return of Christ, so my application of the passage is not an abuse of the context or meaning.

There are three natural events that can cause fire to rain down globally; one is an asteroid impact, the second is a massive meteor shower with large enough stones for them to still be flaming on impact. The third is a large coronal mass ejection (CME) from the sun when our electromagnetic field around Earth is weakened.

When an asteroid impacts earth, it impacts with such force that it literally explodes and sends out pieces of flaming rock in all directions. This is why many scientists believe a very large asteroid destroyed the dinosaurs. Luke 21 continues:

> 33 "Heaven and earth will pass away, but my words will never pass away. 34 Be careful, or your hearts will be weighed down with dissipation, drunkenness and the anxieties of life, and that day will close on you unexpectedly like a trap. 35 For it will come upon all those who live on the face of the whole earth. 36 Be always on the watch, and pray that you may be able to escape all that is about to happen, and that you may be able to stand before the Son of Man." (Luke 21:33-36)

Other words for "dissipation" are *self-indulgence* or *gluttony*. We should not be so consumed with making money and having fun that we fail to see the signs and take warning. Many people live such busy lives that they do not watch the news or scientific documentaries about the universe and worsening natural disasters, and know nothing about the threat of asteroid impacts. Some people will see the events and die from fear, others will pay no attention to them, because they will be too busy playing video games or skate boarding or working. It seems hard to believe that anyone in the latter stages of the GT will be oblivious to what is going on, since World War 3 will be raging, but there will be; especially in villages or countries that don't have much free press or contact with the outside world.

Because of the context of this passage, Jesus is not referring to the Rapture when he said, *"pray that you may escape."* He means, pray that you will escape being killed in the natural disasters so you can physically "stand" before him at his return. This is why we are told to watch the signs in the sun, moon, and stars so we will not be caught unprepared and end up dead. So it refers to those whom will not go in the Rapture. Other translations give a better sense of what the Greek means:

> "But stay awake at all times, praying that you may have strength to escape all these things that are going to take place, and to stand before the Son of Man." (Luke 21:36) (ESV)

> "praying that you may be strong enough to come safely through all that is going to happen . . . (JBP)

> "So be alert at all times, praying that you may have strength to escape all these things that are going to take place. . ." (GNB)

It will require strength to make it through to the end of the GT and especially the Wrath of God, and to be one of the few survivors to enter the Kingdom Age. The reason Jesus spent so much time warning us of the coming Great Tribulation and Wrath of God is because 70-90% of Christians will go through those events. The Rapture is not going to take every Christian, as we will see later in the next chapter.

The Old Testament also predicts that great and wondrous things will happen in this solar system before Judgment Day:

> I will show <u>wonders in the heavens</u> and on the earth, blood and fire and billows of smoke. The sun will be turned to darkness and the

moon to blood before the coming of the great and dreadful day of the LORD. (Joel 2:30-31)

Some first century writings not included in the New Testament also speak of momentous events in this solar system. The letter written by Barnabas says:

> ... when his Son shall come, and abolish the season of the Wicked One, and judge the ungodly; and shall <u>change the sun and the moon, and the stars</u>; then he shall gloriously rest in that seventh day. (13:6) (*The Apocryphal New Testament*, by Jeremiah Jones, William Hone, and William Wake, 1824)

If God is going to change the sun, moon, and planets, then truly unexpected and incredible things are going to take place in this solar system, but most of it will take place after the Rapture. Notice that he will also end the reign of the Wicked One, which likely refers to the beast and false prophet, and / or Satan himself.

By watching the signs we will know when to expect the global destruction and can seek shelter. Of course, this refers to the Christians who do not go in the Rapture.

(2) The Watch Has Begun

There is evidence that the 6th Seal has already opened and the signs of coming destruction have begun. The 6th Seal may have opened with a series of events in the summer of 1994. On June 9, 1994, a massive earthquake shook many areas of the Western hemisphere. It was centered below Bolivia, South America. What makes it unusual is the depth of the quake, 400 miles down in the earth's crust. The great depth spread out the force so it shook most of North and South America, including Canada.

Only six weeks after the deep earthquake, a frightening event took place in this solar system; fragments of the comet Shoemaker-Levy 9 slammed into the planet Jupiter at 130,000 miles per hour, creating explosions greater than nuclear bombs, and triggering fireballs more than 1,500 miles across and rising up more than 600 miles above Jupiter's clouds. If those fragments had hit Earth it would have blanketed the world with dense dark clouds and created a cosmic winter, with freezing temperatures and no crops for years. It would have been the end of the world as we know it with few survivors.

At the same time that the comet fragments were hitting Jupiter, several Southern states were having floods that killed at least 24 people, while most of the western half of the U.S. was having the worst fire season in its history (up to that time). Over 50,000 fires were started, most by lightning strikes. That summer, Europe also had massive flooding. Do you suppose God was trying to tell us something? The deep earthquake was a rare event, and the comet hitting Jupiter was the first such event ever witnessed by humans, plus the floods and the fires. I do not believe that all these things happening together was a coincidence, especially when you consider that the Bible tells us that God's judgment upon the world will come in the form of a massive earthquake, an asteroid impact, and will include large amounts of lightning and global fire.

The comet fragments hitting Jupiter was a wake-up call. Many scientists became alarmed at the possibility that such an event could happen to Earth. Before the comet Shoemaker-Levy hit Jupiter, most scientists did not take the possibility of an asteroid impact seriously. Dr. Shoemaker was perhaps the only scientist who was looking for earth-crossing asteroids. Since the Jupiter impacts, scientists have changed their minds and have begun looking for danger from outer-space. Several scientific organizations were created for one purpose, *to watch for asteroids that could be heading for Earth*. One such project is called NEAT, Near Earth Asteroid Tracking system, in Hawaii. Another is called Sky Watch. These and other sky watchers have found many asteroids, some of which could pose a threat to Earth.

Even though Dr. Shoemaker was looking for such asteroids, it was not a known concern or an ongoing project by many people like it has become since the July, 1994 comet impacts. Therefore, since the comet hitting Jupiter in 1994 is when the world woke up to the danger of asteroid impacts and began watching the skies for asteroids, that is when the "watch" officially began. Therefore, that is likely when the 6th Seal was opened. Remember what Jesus said, the generation that sees the first signs will live to see his return.

But danger is not all we should be looking for from space. The signs Jesus spoke about include strange or unusual events; "*wonders in the heavens*," Joel said. We should keep on the watch because there will be many more cosmic signs that may point to the end of the age. Most likely the signs will become more and more unusual, that is, things will happen that are unexpected and that we have never seen before.

More evidence that the 6th Seal is open is found later in this chapter.

(3) A Command to Keep Watch

We have learned that Jesus told us there will be signs in the sun, moon, and stars; Jesus also told us in several places to "watch" for his coming so that we will not be killed in the coming destruction, which refers to those who do not go in the Rapture.

In Matthew 24, Jesus tells us that when he comes, the world will be destroyed just like it was by the Flood of Noah. That passage ends with the statement, "*Therefore keep watch, because you do not know on what day your Lord will come*" (Matt. 24:42).

In this passage, people were living their lives as usual, and then the flood came and killed them all; some people were eating, others getting married, some were working in the field, and some were grinding grain. Even though Noah warned people of the coming flood, they did not believe him; but it is reasonable to assume that many people on Earth never heard the warning.

Why would someone need to watch for signs of the end if the Rapture is going to catch away every Christian before any of that happens? This reasoning does not make sense.

The reference Jesus makes here does not refer to being spiritually ready for the Rapture, but to being physically ready for the coming destruction after the Rapture. The reason he spends so much time on it is because most of the global Christian population will not go in the Rapture. Most people who are not prepared like

Noah, will die. Noah did not know exactly what day it would start to rain, but he did not wait until it started to rain to start building the ark. Likewise, we should not be caught by surprise like those who died in the Flood, but should be completely ready like Noah.

Jesus could have worded the above passage like this, "*I'm coming with destruction as great as Noah's Flood, therefore you should watch the signs and be ready like Noah, otherwise, you will be taken by surprise and will die.*" People who are watching the signs and the world events will know when to seek shelter like Noah.

The whole developed world watched the comet fragments hit Jupiter in July 1994. Likewise, most everyone will be aware of the events, because you will be able to look up and see them for yourself. People just need to be warned that the cosmic events are indeed signs that point to the approaching end of the world as we know it.

The last verse above refers to both the warning of Noah, and to the next passage, because he continues on the same subject and give us more details:

"Therefore keep watch, because you do not know on what day your Lord will come. 43 But understand this: If the owner of the house had known at what time of night the thief was coming, he would have kept watch and would not have let his house be broken into. 44 So you also must be ready, because the Son of Man will come at an hour when you do not expect him. (Matthew 24:42-44)

Verse 42 begins with "therefore" and refers back to what he just said, which was that a great destruction like Noah's flood will come upon the world. This means that verse 42 tells us that a Noah-like destruction will happen at the coming of Christ. Jesus then helps us to understand what he is saying by giving us a story to illustrate his point.

Jesus said he will come like a thief; since a thief comes only to steal, kill, and destroy, this passage refers to the coming destruction of the Day of Judgment. Jesus will not appear bodily during the destruction, but only in the sky.

Though we will not know in advance the exact day or hour the judgment will begin, we can know when the Day of Judgment is very close. The key to the passage is this; <u>if the owner of the house had known what hour the thief was coming, he would have taken the necessary steps to prevent the thief from breaking into his house</u>. If the owner knew the thief was coming at 1 a.m., he could sleep until 12:30, then awaken and turn on all the lights and do whatever is necessary to keep the thief from breaking in. But since we do not know when the thief will come, we should watch for the coming of the thief-- this means that if we are watching, we will be able to see the thief as he approaches. It means we will be able to see and know that destruction is about to take place if we are watching the signs in the sun, moon, and stars!

We must also pay attention to world events, if we have access to up-to-the-minute news. But at some point during WW3, probably near the end, we will most certainly have all our communication satellites destroyed, and electronics destroyed by an EMP attack. (An Electro Magnetic Pulse will fry everything electronic.)

Watching the signs is kind of like radar. An army general cannot know when the enemy planes are approaching, but if the radar is watching, it will give him advance warning so the air-raid alarm can sound. Civilians and military personnel can then flee into bomb shelters for protection. In like manner we are commanded to watch the cosmic events in this solar system so we will know when to flee to shelters so we can be protected during the time of global destruction from asteroids, nuclear fallout, and more. So, we must watch the skies.

Jesus said that people will die from fear because of what might take place, but those who die from fear have no faith or hope in God. The exact things to look for and what will happen are given in a future book.

(4) When You Do Not Expect Him

But, what about the end of the above passage that says Christ will come when we do not expect him? Notice the first part of that statement:

4. A tetrad of eclipses occurred on Passover and the Day of Atonement in 860 and 861 A.D. Important things happened in these years as well. In 861 the first Russians, sailing in 200 ships, attacked Constantinople but withdrew after the Virgin Mary's robe was carried in procession around the walls of the city. A few years later Russia's first ambassador to Constantinople accepted Christianity, which laid the groundwork for the conversion of Russia. In 863 Saint Cyril and Saint Methodius began translating part of the Bible into the Old Slavonic language, which also helped in the conversion of the Slavs (Russians). This later led to a great persecution of the Jews by the Russian Christians, who were themselves later severely persecuted by the Communists.

Also in 861 Muhammed al-Mudabbir arrived in Egypt and tripled the jizya (tax) on Christians and Jews. Because so many could not pay the tax, they filled the prisons. The churches were looted and confiscated, and the Coptic patriarch, *"unable to pay the taxes demanded from the Coptic episcopate, fled from place to place and went into hiding"* (*The Decline of Eastern Christianity Under Islam*, by Bat Ye'or, page 84).

5. A tetrad occurred on Passover and the Feast of Trumpets in 1493 and 1494. In 1492 King Ferdinand and Queen Isabella of Spain ordered the expulsion of all Jews from Spain, about 200,000. Many fled to Morocco where they were later persecuted. It was also in 1492 that Columbus discovered America; the U.S.A. was to become the home of many Jews and a friend to Israel.

6. The sixth tetrad occurred on Passover and Tabernacles in 1949 and 1950, just after the creation of the Jewish state of Israel in 1948 and the 1st Arab - Israeli War for Independence (May 15, 1948 – March 10, 1949).

7. The seventh tetrad since the time of Christ occurred on Passover and Tabernacles in 1967 and 1968, with the 6-Day War taking place in June of 1967 when Israel captured all of Jerusalem and additional land.

8. The next tetrad will occur on Passover and Tabernacles (Sukkot) in 2014 and 2015. Therefore, we can expect the eighth tetrad to be associated with something important that will affect

Christians and Jews; perhaps the start of the GT and World War 3.

> Passover —   April 15, 2014
> Feast of Tabernacles —   October 8, 2014
>
> Passover —   April 4, 2015
> Feast of Tabernacles —   September 28, 2015

These eclipses of the moon are all in a row, with no partial eclipse in between. Since we know that God expects us to watch the signs in the heavens, these eclipses should clearly not be ignored. They mean that something important is about to happen.

In addition to the four blood moons, there is a total eclipse of the sun on March 20, 2015, which is Adar 29/Nisan 1 of the Jewish calendar, which is the start of the Jewish religious new year. Then there is a partial eclipse of the sun on Sept. 13, 2015, which is the Feast of Trumpets. Mark Biltz said in a recent article in WND:

> Not only that, according to NASA, this total blood moon on 9/28/15 will be at perigee meaning it will be a super moon and seen in Jerusalem during the feast of sukkot while the Jewish people will be dwelling outside in their sukkahs looking up toward the heavens. (*Blood moons expert: Watch 2014 and 2015*, www.wnd. com/2013/10/blood-moons-expert-watch-2014-and-2015/)

According to the Jews, an eclipse of the moon is a bad omen for the Jewish people, but a solar eclipse is a bad omen for the Gentile nations.

Also, some of the four blood moons in 2014-2015 are over Jerusalem, but not all, as often reported; they are merely all on Jewish feast days. At least this is what I have been able to ascertain, but I could be wrong on this.

In addition, there is more information that points to 2015 being a year when something really bad could happen, than the four Blood Moons, such as a book called The Harbinger, by Jonathan Cahn. He said the stock market crashes in 2001 and 2008 both occurred on the same day on the Jewish calendar that occurs only

"So you also must be ready, because the Son of Man will come at an hour when you do not expect him." (Matthew 24:44)

Jesus is talking about destruction coming upon the whole world, so we *"must be ready."* How can we watch for the coming thief and have a shelter ready if he will come when we do not expect him? I believe this passage refers to the length of time that has transpired since the time of Christ. Jesus continues speaking about this same subject in the very next parable, which clearly states, *"My master is staying away a long time."*

The apostles and the early Church were looking for the return of Christ within a few generations. They did not expect it to be 2,000 years before Jesus would return. That is probably what the statement means that Jesus would return when we do not expect him. It does not refer to catching us by surprise, because he is here warning us to be watching so that we are not caught by surprise.

Jesus knew that many Christians would stop expecting his return because he was going to stay away such a long time. And, indeed, many Christians no longer believe in his return to set up his Kingdom on Earth and will not believe any warning of the coming asteroid impacts and nuclear war because it does not fit their faulty theology.

(5) Four Blood Moons

Pastor Mark Biltz, of Tacoma, Washington, teaches that there is going to be four blood red moons in a row in 2014 and 2015 and two solar eclipses. All are on Jewish holidays or feast days. This is very rare. I found many magazines and websites that reported his findings as far back as 2008. The blood moons are caused by eclipses of the moon which result in the moon appearing blood red. Four occurring in a row are called *"astronomical tetrads."*

NASA's web site allows us to go forward to find future tetrads, and back in time to find previous tetrads. No more tetrads will take place in this century. Four blood moons, or a tetrad, is rare; but when they all four fall on Jewish holy days, it is very rare, only seven of these have taken place since the time of Christ.

During past tetrads on Jewish holy days, significant historical events have taken place before, during, or after the blood moons.

1. The first of the seven tetrads occurred on Passover and the Feast of Tabernacles in 162 and 163 A.D., which happened during one of the worst persecutions of Jews and Christians that began in 161 by Marcus Aurelius, emperor of Rome. Also in 161 the Parthians invaded Armenia, a Roman province. About three years later a great plague killed about 10% of the pagan Roman population.

2. The second occurred on Passover and the Day of Atonement (Yom Kippur) in 795 and 796. Pope Leo III was crowned Pope on Christmas day, 795. He was attacked and injured by his enemies in 799, then he fled to Charlemagne for protection. In 800 he and Charlemagne returned to Rome where the Pope was put on trial, but Charlemagne was able to get him acquitted of charges. The Pope then crowned Charlemagne the first Emperor of the Holy Roman Empire, which lasted over 1,000 years. Thus, the Church gave the emperors authority to rule, and the emperors gave the Church protection.

(Prior to this, the only official Christian kingdom had been centered in Constantinople, the Christian Eastern Roman Empire, which historians call the Byzantine Empire, but it was actually a continuation of the Roman Empire, which was divided into east and west before the western half fell.)

3. Another tetrad occurred on Passover and Day of Atonement in 842 and 843 A.D. A lot happened in those years that affected both Christians and Jews. In 842 a synod in the eastern Church reaffirmed the use of icons, which had been banned for the second time in 814. In Europe, Muslims had been attacking Sicily for several years as they attempted to conquer Italy and Europe, and this continued as they attacked and captured Messina in Sicily in 842. In 843 the Treaty of Verdun divided the Holy Roman Empire into three parts. This affected Jews adversely because the French were tolerant of Jews, but when the French no longer had power over most of Europe, then anti-Jewish feelings were allowed to manifest, leading to persecution of the Jews.

once every seven years. That day is called Shemitah, which is a day for wiping out debits. It is the last day of the Shemitah (Sabbatical) year. The next Sabbatical year is Sept. 25, 2014 thru Sept. 28, 2015. So 9/28/15 is the day to watch. Since we had two stock market crashes without the blood moons, I expect something worse, like a dollar collapse, or the start of the Great Tribulation.

(The present version of this book 1.5.4, has a mistake corrected. Previous version 1.5.2 said, "So 9/13/15 is the day to watch." It should have said, "So 9/28/15 is the day to watch.")

An important point concerning the Sixth Seal, is that it mentions an eclipse of the sun and a blood moon. And in Joel 2 we read that the sun will be darkened and the moon turned to blood "*before* the coming of the great and dreadful day of the LORD" (Joel 2:31). In past years I have always believed that the eclipse and blood moon will happen near or at the time that the Wrath of God comes upon the world, at the end of the GT, but since no more tetrads will take place in this century, the ones we are having now could be the very same eclipses mentioned in Joel and the Sixth Seal, which herald the beginning of the end, not the end itself. If so, then Sept. of 2015 is when the Sixth Seal will open.

(6) Birth Pains of the Earth

Jesus spoke about the birth pains of the earth in Matthew 24:

> Nation will rise against nation, and kingdom against kingdom. There will be famines and earthquakes in various places. 8 All these are the beginning of birth pains. (Mat. 24:7-8)

Birth pains get more painful as the birth draws near, and they also become more frequent. So we can expect to see an increase in natural disasters as we near the return of Christ, and the birth pains may have already started (unless they start in Sept. 2015).

One of the Early Church Fathers, Lactantius (240-320 A.D.), spoke about the GT in a manner that can only come from a vision or prophecy, or from direct teaching passed down from the twelve

Apostles; because it agrees with everything in the Bible and agrees with other prophecies and scientific information that are believed to be genuine:

Then, in truth, a detestable and abominable time shall come, in which life shall be pleasant to none of men. Cities shall be utterly overthrown, and shall perish; not only by fire and the sword, but also by <u>continual earthquakes and floods, and by frequent diseases and repeated famines.</u> For the <u>atmosphere will be tainted, and become corrupt and pestilential</u> -- at one time by unseasonable rains, at another by barren drought, <u>now by colds, and now by excessive heats</u>. Nor will the earth give its fruit to man: no field, or tree, or vine will produce anything; but after they have given the greatest hope in the blossom, they will fail in the fruit. Fountains also shall be dried up, together with the rivers; so that there shall not be a sufficient supply for drinking; and waters shall be changed into blood or bitterness. On account of these things, beasts shall fail on the land, and birds in the air, and fishes in the sea.

Wonderful prodigies [signs, wonders] also in heaven shall confound the minds of men with the greatest terrors, and the trains of comets, and the darkness of the sun, and the color of the moon, and the gliding of the falling stars. Nor, however, will these things take place in the accustomed manner; but there <u>will suddenly appear stars unknown and unseen by the eyes</u>; the sun will be perpetually darkened, so that there will be scarcely any distinction between the night and the day; the moon will now fail, not for three hours only, but overspread with perpetual blood, will go through extraordinary movements, so that it will not be easy for man to ascertain the courses of the heavenly bodies or the system of the times; for there will either be summer in the winter, or winter in the summer.

Then the year will be shortened, and the month diminished, and the day contracted into a short space; and stars shall fall in great numbers, so that all the heaven will appear dark without any lights. The loftiest mountains also will fall, and be leveled with the plains; <u>the sea will be rendered un-navigable</u>."

And that nothing may be wanting to the evils of men and the earth, the trumpet shall be heard from heaven, which the Sibyl foretells in this manner: "The trumpet from heaven shall utter its wailing voice. And then all shall tremble and quake at that mournful sound." But then, through the anger of God against the men who have not known righteousness, the sword and fire, famine and disease, shall reign; and, above all things, fear always overhanging. Then they shall call upon God, but He will not hear them; death shall be desired, but it will not come; not even shall night give rest to their fear, nor shall sleep approach to their eyes, but anxiety and watchfulness shall consume the souls of men; they shall deplore and lament, and gnash their teeth; they shall congratulate the dead, and bewail the living. Through these and many other evils there shall be desolation on the earth, and the world shall be disfigured and deserted, which is thus expressed in the verses of the Sibyl: "The world shall be despoiled of beauty, through the destruction of men."

For the human race will be so consumed, that <u>scarcely the tenth part of men will be left</u>; and from whence a thousand had gone forth, scarcely a hundred will go forth. Of the worshippers of God also, two parts will perish; and the third part, which shall have been proved, will remain. (*The Divine Institutes*, Book VII, chapter 16)

And according to Lactantius, not only sinners will die, but also two-thirds of all Christians will die. The oceans becoming unnavigable agrees with what Jesus said about the tossing of the sea in Luke 21:25. Much of what Lactantius describes will take place near the return of Christ, but the wild weather has already started.

According to the National Climate Data Center, there were 12 weather disasters in the 1980s that totaled 1 billion dollars in damage or more. In the 90s there were 36; in the 2000s there were 45; and in the first three years of the 2010s, there were 26. So you can see the increase.

The 9 weather disasters we had in 2008 totaled 150 billion dollars in damage. In 2009 there were 6 with 100 billion in damage. In 2011 there were 12 disasters that totaled an estimated 52.5 billion dollars. In 2012 there were 11 that totaled 147 billion.

In January of 2010, there was a massive ice storm across much of the central U.S. that downed hundreds of power lines, leaving hundreds of thousands of people without electricity for several weeks in freezing temperatures, and causing billions of dollars worth of damage. So many trees lost their branches because of the weight of the ice that some streets were impassable. Then in early

May of 2010 an *"incredible storm"* caused flash flooding in Tennessee, Kentucky, and Mississippi, that brought great destruction to the city of Nashville with 10 feet of water. At least 29 people died and the governor of Tennessee declared half the counties to be disaster areas. This disaster did not get a lot of news coverage because of the Gulf Oil Spill that began on April 20, and the attempted car bombing in New York on May 1. The oil spill was also a mega-billion-dollar disaster and the effects will be with us for years to come.

During the winter of 2010-2011 there were many record snow falls from New York to NE Oklahoma which resulted in record flooding when the snow melted. All along the Mississippi River, cities and whole regions were flooded that had not flooded in generations. During April of 2011 there were hundreds of tornadoes; in May there were 70 tornadoes in 7 states in one day (ABC News), one totally destroyed the town of Joplin, Missouri, and killed 141 people and destroyed 8,000 buildings.

Then in the summer of 2011, we saw a massive heat wave in which all 50 states had record heat, with temperatures up to 112 degrees. The record heat lasted for up to 3 months in some places. Many of the states with the high temperatures were also having a year-long drought that dried up lakes and destroyed crops, including Texas and Oklahoma. The drought brought with it huge brush fires that burned millions of acres and thousands of homes.

Even the desert west did not escape, which had huge dust storms that are normally seen only in the Sahara Desert or the Middle East, that enveloped Phoenix. Five in all: July 5, July 18, August 19, 26, 27. At the same time as the last dust storm, hurricane Irene hit the east coast. God in his mercy reduced the winds, but it still caused more than 10 billion dollars worth of flood damage as it washed out roads, bridges, and homes.

The hurricane hit just days after a 5.8 earthquake in Virginia that cracked the Washington Monument and other Washington D.C. land marks. With 19 aftershocks the following week, the ground was likely quaking while Irene was blowing through.

And yet it continued; tropical storm Lee in early September

2011 went from Louisiana to Maine and left enormous flooding much of the way. Some areas of Louisiana flooded more than they did with hurricane Katrina in 2005. And because the NE was already waterlogged because of hurricane Irene, the rain of Lee caused horrible flooding throughout the region.

Michael Boldea Jr. is an evangelist and chairman of *Hand of Help Ministries*, founded by his late grandfather, Dumitru Duduman, former pastor from Romania. Michael had a dream in 2010 about three men in a wheat field. One man burned up one-third of the field with fire, another flooded one-third of the field. A third man harvested one-third of the field with great care:

> On the third night, the dream began as the previous two nights, with the first man setting fire to one third of the field, the second man flooding one third, and the third man meticulously harvesting the last third, I thought it would be the same dream yet again, until the man with the sickle turned, looked at me and said, "the world will know hunger, the faithful will know the power of their God." I recognized him; I had seen him in both my dreams and my visions before. . . . I received no further insight or interpretation, but this is what I believe in regards to its meaning:
> I believe that a worldwide food shortage is imminent. Whether due to too much sun and not enough rain, or too much rain and unprecedented weather patterns, global agriculture will suffer a severe blow very shortly. I also believe that God has already prepared provision for His children, that He will provide for them, and miraculously so. I do not believe God reveals coming events to His children that they might grow fearful or panic, but rather that they might learn to trust Him . . . (www.handofhelp.com/vision_58.php)

With part of the country having massive floods while other states are in a drought, if this keeps up we will be in a famine.

Michael Boldea Jr. also had a vision of a finger being pushed into a map of the United States. A voice said that God will allow a great event to this country *"to try and wake her up"* because the churches were asleep. It was not long after the vision when 9-11 took place. Then in 2002 he had a vision of a fist into a map of the U.S.. The Holy Spirit said that next time it will not be a finger but a fist that will bring an event greater than 9-11. Several other people have had visions or dreams of destruction upon an entire American city. This destruction most likely will be from a nuclear bomb or an asteroid impact long before the full Wrath of God. (More on this subject later in the book.)

The weather events of 2012 were similar to those of 2011; 2012 was the warmest year on record, and saw a great drought with the 3rd worst fire season in U.S. history. Here is a listing of the worst or out of normal weather for 2012 in the U.S.:

* Warm Winter (2011-2012):

Flowers sprouted in January in New Hampshire, while the Sierra Mountains in California are nearly free of snow.

* Alaska Cold Winter/Snow Record (January):

Several places in Alaska had record cold. The statewide average January temperature was −14°F below average. And record snow (134.5 inches) fell in Anchorage that winter that broke the previous record of 1954 − 55.

* Pacific Northwest Winter Storm (January 18 − 23):

Huge amounts of rain and snow with hurricane-force winds knocked out power to 250,000 customers. Damage estimated at $100 million.

* Hawaiian Hail Storm (March 9):

Heavy rainfall and severe thunderstorms created a rare EF-0 tornado that hit two towns on Oahu, with minor damage. Another storm dropped the largest hailstone on record for Hawaii, that measured 4.25" long, x 2.25", x 2". Damage from all the storms estimated at $37 million.

* Texas, Hail (Apr. 10-11):

Hail storm dumped 4 feet of hail on west Texas, resulting in many photos and videos that some people find hard to believe (see photo on my website).

* Severe Weather Outbreak (April 13 − 14):

An outbreak of tornadoes in the Plains created 98 tornadoes, killed at least 6 people. Damage estimated at $1.75 billion.

* Severe Weather Outbreak (April 30 − May 1):

Bad weather in the Ohio Valley caused 38 tornadoes and did

$4 billion in damage, killing 1 person.

* Severe Weather Outbreak (May 25 – 30):

A strong cold front created 27 tornadoes from Texas to the Northeast. Damage estimated at $2.5 billion, mostly from hail.

* Severe Weather Outbreak (June 6 – 12):

Several severe storms across the SW created 25 tornadoes with major hail damage across the Rocky Mountain Front Range. Estimated damage at $1.75 billion.

* Tropical Storm Debby, Florida (June):

Heavy rains from this storm resulted in damage estimated at $310 million, but the rains were welcome in Florida because of drought, which helped create the wettest summer on record.

* Texas and Mexico (June 11-13):

Severe weather that caused $1.75 billion in damage.

* Duluth, Flooding (June 20):

Thunderstorms caused record flooding in Duluth, Min. with over 8 inches of rain in 24 hours. Damage estimated at $175 million.

* Multi-State Derecho Winds (June 29):

A line of severe thunderstorms with strong Derecho winds swept across the U.S. from Illinois to Virginia damaging houses, toppling trees, and downing power lines. The storms killed 22 people and left 3.4 million people without power.

* Mount Evans Tornado (July):

A rare high-elevation tornado was seen near Mount Evans at 11,900 feet; the second-highest known tornado in the U.S.

* Death Valley Record Temps (July):

Death Valley set a world record high minimum temperature on July 12, with the low temperature at just 107°F (41.7°C), after reaching a high of 128° (53.3°C) the previous day. And the average temperature of 117.5°F was the world's warmest known 24-hour temperature ever recorded.

* Gulf Coast, hurricane (Aug 26-31):

Hurricane Isaac dumped 18 inches of rain in Florida, disrupting the 2012 Republican Convention. It did $2 billion in damage and killed 41 people.

* Alaskan Storms and Flooding (September):

Alaska was hit by several large extra-tropical cyclones that caused major flooding of the Sustina River and its tributaries. It was the worse flooding in 30 years. The storms also resulted in early snowfall in the south.

* Near-Record Low Great Lakes Levels (by end of 2012):

The record high temperatures throughout 2012 and drought along with low winter ice coverage created very low water levels in the Great Lakes, within inches of the record low levels of 1964.

* Midwest (June-Oct.):

A drought and heat wave caused $35 billion in damage.

* Superstorm Sandy (October 29):

Hurricane Sandy hit New Jersey and New York, causing $62 billion in damage and 131 deaths. (Main source for 2012 weather events was http://thinkprogress. org/climate/2012/12/26/ 1375081 /top-ten-us-weather-events-of-2012/)

It is normal to have strange weather occasionally, but not month after month, for several years! Even with all this evidence there are Christians who claim it is just normal weather cycles. Even the secular news media declared 2011 "the year the weather report went biblical" (ABC News), but blind Christians cannot see it. In one respect it is the judgment of God upon this country, but even more to the point, it is just the beginning of the birth pains that Jesus prophesied about in Matthew 24.

You no doubt have experienced some of the weather extremes that have taken place the last few years, but you probably do not know that similar crazy weather events have taken place around the world, not just in North America. The network TV news only occasionally reports on what happens in other nations.

Because of all the weather extremes and other strange occurrences, a fellow Christian has spent a lot of time cataloging these events and posting videos of the disasters on youtube.com. He made a summary video about all the disasters of 2011 and from then on he did a video for every month of 2012, and 2013.

Taking one at random, here are some of the news headlines for March 2013. I give the date listed in the video followed by the event, with a few listings that the video missed:

* 1: Sink holes in Florida and California
* 3: A plague of large locusts in Egypt
* 4: 5.5 earthquake in Yunnan Province, China, destroyed 1,800 homes & damaged 83,000 more
* 4: Flooding in Australia
* 4: Blizzard in Japan that killed 9 people
* 4: Asteroid 2013 EC flew passed Earth
* 5: More sink holes in Florida and California
* 7: East coast snowstorm shut down the U.S. gov. and caused tidal flooding
* 7: Plague of millions of giant rats reported in Tehran, Iran
* 7: Beaches shut down in Florida because of 1,000s of sharks
* 7: A new superbug was reported in U.S. resistant to antibiotics
* 7: Eyre Peninsula, South Australia, 1,000s of dead fish
* 7: Comet Panstarrs is visible to the naked eye
* 9: Small asteroid 2013 EC20 flew passed Earth
* 11: 12,000 dead pigs found floating in a river near Shanghai, China. No one knows why they died or how they got there.
* 11: Plague of locusts of Biblical proportions hit Israel from Egypt, 2 weeks before Passover (8th plague of Egypt)
* 11: Asteroid 2013 ET the size of a city block flew passed Earth
* 11: 5.1 earthquake rattled a large section of S. California
* 12: Record number of dead manatees on SW coast of Florida
* 13: Sinkhole appeared under a golfer that took him down 18 feet, fracturing his shoulder
* 13: Large fish kill in Rio De Janeiro, Brazil
* 14: Nuclear threats from North Korea and Iran
* 17: An asteroid impacts the Moon
* 19: Chemical weapons reportedly used in Syria
* 20: Mud slides in Brazil after 24 hours of heavy rain
* 21: Large fish-kill in Chili
* 22: Fish-kill in South Adelaide, Australia,
* 22: 2 states in Australia had a series of tornadoes, dozens of homes destroyed

* 22: Blizzard in Britain

* 23: A small meteor hit the east coast of U.S.

* 24: Massive snow and ice storm across a dozen states

* 24: S.E. Australia hit by a powerful storm

* 24: Bangladesh, tornadoes killed dozens and injured thousands

* 24: 1/2 of U.S. hit by powerful winter storm (probably a continuation of above mentioned storm)

* 25: Seffner, Florida, more sinkholes

* 25: St. Lewis suffers from massive winter storm (same storm)

* 25: Wales, farmers had many sheep buried in a deep snow storm

* 25: Adelaide, Australia had massive see grass wash up on shore

* 25: 6.2 earthquake hit Guatemala

* 25: Massive fish-kill, Tucuman Lake, Argentina

* 26: 5.5 & 5.1 earthquakes hit S.W. Mexico

* 27: 6.1 earthquake in Taiwan

* 27: Whidbey Island, Washington, mudslide on the coast

* 28: Sinkhole in China

* 28: Melbourne, Australia, a sudden powerful gust of wind hit a wall and slapped it down flat

* 28: Plague of locusts hit Madagascar

* 30: S. Australia, fish-kill

* 31: Mauritian capital, Port Louis, has major flood

* 31: Taiwan, huge dust cloud

(See the youtube user names, Fidockave213 & Sevethvial213.)

In late May 2013, Oklahoma had two EF-5 tornadoes, less than two weeks apart; one was a record 2.6 miles wide, then asteroid 1998 QE2, 1.7 miles across flew passed Earth during May 31— June 1, 2013. This one was large enough to end all life on Earth. June saw flooding on most continents, including North America. The flooding in Eastern Europe was described as the worst in 500 years. Then massive fires throughout the western U.S. during the summer, and many more disasters around the world.

Record winter storms, record heat of 112 degrees, record drought, record fires, month after month. All this wild weather is causing many people to ask, *"Are we in the Great Tribulation?"* Of course the answer that is always given is, *no, we cannot be in the GT because the Rapture has not taken place yet, and the 7-year peace treaty with Israel has not been signed yet.* Both of those will be proven wrong in the next chapters. So the answer to the question is, we are in the birth pains of the Earth, leading up to the Great Tribulation.

In addition to the blood moons, Mark Biltz also discovered that three eclipses of the sun were to take place three years in a row, all on the 1st of Av, 2008, 2009, and 2010. The month of Av has been a dark time for the Jewish people as many bad things happened to them in that month. It was during these years that we saw a huge jump in disasters in 2008 with 9, then 2009 had 6, 2010 only 3, but 2011 had 12, and 2012 had 11. With what has happened thus far in 2013, it will be another record year. So it appears that the disasters made a sudden increase starting in 2008.

The New Jersey Boardwalk that was mostly destroyed by hurricane Sandy, was rebuilt at a cost of eight million dollars, then destroyed by a fire in 2013.

The extreme events just keeps coming in 2013 and early 2014 with a severe drought in California, record setting cold in much of the U.S., floods, mud slides, fires. In Sept. 2013 Colorado had a "1000 year flood."

There is rarely a break between the disasters; they are hitting us one after the other. Some parts of the U.S. saw 40 degrees below zero, which was colder than the North Pole. Over 700,000 people were without electricity for days. The disasters are coming with such frequency I cannot keep track of the ones that are hitting the U.S., not to mention those happening around the world. Tornadoes in Japan, flooding in Mexico, typhoons, earthquakes; there is no end to it the disasters.

Chapter 4
The Chosen

(1) Who are the 144,000?

Revelation chapter 7 takes place after the opening of the 6th Seal, but before the opening of the 7th Seal that starts the Great Tribulation. The events of Rev. 7 take place just before the start of the GT:

> 1 After this I saw four angels standing at the four corners of the earth, holding back the four winds of the earth to prevent any wind from blowing on the land or on the sea or on any tree.
>
> 2 Then I saw another angel coming up from the east, having the seal of the living God. He called out in a loud voice to the four angels who had been given power to harm the land and the sea: 3 "Do not harm the land or the sea or the trees until we put a seal on the foreheads of the servants of our God." 4 Then I heard the number of those who were sealed: 144,000 from all the tribes of Israel.

The four winds represent natural disasters that will come upon the world during the GT. This also tells us that God will not allow any huge natural disasters until this point in time. It means that when a tsunami hits the east coast, then it must be the 2nd Trumpet of Rev. 8, because we are told here that no huge event will happen until the 144,00 are counted and sealed. Rev. 7 continues:

> 5 From the tribe of Judah 12,000 were sealed, from the tribe of Reuben 12,000, from the tribe of Gad 12,000, 6 from the tribe of Asher 12,000, from the tribe of Naphtali 12,000, from the tribe of

Manasseh 12,000, 7 from the tribe of Simeon 12,000, from the tribe of Levi 12,000, from the tribe of Issachar 12,000, 8 from the tribe of Zebulun 12,000, from the tribe of Joseph 12,000, from the tribe of Benjamin 12,000. (Rev. 7:1-8)

The first thing any student of Revelation should understand is that these 12 tribes are not Jews who will preach the Gospel during the GT or flee into the wilderness, which is the usual interpretation. That wrong interpretation results from taking this passage 100% literal face value. Remember what we learned about taking statements 100% literally? It is especially true of prophecy, and even more so of Revelation. Very little of Revelation can be taken literally, 98% of it is <u>not</u> to be understood literally. It has a literal interpretation, but is not directly literal. The lamb represents Christ, the white horse represents the Holy Spirit, are you getting the picture here? Only natural disasters should be taken as actually taking place, such as an earthquake because there is no way to discern a symbolic interpretation for an earthquake. And when it says that people are killed in the quake, then it is even more evidence that it should be taken literally.

So what would the 12 tribes represent, seen figuratively? Paul makes it clear that believing Gentiles have been given citizenship in Israel and are considered Abraham's offspring, so they must be included in Israel as well, spiritually speaking. But the Church is never directly identified as Israel in the Old Testament or the New Testament, with good reason; there would be great confusion about who the passage was talking about, the physical descendants or the spiritual descendants. <u>Here in Revelation, God is speaking symbolically, so it refers to the spiritual descendants.</u>

In Revelation 2, Jesus said, *"I know the slander of those who say they are Jews but are not, but are a synagogue of Satan"* (Rev. 2:9). This refers to nonbelieving Jews. To be a true Jew, you must be a spiritual Jew, by being on the tree of promise. Paul said the Jews who refused to believe in Christ were cut off the tree of promise and the believing Gentiles were grafted on; the Jews *"were broken off because of unbelief, and you stand by faith"* (Romans 11:20). All the branches on the tree of promise are

God's chosen people, not just the Jewish branches, and they all stand by faith. Being born Jews did not make them heirs to the promise; it has always been by faith, or rightness of heart. (Nevertheless, God is still fulfilling his promises to the physical descendants of Israel, which will be discussed shortly.)

The Gentiles that Paul addressed were Christians who were grafted onto the tree of promise, thus making them part of the elect. There is a passage that makes a clear distinction between all groups and calls the collective church of Jews and Gentiles *the chosen people*:

> Here there is no Greek or Jew, circumcised or uncircumcised, barbarian, Scythian, slave or free, but Christ is all, and is in all. Therefore, as God's chosen people, holy and dearly loved ... (Colossians 3:11-12)

Paul also said that Gentiles are *"heirs together with Israel, members together of one body"* (Ephesians 3:6). Paul does not say that the Gentiles have become literal Israelites, but merely that Gentiles now share in all the promises made to the believing Israelites; they are *"together in the promise in Christ Jesus"* (Ibid). Together, the Gentile Christians and Jewish Christians form one body of God's elect. This is not replacement theology, physical Israel is not replaced by the Church. Paul said we are all the *"chosen people,"* therefore we are.

Both the Old and New Testaments say that just being a physical offspring of Abraham does not make you acceptable to God. The true offspring of Abraham, Isaac, and Jacob are those of the promise who are the spiritual offspring, because they believe and follow God. Therefore, spiritual Israel has always been only those who genuinely believe and follow God.

This is also seen in Rev.12, which describes a woman who gives birth to Christ, and represents believing Israel; later it says, *"Then the dragon was enraged at the woman and went off to make war with the rest of her offspring-- those who obey God's commandments and hold to the testimony of Jesus"* (v.17). So the Dragon makes war against Christians, both Jewish and Gentile

Christians. If the woman was physical Israel, then the Dragon would only persecute Christian Jews, but that is not the case.

Since Jewish and Gentile believers are together called the Chosen people, unbelieving Israelites cannot be above them in choosiness. All true Christians are God's elect. Unbelieving Jews can be grafted back onto the tree if they believe in Christ, but until then they are not the "elect" of God, though they are physically Israelites.

So the 12 tribes here in Revelation 7 represent God's elect; in other words, all Christianity. Then who are the 12,000 chosen out of the entire body of Christ? The Bride, which will be proven in the remainder of this chapter.

If the passage should be taken literally, then it would still not refer to 144,000 Jews, because the Jews are only the southern tribes of Israel, the northern tribes were taken away captive by Assyria and never returned. Therefore, it would have to include all the lost tribes; most do not even know they are Israelites.

(2) The Bride of Christ

In Revelation 21, the Bride of Christ is depicted symbolically as a physical city, the New Jerusalem. This tells us that the 144,000 is a symbolic number. The Bride of Christ is not a real woman who will marry Jesus, but is symbolism referring to the Christians who will be in the Rapture. Contrary to popular doctrine, the Bride of Christ is not the Church, the whole body of believers; the Bride is chosen out of the Church.

The city has 12 foundations with the names of the 12 apostles on them, but the gates have the names of the 12 tribes of Israel:

> 9 One of the seven angels who had the seven bowls full of the seven last plagues came and said to me, "Come, I will show you the bride, the wife of the Lamb." 10 And he carried me away in the Spirit to a mountain great and high, and showed me the Holy City, Jerusalem, coming down out of heaven from God. 11 It shone with the glory of God, and its brilliance was like that of a very precious jewel, like a jasper, clear as crystal. 12 It had a great, high wall with twelve gates, and with twelve angels at the gates. On the gates were written the names of the twelve tribes of Israel.

13 There were three gates on the east, three on the north, three on the south and three on the west.14 The wall of the city had twelve foundations, and on them were the names of the twelve apostles of the Lamb.15 The angel who talked with me had a measuring rod of gold to measure the city, its gates and its walls. 16 The city was laid out like a square, as long as it was wide. He measured the city with the rod and found it to be 12,000 stadia b in length, and as wide and high as it is long. 17 He measured its wall and it was 144 cubits thick, by human measurement, which the angel was using.

18 The wall was made of jasper, and the city of pure gold, as pure as glass. 19 The foundations of the city walls were decorated with every kind of precious stone. The first foundation was jasper, the second sapphire, the third agate, the fourth emerald, 20 the fifth onyx, the sixth ruby, the seventh chrysolite, the eighth beryl, the ninth topaz, the tenth turquoise, the eleventh jacinth, and the twelfth amethyst. 21 The twelve gates were twelve pearls, each gate made of a single pearl. The great street of the city was of gold, as pure as transparent glass. (Rev. 21:9-21)

There are several reasons why this cannot be a literal city. For example, the city is so tall that it would stick up through the stratosphere where there is no oxygen and the temperature is below freezing.

The city has 12 foundations with the names of the 12 Apostles. This tells us that you must first be a Christian to enter the city; that is, to be part of the Bride of Christ (Eph. 2:20). And since you must pass through the gates to enter the city, it means you also become a spiritual Israelite.

Contrary to popular belief, just being a Christian does not qualify you to be in the Rapture; but only those who actually live according to the teachings of Christ. Sinful Christians might go to heaven when they die, but they will not be in the Rapture.

This is seen clearly in the letters to the 7 churches in Revelation 2-3. Jesus told one church that unless they repent they will be cast into tribulation ten days, which could be a threat to miss the Rapture, because the Days of Awe lasts for ten days (see chapter 1).

But Jesus promised deliverance from tribulation only to the

church at Philadelphia because they kept his Word and did not deny him (3:8-10). All the seven churches of Revelation exist today throughout the world. How could anyone reading the condemnations of those churches believe that they would go in the Rapture? Nonsense! Some of them might go to heaven if they die, but going in the Rapture is something completely different.

Therefore, the 12-tribes here in Revelation 7 symbolically represent the whole body of believers, the Church. The 144,000 are all those who are spiritually ready to be in the Rapture, to be the Bride of Christ. There is a very important symbolic connection between this city and the 144,000 chosen from the 12 tribes in Rev. 7.

(3) Symbolic Number

Each literal tribe most certainly contains a different population; some will have a large population, some will have a smaller population, so how could there be exactly 12,000 from each tribe who are chosen? A large tribe will have a larger number of righteous than a small tribe. So, the number of those who will be chosen could not be exactly 12,000 from each literal tribe.

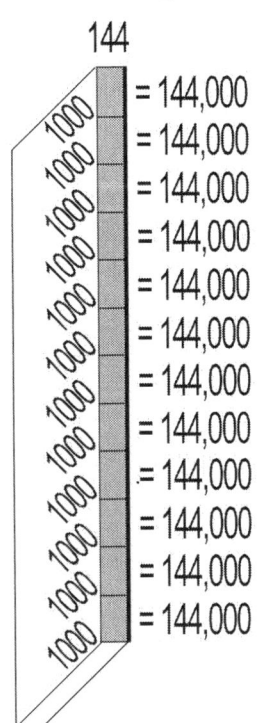

Therefore, this number must be symbolic, which is confirmed in Revelation 21 in the description of the New Jerusalem that has walls that are 144 cubits thick and 12,000 stadia (furlongs) in length; so every 1,000 stadia of wall equals 144,000 (1,000 x 144) x 4 sides. So you cannot figure up how many people will be in the Rapture, it is merely telling us that the number will be many millions.

The actual number of those who will be numbered among the 144,000 will likely be several hundred million, perhaps even a billion. There are more than 2 billion people who claim to be Christian today, but we know that most are not spiritually ready for the Rapture. But the Rapture includes many of those who have lived and died during the past 6,000 years.

(4) Firstfruits
In Revelation 14, the 144,000 are called "firstfruits":

> And they sang a new song before the throne and before the four living creatures and the elders. No one could learn the song except the 144,000 who had been redeemed from the earth. 4 These are those who did not defile themselves with women, for they kept themselves pure. They follow the Lamb wherever he goes. They were purchased from among men and offered as firstfruits to God and the Lamb. (14:3-4)

In the Old Testament, the Firstfruits was an offering to God from the increase of all the land. The harvest could not begin until the Firstfruits offering was given. A small portion of the ripe grain was selected and presented by the priest as an offering. The Firstfruits was not the total harvest, but was to be the choicest portions. Therefore, the Firstfruits represents those in the Bride.

All the professing Christians who have ever lived are the total harvest. The reference to the 144,000 being virgins is a figurative way to show that these are among the most righteous. They are not greedy for money like Christians of Laodicea. Only those who keep God's Word will be in the 144,000. Only this group will be in the Rapture because only this group follows the Lamb wherever he goes. Only this group fully live by the teaching of Jesus.

Therefore, this passage in Revelation 7 means that just before the start of the GT, those whose spiritual condition is right with God will be counted and sealed, "*Do not harm the land or the sea or the trees until we put a seal on the foreheads of the servants of our God*" (Rev. 7:3). The counting represents being chosen to be in the Bride of Christ; the sealing represents divine protection from God's judgments during the Great Tribulation. As we will see in another chapter, the Rapture will not take place until the 7th Trumpet is ready to sound.

The Greek for "servant" in Rev. 7:3 is *doulos*, and means "*bond-servant*," or "bondman." This indicates that the 144,000 are people who are dedicated to serving God. This means their primary concern in this life is doing the will of God. Many Christians are caught up in the things of the world, and they have let their relationship with Christ grow stale, as seen in the letters to the 7 churches. Sadly, a large number of church-going Christians lie, cheat, slander, are hot-tempered, or perhaps they are greedy, or suffer from many other sins. So just being a Christian is not enough to make the Rapture. Catholics and Protestants in Northern Ireland have bombed and murdered each other, so there is more to being a Christian than believing that Jesus Christ is the Son of God and attending church services.

The reason that only those who are ready at the start of the GT will be in the Rapture is because even murderers might repent during the tribulation, and many people will repent because of the events that take place during the GT. Only those who will live right and are serious about God before things get difficult, will be in the Rapture.

Jesus spoke about the future state of the righteous when he said:

> "those who are considered worthy of taking part in that age and in the resurrection from the dead will neither marry nor be given in marriage, and they can no longer die. . ." (Luke 20:35-36)

This indicates that the Rapture will contain a limited number, "*those who are considered worthy.*" He did not say, *those who will believe in me*, but those who *are worthy*, this suggests a special section beyond the average believer. The selection and sealing of those who will be in the Rapture will take place before the start of the GT, which means that the Church will be judged at this time. Judgment begins with Christians (1 Peter 4:17).

Once the GT starts, many of the 144,000 will probably be out preaching and compelling people to get saved because they know that there are only a few years left, and since they are going to become immortal, it does not matter if they are killed. So the Gospel will indeed get preached to the ends of the Earth during the GT. The events of the GT will also cause many people to fill churches, so there will be a great revival during the GT. The idea that 144,000 Jews are going to preach the Gospel around the world after all the Christians have been removed in a pretribulation Rapture is nonsense. The Bible says no one can come to Christ unless the Holy Spirit draws them, and yet we are supposed to believe that people will be saved during the GT after the Holy Spirit has been removed from the planet. You cannot be born-again by the Holy Spirit if the Holy Spirit is not here. More nonsense!

At the start of the Great Tribulation, before any disaster hits, God will speak to each of the 144,000 and tell them where to go and what to do in order to be safe from the disasters, and for their families also. This is how God will protect us from the judgments during the GT. God may say, *"Pack up and move to such-and-such city."* Rick Joyner and Henry Gruver have both said that God said there are seven cities of refuge in the U.S. In these cities Christians will be safe from persecution, natural disasters, and WW3. I am sure that there will be many more places where a family may live, but as far as a large number of Christians being safe, I cannot say that many places in the United States will be totally safe during the GT, because not only will there be World War 3 and nuclear war, but possibly also a civil war.

After the description of the 144,000 in Rev. 7, the angel shows John another group of people, an uncountable multitude.

(5) The Last Great Awakening

This next group that John sees are clearly Christians, but they are not called servants. The 144,000 are the only ones that *"follow the Lamb wherever he goes"* (Rev. 14:4):

> After this I looked and there before me was a great multitude that no one could count, from every nation, tribe, people and language, standing before the throne and in front of the Lamb. They were wearing white robes and were holding palm branches in their hands. 10 And they cried out in a loud voice: "Salvation belongs to our God, who sits on the throne, and to the Lamb."

11 All the angels were standing around the throne and around the elders and the four living creatures. They fell down on their faces before the throne and worshiped God, 12 saying: "Amen! Praise and glory and wisdom and thanks and honor and power and strength be to our God for ever and ever. Amen!" 13 Then one of the elders asked me, "These in white robes--who are they, and where did they come from?" 14 I answered, "Sir, you know." And he said, "These are they who have come out of the great tribulation; they have washed their robes and made them white in the blood of the Lamb.

15 Therefore, "they are before the throne of God and serve him day and night in his temple; and he who sits on the throne will spread his tent over them. 16 Never again will they hunger; never again will they thirst. The sun will not beat upon them, nor any scorching heat. 17 For the Lamb at the center of the throne will be their shepherd; he will lead them to springs of living water. And God will wipe away every tear from their eyes." (Rev. 7:9-17)

Since this group is an uncountable number that will come out of the GT, then they are not the same group as the 144,000. Notice that they have "*washed their robes and made them white.*" This indicates that they are converts, and the wording suggests that they become after the 144,000 are sealed. This group also includes many people who now claim to be Christians, but after the start of the GT they will get serious with God and repent.

When things are going well and people are prosperous, most people feel no need for God, but when times get hard they want to pray and get right with God. This is why there will be a great revival during the Great Tribulation. By the end of the GT there will be very few people who are lukewarm. Getting people to repent is also the reason why God will send the Great Tribulation. God wants people to repent before he sends the Day of Judgment.

The GT will be the greatest hour for Christianity; more miracles and more converts will take place than in the past 2,000 years of Christian history. And yet, the pretrib Rapture theory teaches that the entire Church will be removed before the GT will begin.

The words "great tribulation" only appear in the Bible three times, once in Matthew 24, once in Rev. 2:22, and once here. In this book, I use the term in the classic sense, of several years of global suffering, but it is very possible that the term only refers to the 10 days between the Feast of Trumpets and the Day of Judgment, as mentioned previously. If so, it means that this group will go through those 10 days, which means they will miss the Rapture. Although the scene described appears to take place in heaven, unless you believe that Jesus will be ruling Earth from heaven after his return, then it is here on Earth.

(6) Conclusion

If you want to be counted among the 144,000, you should seek after things that are heavenly, and live a moral life; feed the poor, clothe the naked, and cultivate a personal relationship with God by reading the Bible and praying every day.

We were told the 144,000 are sealed before the four "winds" can blow and harm Earth. The four winds are never actually mentioned again, but they are apparently natural disasters and therefore are most likely the first four Trumpets in Rev. 8, which are all natural disasters. And since the 144,000 are sealed before those events begin, it is safe to assume that the 144,000 are here on Earth during those events. And since they are the Firstfruits, then there is no pretribulation Rapture.

Those who are part of the great multitude who will come out of the GT suffered hunger, thirst, and heat. So we can safely conclude that the GT will include famine and drought, but the worst of it will be the final few months. It is also safe to conclude that God will not perform great miracles to keep the great multitude from this suffering. Though I am sure that some miracles will happen for the great multitude, it will not be as much as the Firstfruits.

Regardless of your belief in the timing of the Rapture, this teaching that says the only people who will go in the Rapture are those who are judged righteous before the start of the Great Tribulation, is a huge change from the teaching that all Christians will go in the Rapture. But I am not the only one who has ever taught this doctrine; my mother was taught it by her parents, so I don't know where it originated.

(7) Additional Evidence

This section contains additional evidence to support my claim that not all Christians will go in the Rapture, but only the truly righteous. I added this three months after this book was originally published, because I did not previously realize that these other passages also support this idea.

In Matthew 25 Jesus gives us a parable of ten virgins, which is familiar to most Christians. In it, the cry goes out that the Bridegroom approaches, they all wakeup and five discover that their lamps had gone out. The five foolish virgins are the Christians who have let their relationship with God grow cold, they are not spiritually ready for the Rapture. The five foolish virgins go off to get oil while the five wise, who have plenty of oil for their lamps, travel with the Bridegroom through the night (the journey through the Great Tribulation) to the wedding banquet, which is the Rapture at the end of the GT.

While the five wise are traveling with the Bridegroom, the five foolish virgins are able to get oil; which means they repent and get full of the Holy Spirit, and they also arrive at the wedding banquet and want to go in the Rapture, but they will not be allowed to take part in the Rapture. They must remain outside, in the world, which means they will be the ones who must remain alive on this earth so that the human race will continue.

The next passage is found in the letters to the seven churches. To the church at Sardis, Jesus said, "*I know your deeds; you have a reputation of being alive, but you are dead*" (Rev. 3:1). Jesus goes on to say that the majority of those at Sardis are not going in the Rapture. He did not say, unless they repent they will not walk with him dressed in white, no. He said unless they repent they will be killed in the Wrath of God:

> But if you do not wake up, I will come like a thief, and you will not know at what time I will come to you. (Rev. 3:3)

The symbolism of Christ coming as a thief refers directly to his coming to destroy the world at the Wrath of God that takes place shortly after the Rapture. So it is as if the judgment of all the seven churches here in Revelation, by Christ, takes place at the same time as the numbering of the 144,000. He appears to be saying that the people of Sardis have already been judged to miss the Rapture, and so they need to repent in order to survive the Wrath of God. The next verse proves it:

> Yet you have a few people in Sardis who have not soiled their clothes. They will walk with me, dressed in white, for they are worthy. (Rev. 3:4)

Jesus here is saying that a few people at Sardis have been judged and found righteous, these righteous will walk with Christ dressed in white, which means they will go in the Rapture. So in this passage in Rev. 3, we have two groups of Christians: one group will be with Christ, dressed in white, the second group needs to repent or they will be killed when Christ comes in judgment. This is exactly what I have been teaching in this chapter.

There are probably other passages that also support my claim, but since I don't have a photographic memory, I cannot just call up any passage and realize that it agrees.

88

Chapter 5
Daniel's 70 Weeks

(1) Daniel 9:25-26

Daniel must be included to disprove any thought that the Antichrist comes to power by bringing world peace; it is a total fiction. This passage also reveals important information about when the Jews will convert to Christianity, and it's not when you may think.

This section contains a detailed analysis of some of the deeper issues within the study of Daniel's prophecies, but it's written as clearly and understandably as possible so that even those who are not familiar with this information can understand it. I will piece together some clues to find out what this passage in Daniel actually means. There is a lot of information that can be expounded upon in Daniel 9, but I will deal only with the main points that relate to the end times, especially Daniel's 70th week.

The angel Gabriel gave Daniel a timeframe of God's unfolding plan for the Jews, but includes some surprising information about the New Covenant. Within this timeframe are three separate periods that add up to 490 years:

> 24 "Seventy `sevens' are decreed for your people and your holy city to finish transgression, to put an end to sin, to atone for wickedness, to bring in everlasting righteousness, to seal up vision and prophecy and to anoint the most holy.
>
> 25 "Know and understand this: From the issuing of the decree to restore and rebuild Jerusalem until the Anointed One, the ruler, comes, there will be seven `sevens,' and sixty-two `sevens.' It will be rebuilt with streets and a trench, but in times of trouble. (Daniel 9:24-25)

Other translations of this passage say "weeks" rather than "sevens." This refers to weeks of years. So one week of years is seven years; (70x7)= 490 years. When those years are completed, the Jews must, and will, have completed the prophesied events.

These seventy 7-year periods are divided into three segments. The period of 7 weeks of years (7 x 7 = 49) and 62 weeks of years (62 x 7 = 434), for a total of 483 years, have already come and gone. These years are biblical years. A biblical year is 12 months of 30 days each, or 360 days. So, 3.5 biblical years = 1,260 days.

Many Bible scholars believe the final 7 years are not accounted for and will be the 7 years prior to the return of Christ, which is the reason they believe the Great Tribulation will last for 7 years. But there is Scriptural evidence that Daniel's 70th week is already one-half completed, which means there remains for the Jews 1,260 days to complete the requirements of the prophecy. And I am not the only one who believes this. Daniel 9 continues:

> "Know and understand this: From the issuing of the decree to re-store and rebuild Jerusalem until the Anointed One, the ruler, comes, there will be seven 'sevens,' and sixty-two 'sevens.' (v25)

At the end of 483 years, *"the Anointed One, the ruler, comes."* The "comes" requires that it refer to the start of Christ's ministry, not the end at the crucifixion. This is an important point which is usually overlooked. Since he began his ministry at this point, then his 3.5 year ministry is the first half of the final 70th week. Daniel 9 continues:

> 26 After the sixty-two 'sevens,' the Anointed One will be cut off and will have nothing. . . . (Daniel 9:26)

It was 483 years to the start of Christ's ministry, and some time "after" that, he was "cut-off" that is, crucified. It does not say Messiah will be cut-off at the end of the 69th week, but after the end of the 69th week. He was cut off 3.5 years after the 69th week, or in the middle of the 70th week as we will see shortly. Verse 26 continues:

> The people of <u>the ruler who will come</u> will destroy the city and the sanctuary. The end will come like a flood: War will continue until the end, and desolations have been decreed. (Daniel 9:26)

The *"ruler who will come"* is not Jesus, although the wording would lead one to that assumption. The people of a future ruler will destroy Jerusalem and the Temple. This must refer to the Romans who destroyed Jerusalem and the Temple in 70 A.D., which means the <u>ruler</u> is Titus and the <u>people</u> of the ruler were the Roman troops under his command. The desolations that were decreed included the scattering of the Jews into other nations because of their rebellion against Rome and God. This scattering is called the Diaspora, or dispersion.

(2) Daniel 9:27

In the above verse 26, reference is made to two different people. The first sentence refers to Jesus, the Anointed One; the second and third sentences to the "ruler" of the Romans and his troops. Likewise, verse 27 also refers first to the Messiah, then the Antichrist:

> 27 <u>He</u> will <u>confirm a covenant</u> with <u>many</u> for one 'seven.' <u>In the middle</u> of the 'seven' he will put an end to sacrifice and offering. . .

The pretribulational view of Daniel 9:27 is that it refers to the Antichrist making a 7-year agreement with Israel, then breaking it in the middle and stopping the Jewish sacrifice in the Temple that is expected to be rebuilt. Only a few Bible interpreters believe that it refers to Jesus instituting the New Covenant and bringing an end to Old Covenant sacrifice and offering; but there is strong evidence for this view.

The covenant will be with "many," but the Jews in Israel are <u>not</u> large in number. According to the *Zondervan NIV Bible Commentary*, the original text *"indicates 'the many' rather than 'many'"* (V.1, p.1389). The NAS translation says *"the many."* If it refers to the Jews, why didn't it just say so? But *"the many"* refers to a particular group that did not exist when Daniel was written.

Isaiah 53 describes Jesus with such well known passages as, *"he was pierced for our transgressions, he was crushed for our iniquities"* (53:5). That chapter goes on to say, *"my righteous servant will justify many . . . For he bore the sins of many"* (53:11-12). Jesus said he came to give his *"life as a ransom for many"* (Matt. 20:28); and *"This is my blood of the covenant, which is poured out for many for the forgiveness of sins"* (Mat. 26:28).

The book of Hebrews says, *"Christ was sacrificed once to take away the sins of many people"* (9:28). And Paul said:

> For just as through the disobedience of the one man the many were made sinners, so also through the obedience of the one man the many will be made righteous. (Rom. 5:19)

> . . . not seeking my own profit, but the profit of the many, that they may be saved. (1 Corinthians 10:33) (NAS)

Christ died for the sins of the whole world, even those who will never be saved, so the covenant with *"the many"* can only refer to those who will be included in the New Covenant.

The pretrib interpretation of Daniel 9 completely skips the Gospel Age by placing Daniel's 70th week after the end of the Gospel Age, that is, after the Rapture. But since Daniel's 70 weeks is the unfolding plan of God and includes *"bring*[ing] *in everlasting righteousness"* and sealing up prophecy, so it must include the Gospel Age. But how could the Gospel Age be within the 70 weeks? This is answered in the next few pages.

The NAS translation says, *"he will make a firm covenant."* Some Bible commentators want us to believe that the Antichrist will make a 7-year agreement with modern Israel and then break it in the middle. That does not sound like a firm covenant. The New Covenant is very firm because it is "everlasting" (Dan. 9:24).

More than one great Bible expositor believed it is Jesus who confirmed the covenant through his miracles and preaching, such as Albert Barnes, author of *Barnes Notes on The Bible*. He said of this passage:

. . . the last one week is again subdivided in such a way, that, while it is said that the whole work of the Messiah in confirming the covenant would occupy the entire week, yet that <u>he would be cut off in the middle of the week</u> . . .

The idea is that of giving strength, or stability; of making firm and sure. The Hebrew word here evidently <u>refers to the "covenant" which God is said to establish with his people</u> . . . to denote the laws and institutions of the true religion - <u>the laws which God has made for his church</u>; . . . <u>The more correct interpretation, therefore, is to refer it to the Messiah</u>, who is the principal subject of the prophecy . . .

The <u>ministry of the Saviour himself</u> was wholly among the Jews, and his work was what would, in their common language, be spoken of as <u>"confirming the covenant;"</u> . . .

Barnes also believed that this passage speaks about the end of the Old Covenant sacrifice and offering, which is why the Jews have not been able to rebuild their Temple. Jesus confirmed the covenant for 3.5 years, then he was crucified, which put an end to the Old Covenant sacrifice and offerings. The New Covenant is now in effect and is an everlasting covenant.

But the text says he will confirm the covenant for seven years; some commentators, like Barnes, believe the 70th week is continuous. But if the Apostles continued confirming the covenant for the last half of the 70th week, then everything mentioned in Daniel 9 would be accomplished, but it is not. The Jews must still *"anoint the Most Holy,"* which is their official acceptance of Jesus as their Messiah. It does not refer to the Holy Place in the Temple; some translations say *"Holy Place"* but they are adding the word "Place." It refers to Messiah, not a literal Temple.

The Keil & Delitzsch Commentary on this verse says:

Much older, more general, and also nearer the truth, is the explanation which refers these words to the anointing of the Messiah, an explanation which is established by various arguments. The translation of the lxx, καὶ εὐφράναι ἅγιον ἁγίων, and of Theod., τοῦ χρῖσαι ἅγιον ἁγίων, the meaning of which is controverted, is generally understood by the church Fathers as referring to the Messiah.

Theodoret sets it forth as undoubtedly correct, and as accepted even by the Jews; and the old Syriac translator has introduced into the text the words, "till the Messiah, the Most Holy."

Other events also must happen in order for all prophecy to become sealed up, or fulfilled. How could all prophecy be fulfilled when the book of Revelation had not been written yet? Not to mention the events of Daniel 7 which predict the final Antichrist. Since those prophecies have not been fulfilled, the remainder of the week cannot have been completed.

Even fewer commentators believe that the 70th week stopped with the crucifixion of Jesus and will continue with the final three and one-half years before the return of Christ, which is the Great Tribulation. *Halley's Bible Handbook* relates this point of view:

The date from which the 70 weeks was to be counted was the decree to re-build Jerusalem, v.25. There were three decrees issued by Persian kings for this purpose, (536 B.C., 457 B.C., 444 B.C., see under Ezra). The principal one of these was 457 B.C.

. . . This 483 years is the period between the decree to re-build Jerusalem and the coming of the "Anointed One" (v25). The decree to re-build Jerusalem, as noted above, was 457 B C. Adding 483 years to 457 B.C. brings us to A.D. 26, the very year that Jesus was baptized and began his public ministry. A most remarkable fulfillment of Daniel's prophecy, even to the year.

Further, within 3 1/2 years Jesus was crucified, that is, "in the midst of the one week" "the Anointed One" was "cut off," "purged away sin and brought in everlasting righteousness," (v24, 26, 27).

Thus Daniel foretold not only the Time at which the Messiah would appear, but also the Duration of his Public Ministry, and his Atoning Death for Human Sin.

Some think that God's chronology was suspended at the death of Christ, to remain so while Israel is scattered, and that the last half of the "one week" belongs to the time of the End. (4th Ed., 1995)

Both Barnes and Hailey likely consulted the Geneva Study Bible (GSB) of 1560, because it presents a similar view, that Christ came at the conclusion of the 69th week and confirmed the covenant for the first half of the 70th week:

. . . In this week of the seventy [the final week], will Christ come
and preach and suffer death.

Concerning *"he will put an end to sacrifice and offering"* the
GSB says, *"Christ accomplished this by his death and resurrection."* Whoever decided to abandon this sound hermeneutic and
make the passage refer to the Antichrist went way off the mark.
But they had to abandon the early view, otherwise they could not
preach their imminent pretribulation Rapture theory.

Since some of the events mentioned in Daniel 9 have not yet
happened, the last half of the week must still be future. Nowhere
in the book of Revelation does it say anything about a seven-year
period, but only three and one-half. This view puts the entire Gospel Age inside of Daniel's 70th week, except for an additional 75
days that will go beyond the 70th week, explained shortly.

Most Bible commentaries say that the Jews will be converted
at the return of Christ, but there is evidence in the Scriptures that a
fair number of them will be converted before the start of the Great
Tribulation. Sir Robert Anderson, in his book, *The Coming Prince*,
first published in 1889, discovered that God's time-clock stopped
anytime the Jews were not in a proper relationship with God.

In 1 Kings 6:1, it says Solomon began to build the temple in
the 480th year after the children of Israel came out of Egypt, which
does not appear to be accurate; but if you include all the years in
which Israel was under judgment, then it accurately adds up to 573
years. Robert Anderson added up the times when the Israelites
were enslaved to foreign powers: 8 years to the king of Mesopotamia, 18 years to Moab, 20 years to Canaan, 7 years to the Midianites, and 40 years to the Philistines; which equals 93. When you
add 93 to 480, it comes to the correct number of 573 years.

It is obvious, therefore, that the 480 years of the book of Kings
from the Exodus to the temple is a mystic era formed by eliminating every period during which the people were cast off by God.
(Chapter 7)

Mr. Anderson believed it means God's time-clock will begin

again when the Jews become a nation again, but the times when Israel were slaves did not refer to being away from the land, because being slaves to a foreign power did not require removal to another land, and did not always include removal. Only the Kings of Assyria and Babylon removed the Israelites.

When we apply the information that God's time-clock stops when the Jews are not in proper relationship with God, then this explains why there is a gap in Daniel's 70 weeks. God's time-clock stopped when the Jews rejected Messiah. Therefore, it means God's prophetic time-clock and the 70th week cannot begin again until a certain number of the Jews accept Messiah.

All of the Jews did not reject Messiah, only a certain number; likewise, a number will accept Messiah before the remainder of the week will begin. There are many Jews around the world who are accepting their Messiah, with hundreds of Messianic Jewish congregations in the U.S. and in Israel. There are already an estimated 1 million Messianic Jews in the world, with 200,000 in the U.S. and 20,000 in Israel. But there will remain a large number who will not accept Messiah until shortly before his return.

It should also be noted that Jesus actually said he will not return until they convert; "*you will not see me again until you say, 'Blessed is he who comes in the name of the Lord*'" (Matt. 23:39). This means they will not see Christ until they convert. The common belief is that they will not convert until they see Christ; this is the exact opposite of what Christ literally said. This is also seen in a prophecy by Hosea:

> I will go back to my place until they admit their guilt. And they will seek my face; in their misery they will earnestly seek me." (Hosea 5:15)

When Peter preached to the Jews in the book of Acts, he said that they will need to convert before Christ will return:

> Repent, then, and turn to God, so that your sins may be wiped out, . . . 20 and that he may send the Messiah, who has been appointed for you— even Jesus. (Acts 3:19-20)

I don't see how anyone can teach that the Jews will not convert until Christ returns with such clear passages as this, that say the exact opposite.

Similarly, Paul said when the Jews convert, it will result in the resurrection of the dead, *"For if their rejection is the reconciliation of the world, what will their acceptance be but life from the dead?"* (Romans 11:15). So the Rapture cannot happen before they convert. More proof against the pretrib theory.

In addition, Paul said that Israel will be blind to the truth *"until the full number of the Gentiles has come in"* (Rom. 11:25). This means that when the full number of Gentiles accepts Christ, then all Israel will be saved. But the pretrib theory says the Rapture will take place 7 years before Israel is saved. No, the Church must be here on Earth at the time the Jews convert.

Even Daniel 9 tells us that they must accept Messiah during the 70 weeks, that is, before the 70 weeks can be finished: *"to put an end to sin . . . to anoint the most holy."* There is no possible way that they can do that after the 70 weeks. All things mentioned in the text must take place before the end of the 70 weeks. Therefore, the Jews in Israel must convert during the final half of the 70th week before Messiah returns.

A footnote in Mr. Anderson's book says, *"The servitude of Judges 10:7, 9 affected only the tribes beyond Jordan, and did not suspend Israel's national position."* This means that all of the Jews do not have to convert, only a large number living in the land of Israel. It only takes a certain number, not the entire population, for them to become in right relationship as a nation again. Plus, there will still be millions of Jews around the world who may not convert until they see Christ split the sky at the Rapture.

This passage of Daniel totally destroys the pretrib Rapture theory and the teaching that there will be a tribulation Temple. The Jews will never rebuild the Temple, and they will not accept the Antichrist as Messiah! That is total nonsense. The Abomination of Desolation is explained in the another chapter, as well as evidence against a tribulation Temple.

John Wesley, the founder of the Methodist church, wrote about Daniel 9:27 before the modern theories about it were developed:

> Christ confirmed the new covenant by the testimony of angels, of John the Baptist, of the wise men, of the saints then living, of Moses and Elias. By his preaching, by signs and wonders, by his holy life, by his resurrection and ascension. By his death and blood shedding. *Shall cause the sacrifice to cease*-- All the Jewish rites, and Levetical worship. By his death he abrogated, and put an end to this laborious service forever. (John Wesley's *Notes on the Bible*)

All the above is powerful evidence that the crucifixion of Christ ended the sacrifice and offering in the middle of the final week. Jesus established the covenant with preaching and miracles. Since Jesus is said to confirm the covenant for 7 years, but his ministry only lasted 3.5 years, it means that the final 3.5 years will be confirmed by one, or likely many, Christians who will be able to perform the same miracles that Jesus performed, as if Jesus were here in person.

(3) The 1,290 Days

John Wesley, John Calvin, and the Geneva Study Bible also agree with my interpretation of the 1,290 days in Daniel 12 because it is related to Daniel 9:27 and refers to the last half of the final seven years:

> "And from the time that the regular sacrifice is abolished, and the abomination of desolation is set up, there will be 1,290 days. How blessed is he who keeps waiting and attains to the 1,335 days!" (Daniel 12:11-12) (NAS)

The abomination is supposedly when the Old Covenant sacrifice is stopped by the Antichrist in the middle of the GT and an image is set up in the Temple. But Daniel 12 tells us that stopping the sacrifice is a totally separate event from the abomination. The passage says that the sacrifice is abolished, then 1,290 days will pass, and then the abomination will take place. So the abomination does not take place in the middle of a seven-year tribulation, but 1,290 days later, so it is not the stopping of the sacrifice.

The NAS version says, *"the regular sacrifice is abolished."* The NIV says *"the daily sacrifice is abolished."* Young's Literal says the *"perpetual sacrifice."* The meaning of the Hebrew word (8548) (tamiyd), translated "regular," "daily," and "perpetual" refers to something that continues for an extended period of time. This refers to the Old Covenant.

The word "sacrifice" is not in the original Hebrew text; it was added for clarification, even by *Young's Literal Translation*. It is *assumed* that it refers to the sacrifice. The LXXE words it this way: *"And from the time of the removal of the perpetual sacrifice"*. The *Jewish Publication Society* version says, *"the continual burnt-offering shall be taken away"*. But since it does not contain the word "sacrifice," and refers to the covenant, it should read, *"the perpetual covenant is abolished."*

And the perpetual, continual, (covenant) is not just stopped, it is "abolished." This again speaks of the original Old Covenant, not the actual sacrifice, although it is included. The Hebrew for *"taken away"* in the KJV, and "abolished" in the NIV, is (5493) (sur), and means to end permanently, not temporarily, thus "abolish" is the better word. Strong's says: *"A primitive root; to turn off (literally or figuratively). . ."* Brown-Driver-Brigg says, *"to turn aside, depart . . . to be removed . . . to come to an end . . . to put aside, leave undone, retract, reject, abolish . . ."*

This passage does not refer to merely stopping the Old Covenant sacrifice temporarily by the order of a mere man, the Antichrist, but to eliminating it forever, which Christ did by his death on the cross. The Antichrist can merely stop it, he cannot put an end to it forever.

So it is now evident how this passage refers to the last half of Daniel's 70th week. The reader now can see that Daniel 9:27 refers to the first half of Daniel's 70th week, and Daniel 12:11-12 refers to the second half.

The 42-month rule of the beast does not end until after the 1,290 days. Those who reach the 1,335th day are blessed because they will have survived World War 3 and the Wrath of God. The Wrath of God will end before the 1,335th day, but the world will not yet be totally safe. God will have to cleanse the air and water which will not be completed until the 1,335th day.

Since the last half of Daniel's 70th week is only 1,260 days long, how do we get 1,290 and 1,335? The reason is the GT lasts longer than 1,260 days. It is at the 1,260 day point that the Jews will accept Messiah and complete everything mentioned in the Daniel 9 prophecy.

In the book of Revelation, the 42-month rule of the beast will not begin at the same point as the final 3.5 years of Daniel. They are separate timelines. Likewise, the 1,260 days mentioned in Revelation is not the last half of Daniel's 70th week, but is the last 3.5 years of the Gospel Age. Daniel's 70 weeks only refers to the Jews, except the final week that includes the New Covenant.

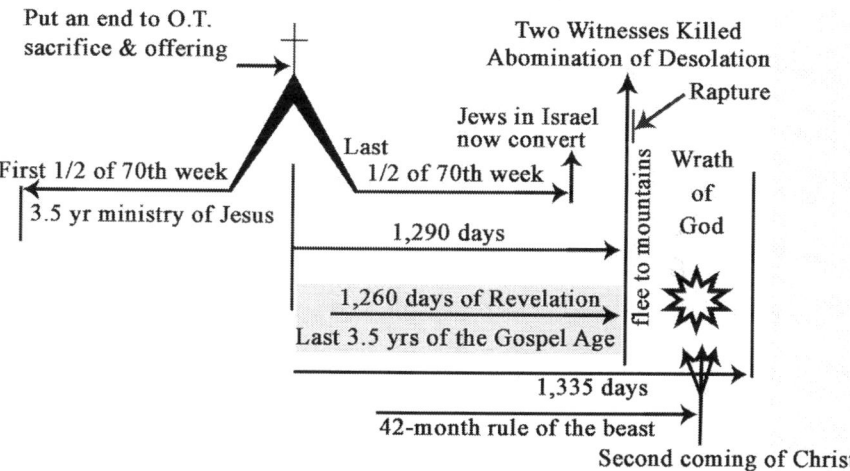

Since this may not be clear to you, I will explain it farther. The last half of Daniel's 70th week comes to an end when they accept Messiah, but the Gospel Age does not end for another 30 days, which brings us to 1,290 days, which is when the Abomination of Desolation takes place and marks the end of the Gospel Age (more proof of this is given in a later chapter). The 1,260 days in Revelation is the last 3.5 years of the Gospel Age, not the last half of the 70th week. So the 1,260 days do not end until the 1,290-day point of Daniel 12. The timeline Daniel 12 continues until the completion of the Wrath of God.

Some people believe that the days in Daniel 12 actually refer to years because the weeks of Daniel 9 refer to years, but they do not. There is no event that took place 1,290 years after the crucifixion of Christ within Jewish or Christian history that qualifies as the final Abomination of Desolation. The same applies to the 1,260 days and 1,335 days; these days must refer to the final half of Daniel's 70th week. The context also shows that these days refer to the final events of the age, because Daniel 12 refers to the GT and the Rapture.

How does the above information destroy the pretrib / imminent return theory? It shows that thousands of Jews in Israel must convert before the last half of Daniel's 70th week can begin. So if they have not yet converted, the final years of Jesus's confirming the covenant cannot take place.

The last half of Daniel 9:27 and the Abomination of Desolation will be discussed later.

(4) Conclusion

We have learned in this chapter that there is no such thing as a 7-year peace treaty. It is this wrong interpretation that has caused people to believe the GT will last for 7 years. Daniel's 70th week refers to Jesus confirming the New Covenant, which will continue for another 3.5 years, which is just the last 3.5 years of the Gospel Age. We will learn shortly that the GT will likely last 4-5 years.

Most modern Bible commentaries say that the Jews will convert at the return of Christ, except for the 144,000 who will be converted not too far into the GT so they can preach the Gospel around the world; both beliefs have been proven wrong. But what about the verses that seem to indicate that the Jews will convert at the return of Christ? Most of the Jews in Israel will convert before the return of Christ, but there will be some Jews around the world that will not convert until they see him return.

Chapter 6
The Great Tribulation

(1) What is The Great Tribulation

The word "tribulation" in Greek is *thlipsis* and *"primarily means a pressing, pressure, anything which burdens the spirit"* (VED). The KJV most often translates it affliction or tribulation, but other translations also use distress, misery, suffering, sorrow, or trouble. A good indication of its meaning is how it is used in the New Testament:

> Religion . . . is . . . to look after orphans and widows in their <u>distress.</u> (James 1:27)

The word is used with the same meaning in several verses, but an especially illuminating one says, *"When <u>trouble</u> or persecution comes because of the word, they quickly fall away"* (Mark 4:17). So tribulation and persecution are not the same. This word does not typically refer to persecution, but to the trials and difficulties anyone could face in this life. Jesus also said, *"In this world <u>you will have trouble</u> [thlipsis]. But take heart! I have overcome the world"* (John 16:33).

Every single day of this life, many people go through great tribulation. What could be worse than losing your family in a house fire along with everything you own, and you get burned? It happens to many people as a regular part of this life. People suffer from floods, tornadoes, and car wrecks. They may become paralyzed from the neck down in a sporting accident or their child overdoses on drugs-- all of these things are great tribulations!

Do you think an Antichrist could be worse than Hitler who burned and gassed millions of Jews and Christians? Thousands of prisoners of war were tortured and starved. Then Stalin and Lenin murdered tens of millions. Or what about the Cambodian holocaust in the 1970s and 80s? What about the millions who died from starvation in Ethiopia in the 1980s including Christians; where was the Rapture for all these people? Could anything be worse than these things? Nothing could be worse for the people involved.

The only thing that will make the GT the greatest tribulation in the history of the world is that billions of people throughout the planet will be experiencing the famine, natural disasters, distress, and warfare. God has never promised Christians that they will be totally protected from tribulation (thlipsis); in fact he said we WILL have tribulation. No one has ever seen flood waters standing up around a Christian's house. It floods on the just and the unjust.

The Christians who think that God has special blessings for them, to make them prosperous and successful, will suffer the most during the GT; because they will do nothing to prepare for the coming hardships, and they are expecting God to give them a great life now.

What about the beast of Rev. 13? Christians are not new to persecution. What makes the Christians in America think they are above persecution? Many millions of Christians have died and are still dying for their faith in Christ. The GT will continue this persecution against Christians, but on a larger scale.

(2) Time of Testing

According to a statement Jesus made, there will be Christians who will not have to suffer during the tribulation. Jesus said:

> "Since you have kept my command to endure patiently, I will also keep you from the hour of trial that is going to come upon the whole world to test those who live on the earth." (Rev. 3:10)

The Greek for "trial" is (peirasmos) (3986), and means, *"Trial, temptation, a putting to the test . . . for the purpose of proving someone, never for the purpose of causing him to fall*" (CWD). This calls the GT a time of testing. This is the same Greek word found in 2 Peter 2:9, "*the Lord knows how to rescue godly men from* [ek] *trials* [peirasmos] *and to hold the unrighteous for the day of judgment.*"

Those who support the pretrib Rapture believe the verse refers to being taken out of the world before the tribulation begins, because the Greek for "from" means "*out of.*" According to Robert Van Kampen in *The Rapture Question Answered*, the Greek *ek* (1537) does not mean "*out of*" in the sense of being outside of a circle, but "*out of the midst of*" which means that it comes out from inside of a circle. The *Complete Word Study Dictionary* says:

> If something is in something else, then the separation from it is expressed with ek, out of, while if it is near it, on it, with it, then apo [(575)] is used.

This means the Christians who are referenced in Rev. 3:10 are delivered while yet in the GT. The same word, *ek*, is found in Rev. 7:14, "*These are they who have come out of the great tribulation.*" These clearly go through the GT, therefore, those in Rev. 3:10 don't have to be Raptured to also be "*out of*" the GT.

Finally, an important word that pretrib proponents skip over, is "keep," which is (tēreō) (5083), and means to keep a close watch over, or guard. So, "*keep you from*" means Jesus will protect the righteous during the GT, and see them all the way through it. God protected the Hebrews from the effects of the ten plagues of Egypt, therefore, he will protect us because Jesus is our Passover lamb, but only if you are included in the Bride of Christ.

As Jesus reveals, the GT is the time of testing for the world, during which it will be revealed whether a society is built using wood and straw (worthless beliefs that result in sin and an unjust society), or whether it is built using stones and metal (right beliefs and laws resulting in proper lives and a just, moral society) (1 Cor. 3:12). This also applies to churches and individuals; all things in this world will be tested. William Barclay states:

God is the great saviour, the great deliverer of his people. And the deliverance which he gives is not the deliverance of escape but the deliverance of conquest. It is not a deliverance which saves a man from trouble but one which brings him triumphantly through trouble. It does not make life easy, but it makes life great. It is not part of the Christian hope to look for a life in which a man is saved from all trouble and distress; the Christian hope is that a man in Christ can endure any kind of trouble and distress, and remain erect all through them, and come out to glory on the other side. (*The Revelation of John*, Vol. 2, Revised Edition, page 27)

That is a powerful truth. How can we have a great victory over our enemies if we are removed from the fight? There is another passage that is very curious; Jesus gave a parable of seed falling on different types of ground:

"This is the meaning of the parable: The seed is the word of God. . . . Those on the rock are the ones who receive the word with joy when they hear it, but they have no root. They believe for a while, but in the time of testing they fall away." (Luke 8:11, 13)

Either Jesus was saying that every person who believes the Gospel will be put through a time of testing, or he was referring to the time that will test the population of Earth, the Great Tribulation. It most likely refers to the GT. So this passage tells us that many people who now believe the Gospel will turn away from God during the GT. Jesus spoke more on this subject:

"Then you will be handed over to be persecuted . . . 10 At that time many will turn away from the faith and will betray and hate each other, 11 and many false prophets will appear and deceive many people. 12 Because of the increase of wickedness, the love of most will grow cold, 13 but he who stands firm to the end will be saved." (Matthew 24:9-13)

The literal translation says, "*And then many will be offended, . . . And many false prophets will be raised, and will cause many to err*" (LIT). The word "offended" (4624) means, "*a trap, stumbling block. To cause to stumble and fall . . . to offend, vex, particularly to scandalize"* (CWD). This tells us that many Christians will have cause to turn away from Christianity during the GT and become bitter at churches and preachers and God. But what could possibly cause that?

Christians today are being promised that they will be removed to heaven before any hardship comes upon the world; others are told the events of Revelation were fulfilled by 70 A.D. Some are being told that God has nothing but wonderful things planned for them. So when the GT starts they will know that they were not taught the truth, and they will leave their churches and follow after others who will lead them away from the essentials of the Gospel, *"will cause many to err."* The word "err" means to *"go astray."*

The pretribulation Rapture doctrine will cause millions of Christians to be spiritually and psychologically unprepared for the GT. Christians will suffer in ways they do not need to suffer and should not suffer, but pushers of the doctrine do everything in their power to silence opposition. Corrie Ten Boom, a survivor of a Nazis prison camp, said:

> I have been in countries where the saints are already suffering terrible persecution. In China the Christians [were] told, "Don't worry, before the tribulation comes, you will be translated--Raptured." Then came the terrible persecution. Millions of Christians were tortured to death. Later I heard a Bishop from China say, sadly, "We have failed. We should have made the people strong for persecution rather than telling them Jesus would come first." (*Tramp for the Lord*, 1974)

Even though the whole GT is a time of great distress, the greatest distress of all will be the final few weeks after the Rapture. The time of testing will be very hard, but *"he who endures to the end shall be saved"* (Matthew 24:13) (NKJ). Bible teacher, Derek Prince says, *"the Greek is more precise: 'He who has endured to the end will be saved.'"* (*Prophetic Destinies*, p. 82). So the word "saved" here refers to being alive and well at the end of the GT.

The *Didache* (also known as *The Teaching of the Twelve Apos-*

tles) speaks about the Great Tribulation:

> 5 Then <u>all</u> created mankind <u>shall come to the fire of testing</u>, and many shall be offended and perish; but <u>they that endure in their faith shall be saved</u> by the Curse Himself. 6 And then shall the signs of the truth appear; first a sign of a rift in the heaven, then a sign of a voice of a trumpet, and thirdly a resurrection of the dead; 7 yet not of all, but as it was said: The Lord shall come and all His saints with Him. 8 Then shall the world see the Lord coming upon the clouds of heaven. (16:5-8) (revised J.B. Lightfoot translation)

Notice that this short prophecy has many of the elements that have already been mentioned and are being discussed in this book: The Great Tribulation is called a *"fire of testing,"* which will cause many people to be offended at God, because they are suffering and will turn away from Christianity. But those who endure to the end will be saved. And it shows that this time of testing will happen right before the return of Christ, because it has the resurrection taking place at the end of the time of testing, not before it begins.

This early Christian book says the whole world will go through the time of testing, followed by the Rapture and return of Christ. This agrees with my interpretation of Bible prophecy. It is strange that theologians have developed an opposite doctrine, that God does not test people, and that the Rapture will take place before the Great Tribulation. God said, *"I will test them and see whether they will follow my instructions"* (Exodus 16:4b). It is really amazing how self-deceived people can become because they do not like the truth or do not agree with the truth!

Finally, the last paragraph of Lactanius quoted earlier, also tells us about the time of testing:

> Of the worshippers of God also, two parts will perish; and the third part, <u>which shall have been proved</u>, will remain. (*The Divine Institutes*, Book VII, chapter 16)

In order to be "proved" we must first be tested. Those who pass the test will survive to enter the Kingdom Age.

(3) Seventh Seal: Seven Trumpets

Revelation 8 describes the first major events of the GT:

> 1 When he opened the seventh seal, there was silence in heaven for about half an hour. 2 And I saw the seven angels who stand before God, and to them were given seven trumpets. 3 Another angel, who had a golden censer, came and stood at the altar. He was given much incense to offer, with the prayers of all the saints, on the golden altar before the throne. 4 The smoke of the incense, together with the prayers of the saints, went up before God from the angel's hand. 5 Then the angel took the censer, filled it with fire from the altar, and hurled it on the earth; and there came peals of thunder, rumblings, flashes of lightning and an earthquake. 6 Then the seven angels who had the seven trumpets prepared to sound them. (8:1-6)

Though it is impossible to say for certain, I believe all the evidence indicates that the 7th Seal may be already open, because we are not told anywhere in Revelation about a length of time that will encompass all the end-time events. It could take 5-8 years for all 7 Trumpets and 7 Bowls of Wrath to take place. We are not told how much time there is between the 1st and 2nd Trumpets, or between the 2nd and 3d Trumpets, but I believe it will not be long. Most likely only 4 to 5 years.

(4) First Trumpet: Natural Disasters

The seven Trumpets of Revelation contain the judgments of God upon the world, but they are not the full Wrath of God that will be poured out at the end of the GT. The Trumpet judgments will only come upon one-third of the world, not the entire world, and not in full strength.

> The first angel sounded his trumpet, and there came hail and fire mixed with blood, and it was hurled down upon the earth. A third of the earth was burned up, a third of the trees were burned up, and all the green grass was burned up. (Rev. 8:7)

There are several possible interpretations of this; one that is often considered is a volcanic eruption. A major problem with this is, how will it burn up all the green grass and one-third of the trees? Even a super-volcano will not literally burn up all the grass and trees globally or even on a whole continent, it would only cover them with ash.

Another possible cause is a global meteor shower with meteors large enough to still be burning hot when they land, and burn all the grass. But there is a problem with this view; if there are enough meteors to burn up all the grass, wouldn't it also burn up all the trees? And the inclusion of hail is another problem, since hail does not fall with meteors, and neither does blood. So the event described here is not 100% literal.

We previously saw an angel fill a censer with fire and throw it on the earth (Rev. 8:5); so the hail and fire are symbolic and refer to excessive cold and heat, and the blood refers to people dying in the weather extremes. Therefore, this Trumpet sounding means we have reached a certain point since the birth pains first began.

We have already discussed the start of the birth pains of the earth, but this Trumpet seems to signal that we have reached a specific point as we progress toward the birth of the Kingdom Age.

Just two years ago I thought we had 20 years to the GT, but with all the crazy weather along with the signs in the heavens, and the signs here on Earth such as the Arab Spring, the war in Syria, the final pope (more shortly), and the Progressive socialists trying to take control of the U.S., we must be in the early years of the GT, not long before or after the opening of the 7th Seal.

A major drought will cause all the green grass to die but only a third of the trees because many trees have roots deep enough to reach underground water, and grass dies much quicker without water than trees do. This is not merely global warming, or even climate change, because the birth pains include earthquakes and other natural disasters. Of course, it can include climate change, but that is just one aspect of the birth pains.

How can this Trumpet represent birth pains and climate change if we are already having them? We would not expect to have great weather then suddenly super freakish weather around the globe. When this Trumpet sounds, it means the birth pains have progressed to the point that one-third of the trees have died and all the grass. But we may have actually reached this point. How?

The drought we have been having is not just in the U.S., but more importantly, it is not merely a stoppage of rain. You can be in the middle of a severe drought and still get rain. A drought means you are not getting enough rain, so the lakes and rivers slowly decline. And if you are talking about a global drought that lasts for several years, then it is entirely possible to have all the grass die during this drought without having all the grass die at the same time. The dead grass can come back fully green after you get some rain, but when a tree dies it stays dead.

Although it is possible that the drought will get worse to the point that all the green grass is dead at the same time, it is also possible that in an extended drought that began at a specific point, that all the green grass will die in the drought without it all having to be dead at the same time. When it is summer in the northern hemisphere it is winter in the southern hemisphere. Therefore, we could actually be at or near this point already. There have been many trees die in my state because of the drought, including the tree in my front yard which had to be cut down.

Since birth pains and climate change are already happening, we will not know at what point this 1st Trumpet sounds; all we will know is that we are having a drought with weather extremes. A drought of this size will eventually bring famine, which is a major reason why we should store food and water. But those who are doing so are being called "extremists" and "doomsday nuts."

(5) Second Trumpet: Volcanic Landslide

8 The second angel sounded his trumpet, and something like a huge mountain, all ablaze, was thrown into the sea. A third of the sea turned into blood, 9 a third of the living creatures in the sea died, and a third of the ships were destroyed. (Rev. 8:8-9)

It is easy to see this as an asteroid impact; however, the next Trumpet says a star falls from the sky, which is clearly an asteroid impact; so why would it not say a star falls here if it is also an asteroid? The wording actually give us information designed to point us to the correct meaning. Something *"like a mountain"* means it is not an ordinary mountain, but is very much like a mountain. What is like a mountain that can also be burning with fire? A volcano. A volcanic mountain will fall into the ocean during an eruption and create a huge tsunami that will destroy the ships.

A good question was asked of this interpretation: *"Since a volcano is a mountain, why would it say that it is like a mountain, if it is a volcano?"* The reason is because a volcano is not an ordinary mountain. It is also symbolism, so it is not going to be so direct.

There are many islands in the Pacific Ocean that were created by volcano eruptions. Any of these that have large mountain volcanoes on them could erupt and send a huge section of the mountain into the ocean. Scientists say that the Hawaiian Islands have sent huge masses of earth into the ocean many times in history:

> These landslides are among the largest on Earth, attaining lengths of 125 miles (200 km) and volumes of 1,200 cubic miles (5,000 cubic km). (http://volcano.und.nodak.edu).

There is also at least one volcano in the Atlantic that could slide into the ocean, located in the Canary Islands:

> A collapsing volcano in the Atlantic could unleash a giant wave of water that would swamp the Caribbean and much of the eastern seaboard of the United States, a scientist has claimed. Dr. Simon Day, of the Benfield Greig Hazard Research Centre at University College London, UK, believes one flank of the Cumbre Vieja volcano on the island of La Palma, in the Canaries archipelago, is unstable and could plunge into the ocean.
>
> Swiss researchers who have modeled the landslide say half a trillion tons of rock falling into the water all at once would create a wave 650 metres high (2,130 feet) that would spread out and travel across the Atlantic at high speed. The wall of water would weaken as it crossed the ocean, but would still be 40-50 metres (130-160 feet) high by the time it hit land. The surge would create havoc in North America as much as 20 kilometres (12 miles) inland. (BBC News Online, 4 October, 2000, *Giant wave could threaten US*, http://news.bbc.co.uk/2/low/ science/nature/ 956280.stm)

I believe this volcano will be the one that goes into the ocean because it already slid several feet, which could have been a warning from God. During the 1949 eruption, several earthquakes occurred on the mountain, creating a fracture about 2.5 kilometers long. The western section slid down approximately one meter. So it is just a matter of time until this section of the volcano slides into the Atlantic Ocean. When the tsunami hits, it will actually be several waves, rather than just one, and could go as far inland as 10-25 miles.

Why does it say the ocean is turned into blood? This does *not* refer to literal blood; it is symbolism. The *Cousteau Almanac* calls the oceans "*the planetary blood system.*" Blood in the Bible represents life, and the shedding of blood represents loss of life, "*For the life of a creature is in the blood*" (Lev. 17:11). *Zondervan's Pictorial Encyc. of the Bible* says:

> Because of its fundamental importance for individual existence, blood was frequently used as a synonym for life itself . . . blood indicates life given up in death, not life set free. (Vol. 1, p. 626-627)

When the ocean is turned into blood it will lose its life; the ocean itself will lose its life-giving ability. Debris and sediment in the water cuts off the oxygen available in the water, thus killing most ocean life. It literally suffocates the fish because they are unable to obtain oxygen from the water. In addition to the sediment, ships with oil and other chemicals will be swamped by the waves, and sewage and other toxic debris will be washed into the water when the waves hit coastal areas.

Whether this Trumpet represents a volcano or not remains to be seen, but something is going into the ocean, and it is going to create a huge tsunami. Wise persons will see that the world cannot long endure its present course and the end is therefore approaching, and they will move away from all coastal areas. Tsunamis such as this in ancient history did little damage in a world that was sparsely inhabited. The death and destruction and global chaos following such a tsunami today will be as bad as WW2. This is still early in the GT, and before the final 3.5 years even begins, as we shall see.

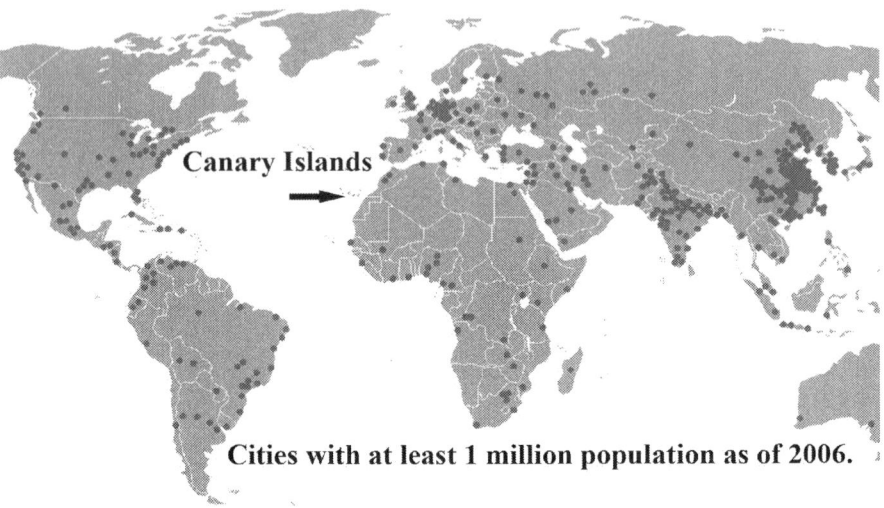

Cities with at least 1 million population as of 2006.

You can see from this map that there are many large cities that will be hit hard by the tsunami. There are many more that are not on the map that are less than 1 million in population, that are between the larger cities. Therefore, the tsunami will be horrific. (A larger copy of the map is on my website.)

(6) The Affect Upon the United States
Whether this tsunami is generated in the Pacific Ocean or the Atlantic Ocean, it will hit the U.S. and cause great devastation. It will be the greatest natural disaster in recorded history. As we will see in the next book, Babylon the Great will fall three times, so this tsunami will be the first fall of Babylon the Great, which is the U.S. It will only take 6-8 hours for the wave to reach the U.S., so there will likely be hundreds of thousands of people who do not get the warning or are unable to flee and are killed, perhaps millions.

The wave will also destroy warehouses full of groceries and manufactured goods. Many businesses will be destroyed and never reopen. The wave will likely also cause the stock market to collapse, and an economic melt-down that will affect the whole world. Many churches will also be destroyed.

This disaster will likely cause the dollar to collapse, which means it will become worthless. Until deals are made in Washington D.C. to restore the dollar, you will not be able to buy anything. Grocery stores will be emptied within hours of the collapse, and gas stations will run out of gasoline. There will likely be rioting and looting, and buildings set on fire by mobs. The long prophesied events by David Wilkerson will finally come to pass.

Many homes will be destroyed and never rebuilt, because it will take many years to rebuild millions of homes. This could cause the price of lumber and other materials to greatly increase. And where are those people going to live until the homes are rebuilt? Some people will just move to another city or state. So there will be millions of people who will have no place to live until they get an insurance payment which renters will not receive, so there will be tent cities throughout the eastern states, perhaps into the Midwest as well. Some people may be put into FEMA camps.

The Sunday after the tsunami will see the churches filled with people, like it was after 9-11, but many preachers will not have an answer. Many preachers will tell the people, *don't worry, this is not the Great Tribulation, it is just a natural disaster*. While a few churches will remain full, those preacher's who are not able to adequately respond to the crisis with solid biblical truth could end up having to close their church doors.

The number one question will be, *how could God allow this to happen?* The answer, of course, is sin. Sin has increased to the point that God will no longer allow it to continue without taking action to bring people to repentance. The second question will be, *why did God allow many Christians to die or suffer total loss with the tsunami?* And *where was the Rapture?* But we have already learned that God will seal and protect all those who are right with him, so it is only Christians who are not right with God who will suffer in this disaster. These questions and more will result in many people questioning their faith and questioning their church, which will cause Christianity to suffer a major crisis.

But at the same time, this will be an opportunity for some Christians to reach out to the crowds of suffering people. Some

Christians will preach from the back of flatbed trailers or on street corners, and a great revival will take place. There have been many prophecies, dreams, and visions over the past 30 years about a great shaking that is coming to Christianity, and also another Reformation and a street revival, all of which could be one and the same movement, and all triggered by this tsunami. (I say, could be, because it could be caused by something else, such as the next Trumpet.)

In February 2011, a 6.3 earthquake hit Christchurch, New Zealand that killed 185 people. The quake badly damaged the historic Christchurch Cathedral. This quake was given spiritual significance by more than one prophet. Cindy deVille of *Shekinah Today Ministries* reported that she had a vision of shaking pulpits just before the Christchurch earthquake:

> While in prayer two weeks ago, I kept seeing a vision of a pulpit that was shaking intensely, as if there was a long and intense earthquake. The pastor behind the pulpit could not stand up, and he started to frantically grasp the pulpit for something solid to hold onto. Everything was crumbling around him, and the only thing that was not shaking, crumbling or changing was the truth of God's Word. In desperation, the pastor fell to his knees, and seemed to be asking himself: "What do I really believe? What is truth?" This caused him to dig deep on his knees in search for truth he could take hold of and stand upon. We know God's Word is everlasting truth: "Thy word is truth" (John 17:17); "The Word of our God shall stand forever." (Is. 40:8).
>
> . . . In light of the vision, we realized this earthquake could have prophetic significance. While I do not believe everything that happens is a prophetic sign, I do believe God uses some things to symbolize what He is doing or will do; we see this throughout holy Scripture. So, I do believe the recent earthquake at Christchurch in New Zealand could be symbolic. (www.charisma mag.com/blogs/prophetic-insight/12937-the-pulpits-are-shaking)

Cindy deVille says that the shaking that is coming will cause some pastors to even *"fall away"* while others will dig deeper and turn to prayer. There was also a 5.8 quake on August 23, 2011 in

Virginia that shook Washington D.C. and damaged the National Cathedral and cracked the Washington Monument. Was this an omen, or sign that the foundation of our nation has cracked?

Andrew Strom, a New Zealander, has studied many prophecies from around the world that predict a Reformation and a street revival, and gives us a summary:

> Just as with many previous moves of God right down through the ages, God has made it very clear that once again, only a "remnant" of believers, who have willingly gone through the necessary preparation, will have a part in the coming Revival. Those who refuse to submit to this preparation process, preferring to remain in their present 'Laodicean' state - will clearly have no part whatsoever in the coming move of God. Rather, just as Jesus has promised, the lukewarm are to be "spewed" out of the mouth of God (Rev 3:16).
>
> The Bible makes it very clear that God cannot live with a 'blessings' -obsessed, Laodicean-type church. And in this world of increasing darkness, it becomes doubly imperative that God has a people in the earth who are shining forth His light with the greatest possible effectiveness. This is what the coming Reformation is all about - finding and cleansing and anointing such a people so that they can shine forth His light in all the earth. This is why such a massive 'shaking' and repentance must first come upon the church. God must find and raise up such a people. . . .
>
> It is my belief that God is going to delight in using the "foolish things of this world to confound the wise" in this Revival. As always, He is going to use the "little" people - the people who are of no account - to humble the powerful, the successful and the mighty. He is going to take the unknowns and the outcasts, the praying solo mothers and the ex-gang-members, the "fishermen and the tax-collectors", and He is going to anoint them and raise them up into the mightiest army of miracle-working apostles, prophets, evangelists, etc., that this world has ever known. And all they will be interested in doing is glorifying Him in every conceivable way. . . .
>
> Be assured of this: Jesus must have His virgin Bride. He cannot return until a Bride is prepared for Him that is literally "without spot, or wrinkle, or any such thing". That is what this Revival is all about: to bring into being and display His beautiful Bride to all the world. In physical terms, this 'Bridal' company of saints will not

look particularly amazing or special. Like the original apostles, they will be ordinary people with an extraordinary calling and anointing. Many of them will no doubt seem a little rough or 'ill-suited' (from an outward point of view) to be endued with such power, but this will only serve to bring God all the more glory. They may not look like much on the outside, but these men and women will have hearts that are literally "as pure as snow". They will be a people who know exactly what it means to walk in total heart purity before God. To Him, they will be vastly more precious than all of the "gold or pearls or costly array" of this entire Universe. And they will go forth with great power, "destroying the works of the devil" in His name. (*The Coming Great Reformation: New Insights into the Coming Worldwide "Shaking", Reformation and Revival*, Andrew Strom).

He goes on to say that the Reformation/Revival will be opposed by many established Christian leaders. All the new movements of the past were opposed by the established church, "*true Reformation and Revival are often the most controversial and the most persecuted spiritual events of their time.*" He goes on to say:

Something that God has made very clear to us in NZ is that the coming Revival is to be a "street-based" (or 'open-air' based) move of God. . . . like the early church (where they met daily in the huge open-air temple courtyard - probably the most public place in all Jerusalem), and also like the mighty Wesley and Salvation Army Revivals, the coming move of God is to be truly street-based. (There will also, like the early church, be gatherings of the saints from "house to house" (Acts 2:41-47)). (Ibid)

Strom says this revival will bring down the walls dividing Christians, because the Bride of Christ will be united, "*By bringing His people out from underneath all these 'labels'!*" Strom says:

[This] has occurred many times down through history, God is going to bring a cleansed and purified "remnant" out from the current church system . . . What we have today is really a whole bunch of "happiness clubs" rather than real churches. (Ibid)

One of the reasons this will be a street revival is because people will run out of gasoline, so they will be on foot and many Christians will be out there reaching them on the street. So we all need to be prepared to witness and lead people to Christ.

Two prophecies by Rick Joyner most likely refer to the tsunami of the 2nd Trumpet and the above quotes. His prophecies refer to a huge tsunami wave of the Spirit that will result in great revival to the point that Christians will be meeting in stadiums. He also predicts a Christian spiritual civil war:

> What is coming will be dark. At times Christians almost universally will be loath to even call themselves Christians. Believers and unbelievers alike will think that it is the end of Christianity as we know it, and it will be. Through this the very definition of Christianity will be changed, for the better. The church that emerges from what is coming will be full of unprecedented grace, truth, and unprecedented power. . . .
>
> Nearly half of the believers in the world today are held under a spiritual "plantation mentality"; leaders are only seeking to build and maintain their own spiritual estates . . .
>
> A god is not just something you bow down to, but what you trust in. Many of the coming conflicts between movements, denominations and individual churches will be deeply rooted in the power that money now has over the church. Many will use doctrinal differences or other issues as justification for their attacks on their brothers, but the real cause will be over a loss, or potential loss, of money. . . .
>
> This will be a conflict between those who may be genuine Christians, but who live mostly according to their natural minds and human wisdom, and those who follow the Holy Spirit. . . . What will for a time look like a total meltdown of Christianity will ultimately result in one of her greatest victories. . . .
>
> After this great spiritual civil war, there will no longer be a white church and a black church. Neither will many of the present distinguishing characteristics that categorize Christians into groups continue to exist. There will be an entirely new definition of Christianity, which the Lord Jesus Himself has already written. The world will know us by our love. . . .
>
> Those who have built their spiritual lives, or positions of lead-

ership, on obeying an organization rather than always seeking to follow the Lord, are in the most serious jeopardy at this time of becoming stumbling blocks. (*MorningStar Prophetic Bulletin* #16)

So, it looks to me that when this physical tsunami hits America, and it causes many people to question their faith, this will bring the spiritual tsunami. It will result in great conflict within denominations and churches about their view of eschatology and other important doctrines. Many Christians will leave the established Church because they don't like the answers they are getting, and will begin living out their faith by sharing their worldly goods with the hungry and naked victims of the physical tsunami.

The Protestants will not be the only ones rocked by the tsunami; in 2003 J. Lee Grady, then editor of Charisma Magazine, had a dream of a spiritual tsunami that will hit the Catholic Church:

> When the wave hit, the palatial building began creaking and tilting. Antique tables, chairs, candelabra and statues began sliding to one side as the floor moved. Chandeliers were hanging at odd angles. Within minutes the floor was perpendicular to the ground and more furniture came crashing down. The movement continued until the floor became the ceiling. More religious icons, statues and paintings fell and broke into pieces....
>
> [He saw Catholics with] their hands raised and they were worshiping God fervently, as if they had experienced another Pentecost. . . . . And I felt the Holy Spirit say to me: "I am going to turn the Catholic Church upside down." (www.charismanews.com/opinion/38632-the-coming-tsunami-in-the-catholic-church)

But it was a *spiritual* tsunami, right? Yes, but from the buildings and objects being broken, it would have been just as effective to say that a spiritual earthquake was going to hit. Why did Joyner and Grady both hear from God about a spiritual *tsunami*? Even though the Catholics were acting "Pentecostal," that is not new; it has happened before during the original Charismatic Renewal. This is not a renewal, it is a shakeup, and the real tsunami has the very real power to also cause a spiritual tsunami within Catholicism the same as Protestantism.

Finally, while in the middle of this crisis and reformation, another major disaster will take place, an asteroid impact. But we are not given any indication how much time will pass between these two disasters.

(7) Third Trumpet: Asteroid Impact

10 The third angel sounded his trumpet, and a great star, blazing like a torch, fell from the sky on a third of the rivers and on the springs of water-- 11 the name of the star is Wormwood. A third of the waters turned bitter, and many people died from the waters that had become bitter. (Rev. 8:10-11)

The Greek for "star" in the Gospels and here is "aster" (792), and is the word from which we get "asteroid." So this means the star is in fact an asteroid.

Wormwood is common in Europe, Russia, the Middle East, and the United States. When the Hebrews were wandering in the desert they were given bitter water to drink as a punishment from God; the water was made bitter by Wormwood. In Jeremiah, God threatens to give them Wormwood to drink (Jer. 9:15; 23:15). William Barclay in his commentary on Revelation states; "*Wormwood always stood for the bitterness of the judgment of God on the disobedient*" (page 44).

Since wormwood is used symbolically in the Bible to refer to the bitterness of God's judgment, it is not literally the name of this asteroid. Therefore, the name of this asteroid signifies that it comes as God's judgment upon those directly affected by the impact, but also the whole world, because it will have global effects.

However, it also may have a secondary meaning. Since Wormwood means bitter and people will die from drinking the water, it may mean that the asteroid will impact in a city. If the asteroid impacts in a forest there won't be any chemicals ejected into the atmosphere to fall into the water, but if it hits a city it will vaporize tons of man-made products that contain chemicals that will enter the lakes and rivers. It could even destroy a chemical or nuclear power plant. At this writing there are about 15,000 chemical plants worldwide, and according to www.euronuclear.org there are 437 nuclear power plants, with 68 more under construction. So, hitting a modern city is probably what will cause people to die from drinking the water.

When the two towers of the World Trade Center in New York City fell, huge clouds of dust filled the air and covered everything for blocks, like ash from a volcano. All kinds of products were burned or crushed and mixed together, such as plastics, floor cleaner, burned jet fuel, brake fluid and gasoline in parked cars under the towers, and all the office equipment and furniture. All this created a toxic soup that people breathed and absorbed into their bodies. As a result, many of the people who worked to clean up the mess became sick, and several died. But this asteroid impact will create conditions far worse than 9-11.

There was a stir back in 1986 when a nuclear power plant in Chernobyl, Ukraine had a meltdown. Information spread that Chernobyl was Russian for "wormwood." The name Chernobyl comes from chornobyl which is mugwort, one of over 160 species of wormwood, though sometimes thought of as *common worm-wood*." So it is easy to see why Chernobyl was said to mean "wormwood," (because it refers to mugwort, which is a type of wormwood). However, the word does not literally mean "wormwood," but it is given as a secondary meaning in Russian dictionaries. Even so, the events of the 3rd Trumpet do not fit the Chernobyl disaster, and this event did not destroy 1/3rd of the ships. Also, the GT is not going to drag on for 25+ years.

Several large impact craters have been found on Earth which is proof positive that Earth has been hit in the past and will be hit again. A 6-mile wide asteroid is believed to have wiped out the dinosaurs. In the late 90s, scientists discovered a chain of craters, named the Aorounga craters, in the central African country of Chad. *"The Aorounga craters are only the second chain of large craters known on Earth,"* said Adriana Ocampo, geologist with NASA's Jet Propulsion Lab, *"and were apparently formed by the break-up of a large comet or asteroid prior to impact"* (Hague, *Final Frontier Magazine*, p.41).

Dr. Eugene Shoemaker has found several impact craters; one

in Germany has a town built inside the earthen ring of the crater. There are over 160 recognized impact sights throughout the world with more being identified on a regular basis. Among the largest are: Sudbury, Ontario, Canada, 140 KM (87 miles) in diameter; Vredefort, South Africa, 140 KM (87 miles); Manicouagan, Quebec, Canada, 100 KM (62 miles); Popigai, Russia, 100 KM. The largest impact sight in the United States is about 18 miles wide in Manson, Iowa. Perhaps the most recognizable sight is Meteor Crater in Arizona that is a mile across and 600 feet deep. This evidence means that no rational person can argue against the likelihood of an asteroid impact; the facts are undeniable.

Though some scientists are taking the threat seriously, many still say the chances of an asteroid hitting Earth are very remote. They use terms and numbers like millions of years and a million to one. They also make the boast that if an asteroid were to head toward Earth that scientists will be able to save the planet by nudging it and changing its course, but they are wrong because the Bible tells us that this asteroid will impact.

Many asteroids now travel in wide-ranging and erratic paths through the solar system and cross paths with Earth on a regular basis. So it would not take much of an orbital change of an asteroid to send it on a collision course with Earth. The gravitational pull from a comet passing through the solar system could easily change the course of several asteroids as it passes them. Scientists say it is just a matter of time until it happens, and this is the time. Comets were regarded throughout ancient history, even into the modern era, as messengers of god and omens of disaster. This asteroid is not a coincidental event, but it will impact when and where God wants it to impact. (Comets and asteroids are similar, and comets can become asteroids after they burn off all their ice.)

This asteroid will not, I repeat, not, be a global killer, but it will be large enough to destroy an entire city, somewhere in the world. My guess is that it will impact either in the U.S. or Western Europe; the reason being that the U.S. and EU are keeping aggressive nations in check, but the U.S. will be hurt more by the tsunami than Western Europe because of all the coastal cliffs in Europe, so if Western Europe were hit by the asteroid, then that will be even more of an opportunity for aggressive nations to begin attacking other nations.

However, because of the prophecies about a U.S. city suffering destruction, I would not be surprised if it hit southern California. Hollywood is intentionally spewing vomit upon the world as it denigrates Christian moral values and pollutes the minds of everyone watching the TV shows and movies it produces.

(8) Fourth Trumpet: Darkness

The fourth angel sounded his trumpet, and a third of the sun was struck, a third of the moon, and a third of the stars, so that a third of them turned dark. A third of the day was without light, and also a third of the night. (Rev. 8:12)

The wording of this passage is cryptic; while the sun is shining on one part of the globe, the moon is shining on another. If a third of the light from the sun, moon, and stars is darkened, it could mean there will be no light upon the whole planet for eight hours; or that a third of the planet will be in complete darkness.

There are many possible causes for the darkness, but the most obvious are the dark clouds caused by the asteroid impact of the 3rd Trumpet. If caused by the asteroid, the dark cloud will eventually spread out thinner so that it covers the entire globe, thus dimming the sun with a haze and lowering global temperatures for a year, which will affect crop yields. We are already having reduced crops because of all the floods and droughts, so this will make the global food production even less.

The eruption of Krakatoa in 1883 in the Pacific Ocean was about 200 megatons. The explosion was heard 3,000 miles away, and ash from it fell on New York City. The dust cloud darkened the sky and spread around the globe lowering global temperatures about 2 degrees Fahrenheit (1.2 degrees Celsius). The ash in the atmosphere caused spectacular red sunsets for several years afterwards. But the 4th Trumpet could be worse than Krakatoa.

The 1815 volcanic eruption on the island of Tambora, Indonesia was three times greater than the eruption of Krakatoa. The

Tambora eruption sent about 1.5 million metric tons of dirt into the atmosphere, darkening the sky and lowering global temperatures for more than a year. The following year was known as the year without a summer in Europe and North America. There were freezing temperatures even during August; the result was numerous crop failures. The price of a bushel of Oats rose from 12¢ in 1815 to 92¢ in 1816. Today there are more than 7 billion people on Earth; with many crop failures, great famine will likely ravage the world.

If the natural disasters of the first four Trumpets are not bad enough, there will likely be many more smaller, local disasters. The Trumpet events mentioned here in Revelation do not mean that only these events will take place and no more, but these are the only ones that are large enough to justify being singled out for special mention. The birth pains will continue to increase in severity.

The events of the Trumpets are mentioned in Revelation so we can know where we are on the time clock that is counting down to the rise of the beast and the start of World War 3, and ultimately the Wrath of God at the end of the age. Each of the Trumpet events is a warning; God wants us to repent before WW3 and the full Wrath of God destroys the world.

Therefore, there certainly will be many other natural disasters as described by Lactantius and other prophets. There will be volcanic eruptions, hurricanes, earthquakes, droughts, floods, tsunamis, tornadoes, and more. Be warned and be ready.

(9) Three Woes

As I watched, I heard an <u>eagle that was flying in midair</u> call out in a loud voice: "Woe! Woe! Woe! To the inhabitants of the earth, because of the trumpet blasts about to be sounded by the other three angels!" (Rev. 8:13)

Almost all translations have "eagle" rather than "angel" as the King James Version does. Adam Clarke's commentary corrects the KJV:

Instead of αγγελου πετωμενου, an angel flying, almost every MS [manuscript of the Bible] and version of note has αετου πετωμενον, an eagle flying.

William Barclay's commentary agrees with Clarke. This passage tells us that the three woes are events that take place within the next three Trumpet blasts. The eagle may refer to the United States warning the world of what is about to happen. Since the United States will suffer a crippling hit from the tsunami, and possibly from the asteroid impact, it makes sense that the U.S. will warn aggressive nations not to try to take advantage of the situation and attack the U.S. while we are thus wounded. But since the U.S. is partly responsible with other nations like Britain and France to help keep the global peace, it may be warning aggressive nations not to attack other nations while we are thus wounded and less able to maintain the global peace.

The tsunami of the 2nd Trumpet will sink one-third of the world's ships, thus weakening the American and European militaries. The tsunamis will kill millions of people and create millions of hungry, homeless refugees in both North and South America and even Europe and Africa. Add to this the effects of the asteroid impact of the 3rd Trumpet, and human suffering will be at its highest level short of nuclear war.

Despite the warning, the door of the Abyss is about to open and the beast is going to rise to power. Since there will never be a better time to conquer Europe, the U.S.A., or the people next door, World War 3 will begin. Contrary to most teaching on the beast, the Antichrist will not bring global peace or rule the world, its purpose is to "*make war*" (Rev. 13:4, 7), as proven in chapter 1. So it should be no surprise that the 5th Trumpet signals the rise of the beast, followed by the start of World War 3 (6th Trumpet) that we are told will directly kill one-third of the world's population.

(10) Other Prophecies of Great Tribulation

Here are a few prophecies not found in the Bible, but which agree with the interpretation of Bible prophecy as presented in this book. Here is an excerpt from a vision Rick Joyner had, called *A*

Vision of The Harvest, which can only be about the Great Tribulation:

> . . . Wars will increase. There will even be some nuclear exchanges, but on a limited basis, mostly between Third World nations. Far more will perish by plagues and natural disasters than by wars during the period of this vision. The very foundations of civilization will shake and erode. Even the world's most stable governments will be melting like wax, losing authority and control over their populations. Eventually it will be hard to find anyone with the courage to assume authority. This will cause sweeping paranoia throughout the entire earth.
>
> Huge mobs will attack everything in their path. The infrastructure of the great denominational churches and large visible ministries will be one of their primary targets and will vanish almost overnight. Pagan religions, cults and witchcraft will spread like plagues but these will also become targets of the mobs. By this time governments will have broken down to the point that lynching and mass executions, perpetrated by these mobs, will be ignored by the authorities. Fear and deep darkness cover the earth, but this just makes the glory which is appearing upon the saints more striking. Huge masses of people will be streaming to the Lord; the inflow so great in places that very young Christians will be pastoring large bodies of believers. Arenas and stadiums will overflow nightly as the believers come together to hear the apostles and teachers. . . . What I was allowed to foresee ended with increasing chaos and increasing revival.

In 1986, a prophecy was given out at a prophetic conference in Jerusalem where 153 prophets from around the world had gathered to wait upon and hear from God. A prophecy by Lance Lambert clearly describes what can only be the Great Tribulation. I found it on the TBN web site, yet TBN still teaches that Christians will *not* go through the GT:

> "It will not be long before there will come upon the world a time of unparalleled upheaval and turmoil. Do not fear for it is I the Lord who am shaking all things. I began this shaking with the first world war and I greatly increased it through the second world war. Since 1973 I have given it an even greater impetus. In the last stage, I

plan to complete it with the <u>shaking of the universe itself, with</u> <u>signs in sun and moon and stars</u>. But before that point is reached, I will judge the nations and the time is near. It will not only be by war and civil war, by anarchy and terrorism, and by monetary collapses that I will judge the nations, but also by natural disasters: by earthquakes, by shortages and famines and by old and new plague diseases.

"I will also judge them by giving them over to their own ways, the lawlessness, to loveless selfishness, to delusion and to believing a lie; to false religion and an apostate church, even to a Christianity without me. Do not fear when these things begin to happen, for I disclose these things to you before they commence in order that you might be prepared, and that in the day of trouble and of evil you may stand firm and overcome. For I purpose that you may become the means of encouraging and strengthening many who love me but who are weak. I desire that through you many may become strong in me, and that multitudes of others might find my salvation through you. . . .

"For in the midst of these judgments multitudes upon multitudes will be saved from the nations. You will hardly know how to bring the harvest in, but my Spirit will equip you for the task. <u>And to Israel, will I also turn in that day, and I will melt the</u> <u>hardening which has befallen her. I will turn their blindness into</u> <u>clear sight, and tear away the veil on their heart. Then shall they be</u> <u>redeemed with heart bursting joy, and it will become a fountain of</u> <u>new and resurrection life to the whole company of the redeemed</u>.

Do not fear for these days, for I have purposed that you shall stand with Me and serve Me in them. Fear not, for I love you and I will protect you and equip you. I, the Lord, will anoint you with a new anointing and you will work My works and fulfill My counsel. You shall stand before Me, the Lord of the whole earth and serve Me with understanding and with power and you shall reign with Me during these days. Above all, I call you to be intercessors."

These prophecies indicate that many people will turn to Jesus during the trouble of the GT, which is to be expected. At the same time, other people will be turning away from God because of their sufferings and the spread of evil. Notice that there was not one mention of world government. But it did mention that Israel will turn to God during this time, not after it. The wording actually suggests that they will turn to God shortly before the Rapture, because their turning to God will result in *"a fountain of new and resurrection life."*

2 Ezra 16, part of the Apocrypha of the *New English Bible,* is quoted below. This chapter of 2 Ezra is not about some general time of suffering; it refers to the Great Tribulation and no other. All the elements are there: sword, famine, so much death that few people will be left alive, and then finally, after all these things, *"the reign of justice over us will begin"* which of course refers to the rule of Christ, the Kingdom Age:

> The sword is let loose against you, and who will (4, 5) turn it aside? Fire is let loose upon you, and who will put it out? Calamities have been let loose against you, and who is there to stop them? . . .
>
> When the Lord God sends calamities, who can stop them? (9, 10) When his <u>anger overflows in fire</u>, who can put it out? When the <u>lightning flashes</u>, who will not tremble? When it thunders, who will not shake with 11 dread? When it is the Lord who utters his threats, is there any man who 12 will not be crushed to the ground at his approach?
>
> <u>The earth is shaken to its very foundations</u>, and the sea is churned up from its depths; the waves and all the fish with them are in turmoil before the presence of the Lord 13 and the majesty of his strength. For strong is his arm which bends the bow, and sharp the arrows which he shoots; once they are on their way, they 14 will not stop before they reach the ends of the earth. Calamities are let loose, 15 and will not turn back before they strike the earth.
>
> The fire is alight and 16 will not be put out until it has burnt up earth's foundations. An arrow shot by a powerful archer does not turn back; no more will the calamities be recalled which are let loose against the earth.
>
> 17 18 Alas, alas for me! Who will rescue me on that day? When troubles come, many will groan; when famine strikes, many will die; when wars break out, empires will tremble; when the calamities come, all will be filled with 19 terror. What will men do then, in the face of calamity? Famine and plague 20 suffering and hardship, are scourges sent to teach men better ways. But even so they will not abandon their crimes, nor keep in mind their scourging. 21 <u>A time will come when food grows cheap, so cheap</u>

that they will imagine they have been sent peace and prosperity. But at that very moment the earth will become a hotbed of disasters -- sword, famine, and anarchy.

22 Most of its inhabitants will die in the famine; and those who survive the 23 famine will be destroyed by the sword. The dead will be tossed out like dung, and there will be no one to offer any comfort. For the earth will be 24 left empty, and its cities a ruin. None will be left to till the ground and sow 25 26 it. The trees will bear their fruits, but who will pick them? The grapes will ripen, but who will tread them? There will be vast desolation everywhere. 27 28 A man will long to see a human face or hear a human voice. For out a whole city, only ten will survive; in the country-side, only two will be left, 29 hiding in the forest or in holes in the rocks. Just as in an olive-grove three 30 or four olives might be left on each trees or as a few grapes in a vineyard 31 might be overlooked by the sharp-eyed pickers, so also in those days three 32 or four will be overlooked by those who search the houses to kill. The earth will be left a desert, and the fields will be overrun with briers; thorns will grow over all the roads and paths, because there will be no sheep to 33 tread them. Girls will live in mourning with none to marry them, women will mourn because they have no husbands, their daughters will mourn 34 because they have no one to support them. The young men who should have married them will be killed in the war, and the husbands wiped out by the famine.

35 BUT LISTEN TO ME, you who are the Lord's servants, and take my 36 words to heart. This is the word of the Lord. Receive it, and do not disbelieve 37 what he says. Calamities are here, close at hand, and will not delay. . . .

The more care they 48 lavish on their cities, houses, and property, and on their own persons, the 49 fiercer will be my indignation against their sins, says the Lord. Like the 50 indignation of a virtuous woman towards a prostitute, so will be the indignation of justice towards wickedness with all her finery; she will accuse her to her face, when the champion arrives to expose all sin upon 51 52 earth. Do not imitate wickedness, therefore, and her actions. For in a very short time she will be swept from the earth, and the reign of justice over us will begin. 53 . . .

Abandon your sins, and have done with your wicked deeds for ever! Then God will set you free from all distress. 68 Fierce flames are being kindled to bum you. A great horde will descend on you; they will seize some of you and make you eat pagan sacrifices. 69

70 Those who give in to them will be derided, taunted, and trampled on. In place after place and in all the neighbourhood there will be a violent 71 attack on those who fear the Lord. Their enemies will be like madmen, 72 plundering and destroying without mercy all who still fear the Lord. They will destroy and plunder their property, and throw them out of their homes. 73 Then it will be seen that my chosen people have stood the test like gold in the assayer's fire.

74 Listen, you whom I have chosen, says the Lord; the days of harsh suffering 75 are close at hand, but I will rescue you from them. Away with your 76 fears and doubts! For God is your leader. You who follow my commandments and instructions, says the Lord God, must not let your sins weigh 77 you down, nor your wicked deeds get the better of you. Alas for those who are entangled in their sins, and overrun with their wicked deeds! They are like a field overrun by bushes, with brambles across the path and no 78 way through, completely shut off and doomed to destruction by fire. (2 Ezra 16) (NEB)

Did you notice verse 21? It says food will be very cheap, then many disasters begin taking place, "*sword, famine, and anarchy.*" Notice also verse 73 that says this suffering will be a test for God's elect, which will be like a refiner's fire.

St. Columba (Columbkille) (521-597 A.D.) also prophesied about the GT and Wrath of God:

Hearken, thou, until I relate things that shall come to pass in the latter ages of the world. Great carnage shall be made, justice shall be outraged, multitudinous evils, great suffering shall prevail, and many unjust laws will be administered. . . .

The changes of seasons shall produce only half their verdure [foliage] . . . Such is the description of the people who shall live in the ages to come; more unjust and iniquitous shall be every succeeding race of men. The trees shall not bear the usual quantity of fruit, fisheries shall become unproductive and the earth shall not yield its usual abundance. Inclement weather and famine shall come and fishes shall forsake the rivers. The people oppressed for want of food, shall pine to death. Dreadful storms and hurricanes shall afflict them. Numberless diseases shall then prevail. Fortifications shall be built narrow during those times of dreadful danger.

Then a great event shall happen. I fail not to notice it: rectitude shall be its specious motive, and if ye be not truly holy, a more sorrowful event could not possibly happen. (*The Prophets And Our Times*, Rev. R. Gerald Culleton. Tan Books, 1974, page 129-131)

This prophecy refers to famine, weather extremes, and reduction in the fish population which is already taking place. The "*great event*" must be the huge asteroid impact that will take place during the full Wrath of God at the end of the GT. The word "rectitude" means moral rightness, which means God is going to set things right with the asteroid.

Jesus said through the prophet Shirley Lise:

"Life as man has known it, will not be the same. Changes in the earth's atmosphere shall usher in changes to seasons. Drought, cold, floods, these will be the norm. These are signs of My coming and the thoughts of men shall be on these things and all will know of the change. Even those who are in far away places will know and acknowledge that the end is near. Yet, all these things will work together for good, for in them, I shall make a way for multitudes to come into the ark prepared as a place of safety." (1-13-03) (River of Life, http://ns1.sgci.com/~riverpub/)

St. Hildegard (d. 1179), prophesied:

Toward the end of the world, mankind will be purified through sufferings. This will be true especially of the clergy, who will be robbed of all property. . . . When the clergy has adopted a simple manner of living, conditions will improve....

Before the Comet comes, many nations, the good excepted, will be scoured with want and famine. The great nation in the ocean [England] that is inhabited by people of different tribes and descent by an earthquake, storm and tidal waves will be devastated. It will be divided, and in great part be submerged. . . . (*The Prophets and Our Times*, R. Gerald Culleton, Tan Books, 1974, p.140)

A nun at the monastery of Vals in Caalonia wrote a prophecy on January 21, 1868:

There are four years that I see which will be terrible with the calamities and punishments which will menace the world: it will be like another flood, not of water but of a thousand other calamities . . . (*After Nostradamus*, by A. Woldben, page 123)

So even Catholic prophecies confirm that the GT will be a time of great trouble, and no mention of global government under a dictator. Jesus will be with us, and afterwards, we will all witness the victory of Christianity at the Rapture, followed by God's Kingdom on Earth. There are dozens of Catholic prophecies about the last days, but many of them are contradictory, even the officially accepted ones, so they are not all genuine, the same as the Protestant prophecies.

Finally, there is an early 12th century prophecy by St. Malachy that says we now have the last pope. St. Malachy predicted 112 popes to the return of Christ; the 111th was *"The Glory of the Olive."* Cardinal Joseph Ratzinger chose the name Benedict XVI. The Order of St. Benedict is associated with the olive branch. Pope Francis, elected in 2013, is the final pope. St. Malachy wrote:

> In the final persecution of the Holy Roman Church there will reign Peter the Roman, who will feed his flock among many tribulations; after which the seven-hilled city will be destroyed and the dreadful Judge will judge the people.

So this speaks of the GT in which Rome will be destroyed in WW3 or a massive earthquake, and then Christ will judge the world.

Though the 112th pope was born in Argentina, his parents came from Italy, so technically he is a Roman. And he took the name Francis after St. Francis of Assisi, who was an Italian. What's more, St. Francis' full name was, "Francesco di Pietro (Peter) di Bernardone" (wnd.com, History's Final Pontiff, 2013).

Also, all popes are said to sit in Peter's chair, and Pope Francis is wearing a ring with St. Peter inscribed on it. The same evening that Pope Benedict resigned, a huge lightning bolt hit the top of the Vatican.

Chapter 7
The Statue of Liberty Prophecy

(1) The Woman in A Basket

There is a prophecy in the book of Zechariah that no one is even trying to interpret. It is a vision the prophet had of a woman placed in a basket with a thin metal cover. I had previously tried to understand this vision without success. Then one day I was watching a video and saw all the pieces being explained to me in a documentary about the most famous woman in American history; she is mounted on a pedestal high in the air, the *Statue of Liberty*.

Let's examine the prophecy in detail to see what it shows:

5 Then the angel who was speaking to me came forward and said to me, "Look up and see what is appearing."

6 I asked, "What is it?" He replied, "It is a basket." And he added, "This is the iniquity [literally, appearance] of the people throughout the land."

7 Then the cover of lead was raised, and there in the basket sat a woman! 8 He said, "This is wickedness," and he pushed her back into the basket and pushed its lead cover down on it.

9 Then I looked up—and there before me were two women, with the wind in their wings! They had wings like those of a stork, and they lifted up the basket between heaven and earth.

10 "Where are they taking the basket?" I asked the angel who was speaking to me.

11 He replied, "To the country of Babylonia [literally, Shinar, a plain of Babylon] to build a house for it. When the house is ready, the basket will be set there in its place." (5:5-11)

Ok, we know that a woman cannot fit into a basket of this size, which is only a few gallons or liters in size. So we know this is symbolism. What we have here is:

* Two women with wings
* A thin metal covering
* A basket
* A woman
* Lifted up between heaven and earth (v.9)
* Set in place, literally set on a base; some translations say *pedestal* (HCSB, NASB)

The two women that lift and carry the basket represent the two nations that took part in the construction of the statue and its base, France and America. The statue was paid for and built in France, but the pedestal was paid for and built in the United States.

The metal lid represents the thin metal covering that makes up the body of the statue, which is made of 310 sheets of copper, molded into the shape we see. Even the type of metal is significant; the lid is said to be made of lead, which is a soft metal. The metal of the statue, copper, is also a soft metal, though not as soft as lead, but a lot softer than iron.

Notice that the woman in a basket is to be lift up *"between heaven and earth."* Lady Liberty is 151 feet tall on a pedestal that is 89 feet tall, and built on a larger earthen foundation that is 65 feet tall. This makes the tip of her torch 305 feet in the air, taller than any structure in the Western Hemisphere at its construction, probably the world.

The above photo that shows wood slats which are very much like the weaving of a basket. The wood was only used during the first stage of the construction before shaping the copper sheets for the exterior. But even in the final construction as it now stands, there is metal weaving inside the statue. (See photo below; there are more photos and a video on my website.)

Thin metal bands that form a loose weave all through the statue on the inside of the copper sheets. These bands hold the copper sheets together and hold them to the metal framework.

Yes, but you may say that is not exactly like a basket because you cannot pick it up and carry it around. It is not meant to be the size of a basket because a woman cannot fit into such a basket. It is not exactly like a basket because the weave is loose, but when interpreting symbolism it does not have to be exact, just close, and it is very close.

The last part of the passage even describes the pedestal of the statue, and the ESV is more literal on these verses:

> Then I said to the angel who talked with me, "Where are they taking the basket?" 11 He said to me, "To the land of Shinar, <u>to build a house for it. And when this is prepared, they will set the basket down there on its base.</u>" (5:10-11) (ESV)

The *New American Standard Bible* says, "*she will be set there on her own pedestal.*" I was surprised to find the following statement in the notes of *The New Oxford Annotated Bible*; "*On its base, as though the ephah* [basket] *were an image.*" Yes, it is an image, a very large statue.

Can you see what this passage says? First, it is taken to the land of Shinar, "*to build a house for it.*" This means it is taken to the land of Shinar before the house is built. So it actually says that the statue will be ready before the base is ready, and that "*when this is prepared*" then it will be placed there. And this is exactly what happened.

The statue was ready long before the base was ready. The Lady arrived in June of 1885, but the base was not ready because the funds had not been raised. So when the funds were finally raised, the base was built, but it was not finished until April of 1886, then the body of the Lady was assembled on the base.

Notice that a house is built for it, but then the wording changes to base or pedestal; "*to build <u>a house for it</u>. And when this is prepared, they will set the basket down there <u>on its base</u>.*" The concrete foundation covered with earth contains many rooms that house the Statue of Liberty Museum, this is the house. She also sits on a pedestal that sits on the house. An astonishing prophecy.

Not all translations read the same as the ESV above, so I consulted many different translations, and the most literal translations, including the KJV, refer to a house and then a base.

However, what about the two statements about the woman in a basket being wickedness? Some translations say *iniquity*. The original Hebrew is difficult to correctly translate. Here is what a few other translations of 5:6 say:

> And he said, This is their *form* in all the earth. LIT
> This is their *eye* in all the land — JPS
> This is their *aspect* in all the land. Young's Literal Trans.

The KJV says, "*This is their <u>resemblance</u>.*" The Geneva says, "*This is the <u>sight</u> of them through all the earth.*" The CEV says, "*A*nd *it shows what everyone in the land <u>has in mind</u>.*"

The Hebrew is (5869) (עין) (ayin); the BDB dictionary says:

> 1) eye 1a) eye
>   1a1) of physical eye
>   1a2) as showing mental qualities
>   1a3) of mental and spiritual faculties (figuratively)
> 2) spring, fountain

Strong's dictionary says:

> Probably a primitive word; an *eye* (literally or figuratively); by analogy a *fountain* (as the *eye* of the landscape): - affliction, outward appearance, + before, + think best, colour, conceit, + be content, countenance, + displease, eye ([-brow], [-d], -sight), face, + favour, fountain . . .

Gill's Bible commentary says, "'*this is their eye' - what they are looking at, and intent upon . . .*" However, K&D says, "*does not mean the eye, but adspectus* [aspect]*, appearance, or shape.*"

Since this is a vision, which is like a dream, it is hard to know how that word should be translated. However, based on the above information, and knowing what the woman in a basket represents, we can more easily ascertain the meaning of the word.

So it is telling us that the woman represents what is in the mind and thoughts of the people of America, our point of view. What does the Lady represent to us? In one word, Liberty, which is clearly the word that best describes America and all those who come here seeking freedom. *It is also the name of the statue.*

The final information to note is that the angel made a point of telling Zechariah that the basket was being taken to Shinar, a plain in Babylonia. Many people believe that Mystery Babylon the Great in Revelation 17 and 18 represents the United States, and I do as well. This passage in Zechariah proves it. This passage is saying that America is the end time Babylon.

Lastly, the prophecy proves that the doctrine of imminent return is totally false because the end could never arrive before this prophecy was fulfilled; that is, before Lady Liberty was constructed.

(2) The Future Destruction of the Statue of Liberty

A poem mounted inside the base of Lady Liberty, written by Emma Lazarus, is titled, *"The New Colossus."* The original *Colossus of Rhodes* was also a large statue at the harbor of Rhodes, one of the Greek islands. It stood 110 feet tall for 56 years, then it was felled by an earthquake in 226 B.C. Even so, people continued to travel long distances for centuries to see the fallen Colossus.

About 1500 years ago, during the end of the 5th century, Rabbi Pinhas lived in the village of Baram in upper Galilee. He was known as a holy man; his wife, Rachel was also devoted to God, but the couple was childless. After much fasting and prayer she gave birth to a boy named Nahman. With a crowd of people gathered around the infant, he began speaking, or so the story goes.

The boy reportedly spoke about heaven, 2nd heaven, 3rd heaven, all the way through the 7th heaven, and spoke about the Throne. And when he began to speak about God, his father told him to shut up; he did not feel that those present were worthy to hear the secrets of heaven. After twelve years of not speaking, the boy's mother asked the Rabbi to allow the boy to speak. He agreed as long as he did not speak clearly about the secret things.

The boy then proceeded to give forth five prophecies in a mixture of Hebrew, Aramaic, Arabic, and possibly some Greek, making them very hard to know what they say or what they mean. When he finished, he told his parents that he would soon die. His grave is known to this day under the name Rabbi Nahman "Katofa".

The prophecies, which are called *"The Child's Prophecy,"* were written down and published several times in books over the centuries, such as *"Naggid uMetzave"* in the 20th century, and included in *"Otzar HaMidrashim."* The prophecies have always been thought of as genuine. About 500 years ago, a commentary was written about the prophecies by Rabbi Avrabam Ben Eliezer HaLevi, that was recently republished.

As a result of this newly republished commentary, an American Hassidic Jew named R'Yaakov Nathan studied the prophecies. He discovered a way to translate the prophecies, and to understand them. From the 4th prophecy we have these interesting lines:

When the idol of Rhodes will be destroyed,
Know that the end of the
Wicked Kingdom is near.

Since the original Colossus fell more than 700 years before this prophecy was given, it cannot refer to the original Colossus, but to *The New Colossus*, which is the *Statue of Liberty*.

In all probability, the Statue of Liberty will be destroyed when the huge tsunami of the 2nd Trumpet hits the east coast of the U.S., which is shortly before the rise of the beast. I believe the evil kingdom refers to *the power behind* the beast of Revelation. This power is now in the world and will come to an end only a few years after the destruction of the statue, at the same time the beast itself comes to an end, never to be revived again (this is discussed fully in my next book).

(Sources for the Jewish child prophecy:

http://tamaryonahshow. blogspot.com/2007/01/video-end-times-prophecies-statue-of.html

www.youtube.com/watch?v=7mncBPJb2hI

http://academysounds. blogspot.com/2009/05/child-prophecy-statue-of-liberty.html

If these files are ever deleted, I have a copy of the video.)

Chapter 8
World War 3

(1) Fifth Trumpet: The Abyss is Opened

Revelation itself tells us when the beast of Rev. chapter 13 will rise to power within the framework of the Seals and Trumpets, and it's not Rev. 6:1, with the white horse. Notice what chapter 11 says about the beast:

> Now when they have finished their testimony, the beast that <u>comes up from the Abyss</u> will attack them, and overpower and kill them. (Rev. 11:7)

It says the beast will come up out of the Abyss. Coming up out of the Abyss is a way to metaphorically describe its rise to power. This is also seen in Rev. 17:

> The beast, which you saw, once was, now is not, and <u>will come up out of the Abyss</u> and go to his destruction. (Rev. 17:8)

Therefore, there can be no doubt that the beast will rise up out of the Abyss. At the present time the Abyss is closed and locked. Revelation tells us when the Abyss will be opened:

> The fifth angel sounded his trumpet, and I saw a star that had fallen from the sky to the earth. The star was <u>given the key</u> to the shaft of the Abyss. 2 When <u>he opened the Abyss</u>, smoke rose from it like the smoke from a gigantic furnace. The sun and sky were darkened by the smoke from the Abyss. (Rev. 9:1-2)

Some translations say the key was given "*to him*," making the star a person, but in the Greek it says "it."

Some translations of this passage say that John saw a star fall from heaven, but the original Greek indicates that he saw a star that had already fallen. *Roberts Word Pictures* says, "*Fallen (πεπτωκοτα). Perfect active participle of πιπτω, already down.*" Young's Literal Translation says, "*I saw a star out of the heaven having fallen to the earth.*" Therefore, it refers back to the asteroid of the 3rd Trumpet.

The asteroid of the 3rd Trumpet is called a star, as this is called. The smoke of the 4th Trumpet is doubtless the result of the 3rd Trumpet asteroid, but the smoke spoken of here in Revelation 9 is symbolic. The Abyss refers to hell, bottomless pit, or abode of darkness in the spirit world. This asteroid opens the Abyss, figuratively speaking. It means this asteroid will be responsible for evil being unleashed upon the world, which is the start of WW3.

Because the Abyss is not opened until the 5th Trumpet, this proves that the beast and Antichrist do not rise to power with the rider of the white horse of the 1st Seal. This one point destroys one of the major points on which the pretribulation Rapture theory is built, that all of Rev. 4 onwards takes place after the Rapture, and that the Antichrist comes to power with the 1st Seal.

The Seals and Trumpets are not concurrent; the 1st Seal does not take place at the same time as the 1st Trumpet. The events of the Seals take place before the events of the Trumpets.

So the events that take place after the 5th Trumpet, take place as a result of the asteroid impact and includes the rise of the beast with ten horns. The events of the other Trumpets also are important in allowing the rise of the beast, but the asteroid impact is just the final event that will ultimately open the Abyss and allow the beast to rise again. Revelation 9 continues:

> 3 And out of the smoke locusts came down upon the earth and were given power like that of scorpions of the earth. 4 They were told not to harm the grass of the earth or any plant or tree, but only those people <u>who did not</u> have the seal of God on their foreheads. 5

They were not given power to kill them, but only to <u>torture them for five months</u>. And the agony they suffered was like that of the sting of a scorpion when it strikes a man. 6 During those days men will seek death, but will not find it; they will long to die, but death will elude them. (9:3-6)

The locusts would have to be giant in size to represent helicopters, as some interpreters have suggested. But no one is killed, so the locusts cannot represent warfare. Notice also that no Christians (or Jews) are stung. More interpretation will be given shortly, but pay careful attention to the next block of verses, as they are important to understand the meaning of the above passage. Rev. 9 continues:

7 The locusts looked like horses <u>prepared for battle</u>. On their heads they wore something like crowns of gold, and their faces resembled human faces. 8 Their hair was like women's hair, and their teeth were like lions' teeth. 9 They had breastplates like <u>breastplates of iron</u>, and the sound of their wings was like the thundering of many horses and chariots <u>rushing into battle</u>.

10 They had tails and stings like scorpions, and in their tails they had <u>power to torment people</u> for <u>five months</u>. 11 They had as king over them the angel of the Abyss, whose name in Hebrew is Abaddon, and in Greek, Apollyon. 12 The first woe is past; two other woes are yet to come. (9:7-12)

Abaddon and Apollyon mean *"the Destroyer."* How could their king be called "the Destroyer" if they do not kill people? This is very puzzling. The locusts appear to describe an army of soldiers with breastplates and helmets, with *"power to hurt people"* (v10)(ISV, ESV, GNB); an army has power to hurt people. The key to understanding the passage is the statement that they are *"prepared for battle."* This means the war has not yet started. These verses describe five months of preparation for war.

1 Kings says, *"My father scourged you with whips; I will scourge you with scorpions"* (12:11). The *NIV Study Bible* says scorpions refers to, *"Metal-spiked leather lashes."* The main emphasis of the 5th Trumpet is preparation for war; therefore the

scorpion stings represent governments forcing people into their armies. Since the locusts will only sting people for five months, it means they will spend five months drafting men into the army and getting ready for war. So there will be five months between the 5th and 6th Trumpets, the 6th being the start of World War 3.

It does *not* say that all people without the seal of God are stung; it says the only people who are stung do not have the seal. The reason that those with the seal of God are not stung is because they are Christians who are not allowed in the armies of Islamic nations. The beast of Rev. 13 will be a revived Ottoman Empire (Turkey) that was wounded in the 1800s and given the death blow in World War 1. It will likely be led by the Mahdi, which is a mythical future leader of the Muslims who is supposed to rise to power during a time of chaos and confusion, which is what we have here in Revelation 8 and 9.

It is possible that the ten horns will have already formed a commonwealth before this; if so, they will be an association of ten independent nations. But at this point they will appoint a single leader who will call all Muslims to join in jihad. So even if a commonwealth exists before this, they do not actually form an empire until this point. This is the point in time when the beast rises out of the Abyss and not before. Rev. 9 continues:

> During those days men will seek death, but will not find it; they will long to die, but death will elude them. (Rev. 9:6)

It helps to see the meaning of this by reading it in another translation:

> And in those days men will be hoping for death, and it will not come to them; and they will have a great desire for death, and death will go in flight from them. (BBE)

Even though some Muslims who oppose Islamic law will be forced against their will to join the army, others will join eagerly. Do you know a group of people who desire to die and look forward to dying? Yes, we all know who they are, the Muslim jihad warriors who believe if they die in war they are guaranteed a ticket to heaven where they will get 70 virgins each. But they are not able to die yet, because the war has not yet started.

On their heads they wore something like crowns of gold, and their faces resembled human faces. (Rev. 9:7)

Arabic headdress worn by Edward Lawrence of Arabia.

Muslims have always worn various types of headdresses, which they still wear. In addition, the Janissaries of the Ottoman Empire wore elaborate head coverings that looked even more like crowns.

(2) The Destroyer

They had as king over them the angel of the Abyss, whose name in Hebrew is <u>Abaddon</u>, and in Greek, <u>Apollyon</u>. 12 The first woe is past; two other woes are yet to come. (9:11-12)

Abaddon and Apollon both mean *"the Destroyer,"* therefore, the name of the ruler of this revived empire is *"the Destroyer."* In the Quran, Allah is described using many different names, much the way that Yahweh has many names in the Bible such as El-Shaddai, God Almighty. One of the names of Allah, depending on who does the translation from Arabic, is "Destroyer." I will not include all 99 names, but here is a sampling:

1. Ar-Rahman- The All-Merciful
9. Al-JaKhaliq- The Creator
15. Al-bbar- The Compeller

11. Al-Qahhar- The Subduer
62. Al-Mumeet- The Creator of Death, The Destroyer, The One who renders the living dead. (www.faizani.com/articles/names. html www.ahadith.co.uk/99 names of Allah.php?)

Some websites have the names numbered one digit differently and spelled differently; wikipedia.org has it this way:

61. Al-Mumit- The Destroyer, The Bringer of Death . . .
(en. wikipedia.org/wiki/Names_of_God_in_Islam)

So this passage in Revelation 9 literally names *Allah* as being the power behind the beast of Revelation! Given the history of what Islam has done to the nations it invaded and conquered, and is still doing today, "destroyer" exactly describes Islam.

The word "angel" does not mean only spiritual beings from God, but it literally means "*a messenger.*" So, this passage says the messenger of the Abyss is the king of the Abyss, and therefore of the army that is released. Muhammad is called "*the Messenger of Allah.*" Many of the names and attributes of Allah also fit Muhammad.

(Rev. 9:11 points us to Allah, and it was the followers of Allah who carried out the 9/11 attacks in the U.S.)

(3) The Abyss in Arabia

The Greek for "shaft" is *phrear* (5421), usually translated "pit," and means "*A well or pit dug in the earth for water or other purposes*" (CWD). Even though the Abyss in Rev. 9 is not a literal earthly location, it is truly amazing that the Ka'ba actually covers a pit where a snake once lived! Yes, it's true. (The Ka'ba is Islam's holiest temple, which is just a small cube-shaped building covered with a black cloth.) F.E. Peters wrote about this in his book, *The Hajj: The Muslim Pilgrimage to Mecca and The Holy Places*, Princeton Univ. Press, 1994.

He quotes two Muslim historians:

In a chapter entitled "The Building of the Ka'ba by the Quraysh in the Age of Barbarism," the Meccan historian al-Azraqi (d. 834 C.E.) collected some of the traditions still extent on the early appearance of the House before its substantial reconstruction during the early manhood of Muhammad. ... On the right as one entered the Ka'ba there was a pit where gifts of money and goods for the Ka'ba were deposited. In this pit sat a snake to guard it, which God had sent at the time of the (tribe of) Jurhum.... The horns of the ram that Abraham had slaughtered (in place of Isaac or Ishmael) were hanging on the wall facing the entrance.... (Azraqi 1858, p. 106) (Peters, p. 12)

Peters goes on to say:

In 605 C.E., when, if we follow the traditional chronology, Muhammad was thirty-five years old, a memorable event occurred in Mecca: the reconstruction of the Ka'ba, the only stone building in that town. We follow Ibn Ishaq's account:

. . . Now a snake used to come out of the well in which the sacred offerings were thrown and sun itself every day on the wall of the Ka'ba. It was an object of terror because whenever anyone came near it, it raised its head and made a rustling noise and opened its mouth, so that they were terrified of it. While it was thus sunning itself one day, God sent a bird which seized it and flew off with it.... (Ibn Ishaq 1955: p. 84-85) (Peters, page 46)

I do not believe it is a coincidence that there was a pit inside Islam's most holy temple, or that a snake lived in it, or that it terrorized people, since Islam has many terrorists. Peters also states that there is even a location in Arabia named, *Valley of the Abyss*" (Peters, p. 102)!

(4) The Dogs of War

In Revelation chapters 8 and 9 we have the first 6 of 7 Trumpets that will herald terrible events during the Great Tribulation; the first four are natural disasters. Rev. 7:16 says those who come out of the Great Tribulation will suffer hunger and thirst, so we know there will be famine, which is common in times of war.

If billions could die in famine, why not just kill your neighbors and take what food they may have so that your country or village will not starve? Famine has historically been an instigator of war, and it will at least be a contributing factor in WW3.

It is a little known fact that war does not increase mortality; mortality is 100% in every generation, it just brings death a few years sooner. Since some nations may be facing starvation, they will think to themselves that it is better to go out in a blaze of glory by dying for a cause they believe in such as the spread of Islam, the annihilation of Christians and Jews, the annihilation of Capitalism, the destruction of a neighboring country or city, or just the people next door. So the dogs of war will be unleashed upon the world as wars break out among many of the nations.

The natural disasters of the 2nd and 3rd Trumpets will open the door for the beast of Revelation to rise again. There will be no better time to invade Western Europe, the United States, or the country next door. Muslims may think to themselves that Allah has provided this opportunity for them to conquer the world.

Several passages in the Bible that refer to World War 3 say that war will rage between nations, cities, even neighbors, and relatives. It will be like a city with a hostile population that has suffered a power failure or government collapse, the populace then goes on a rampage of looting and killing and setting fires, only it will be global, *"Every man's sword will be against his brother"* (Ezekiel 38:21). This is not merely battlefield confusion, because other passages make it clear:

"I will stir up Egyptian against Egyptian-- brother will fight against brother, neighbor against neighbor, city against city, kingdom against kingdom." (Is. 19:2)

Every man will seize the hand of another, and they will attack each other. (Zechariah 14:13)

People will oppress each other-- man against man, neighbor against neighbor. The young will rise up against the old, the base against the honorable. (Is. 3:5)

This concept is also found in the writings of the Apocrypha:

> Behold, the days are coming when the Most High will deliver those who are on the earth. 30 And bewilderment of mind shall come over those who dwell on the earth. 31 And they shall plan to make war against one another, city against city, place against place, people against people, and kingdom against kingdom. (2 Ezra 13:29-31)

The deliverance prophesied above takes place after the war. This next verse does in fact refer to confusion during war, probably the Battle of Armageddon that will be the last battle of WW3:

> "On that day I will strike every horse with panic and its rider with madness," declares the LORD. (Zech. 12:4)

Jesus said that strange things will take place in this solar system before he returns (Luke 21:25-26), so the battlefield confusion could be caused when people see something like the light of the sun change color, or something else odd. Whatever happens could really mess with people's minds. It will also affect horses and other animals, because animals are actually more sensitive to changes in nature than humans, such as knowing that an earthquake is about to take place.

(5) Sixth Trumpet: Missiles and Rockets

When the angel blows the 6th Trumpet in Rev. 9, John sees fire-breathing horses. John's description was not an attempt to describe a modern weapon. John described exactly what he saw, but it is symbolism that must be interpreted; but when properly interpreted it turns out to be modern missiles and rockets:

> 13 The sixth angel sounded his trumpet, and I heard a voice coming from the horns of the golden altar that is before God. 14 It said to the sixth angel who had the trumpet, "Release the four angels who are bound at the great river Euphrates." 15 And the four angels who had been kept ready for this very hour and day and month and year were released to kill a third of mankind. 16 The number of

the mounted troops was two hundred million. I heard their number. (Rev. 9:13-16)

The Euphrates River begins in Turkey and flows through Syria and Iraq, but the major portion is in Iraq. The four angels of destruction being released from the Euphrates tells us that the final war of this age will begin in Turkey, Syria, or Iraq, or at least be caused by the people living in that region. It also tells us that the beast will be based in Islam. Armageddon will be the last battle of this war and is seen in Rev. 16. Rev. 9 continues:

> 17 The horses and riders I saw in my vision looked like this: Their breastplates were fiery red, dark blue, and yellow as sulfur. The heads of the horses resembled the heads of lions, and out of their mouths came fire, smoke and sulfur. 18 A third of mankind was killed by the three plagues of fire, smoke and sulfur that came out of their mouths. 19 The power of the horses was in their mouths and in their tails; for their tails were like snakes, having heads with which they inflict injury. (Rev. 9:17-19)

One-third of all people on Earth will be killed in this war. Therefore, it must include a nuclear war, because a regular war cannot kill between 2 and 3 billion people.

This is what John saw.

head that kills

Notice that it says the *"power of the horses was in their mouths and in their tails."* This describes two different power sources. It is the power at the tail that kills people.

The rider (not shown in the drawings) tells us it is controlled by humans. The verse says the tails have heads on them like snakes; and since the tail's head inflicts injury with fire, smoke and sulfur, then the head of the tail must explode. So it is the heads on the tails that explode. A missile's payload of explosives is in the nose-cone and is called a *warhead.*

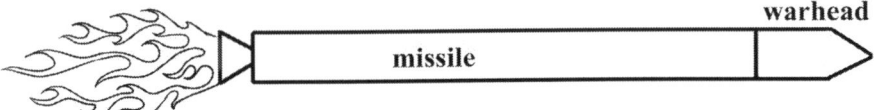

The power of the mouth is at the opposite end and propels the missile to its target. The metal breastplate of the rider represents the outer metal covering of the missile. The breastplates have colors on them, as do missiles that identify their intended purpose, and the type of explosive they are carrying, and so forth.

Rockets travel up then down as they travel toward their targets, like an artillery shell; but guided missiles have the ability to make turns as they travel. Consider the tail of these horses that are like snakes. The snake-like tail is what turns the tail's head. Directly behind the missile's warhead is the guidance and control section.

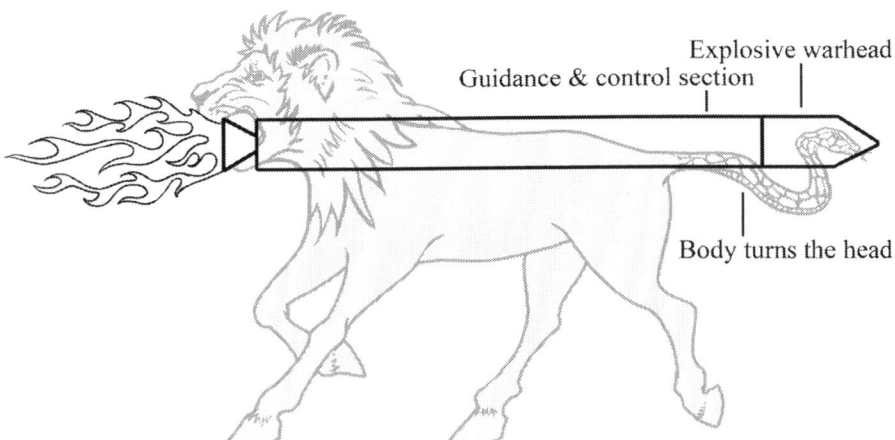

John's description is not specific enough to refer to one particular missile; it refers to all self-propelled missiles and rockets regardless of size, from the small shoulder-launched missiles to the intercontinental. There will be 200 million missiles and rockets used in this war; rockets do not have guidance systems.

Notice that the command to release the angels of destruction come from the altar before God. Because of the large number killed and the specific date given, *"this very hour and day and year,"* we know that this war will not and cannot start until this exact point in time. There is security in knowing that World War 3 and nuclear war cannot happen today, except the specific day and hour that God has appointed. The 6th Trumpet blast signals the start of WW3. The nuclear war described in the 7 Bowls of Wrath takes place near the end of the war. However, it is *possible* the U.S. will be hit by a nuclear strike before then, because the nuclear effects described there are said to hit the beast of Rev. 13, and may not be a global nuclear war at that time.

(6) The Prophet Joel

The prophet Joel in the Old Testament saw the same army of horses that John saw. In the following Scripture, notice that the horses leap over the mountain tops, destroy with fire, cause the earth to shake, and cause clouds and darkness that will darken the sun and moon. The army of the Lord here in Joel is not resurrected saints, or angels, it is missiles and rockets. Also notice the term *"the day of the Lord,"* which is the time of God's Wrath, so it refers to the final battles of WW3 that will include nuclear weapons:

> 1 Blow the trumpet in Zion; sound the alarm on my holy hill. Let all who live in the land tremble, for the day of the LORD is coming. It is close at hand-- 2 a day of darkness and gloom, a day of clouds and blackness. Like dawn spreading across the mountains a large and mighty army comes, such as never was of old nor ever will be in ages to come. 3 <u>Before them fire devours, behind them a flame blazes</u>. (Joel 2:1-3a)

This describes the same two power sources that John described. The fire that devours is caused by the explosion of the rocket; the flame that blazes behind them is the burning fuel that propels the rocket. Joel 2 continues:

Before them the land is like the Garden of Eden, behind them, a desert waste-- nothing escapes them. 4 They have the appearance of horses; they gallop along like cavalry. 5 With a noise like that of chariots they leap over the mountaintops, like a crackling fire consuming stubble, like a mighty army drawn up for battle. 6 At the sight of them, nations are in anguish; every face turns pale.

7 They charge like warriors; they scale walls like soldiers. They all march in line, not swerving from their course. 8 They do not jostle each other; each marches straight ahead. They plunge through defenses without breaking ranks. 9 They rush upon the city; they run along the wall. They climb into the houses; like thieves they enter through the windows. (Joel 2:3-9)

This can only describe nuclear missiles. The statement that the land is like the Garden of Eden before them and after them is like a desert waste, refers to the great destructive ability of these symbolic horses; it does not literally mean that the land will be like the Garden of Eden before the destruction. The fact that *"nothing escapes them"* also refers to their destructive ability. A nuclear explosion can turn steel beams into fine dust!

Notice that it says they *"march in line, not swerving from their course . . . each marches straight ahead."* Missiles have guidance systems but rockets do not, so rockets can only go straight. It also says that never before has there been such an army, and there will never be another; World War 3 and nuclear war will only happen once. Humanity will never again build nuclear weapons, and they will never again build rockets and missiles of any type.

Before them the earth shakes, the sky trembles, the sun and moon are darkened, and the stars no longer shine. (Joel 2:10)

It is a known fact that earthquakes accompany nuclear explosions. What is not known is whether the explosions create earthquakes or trigger earthquakes waiting to happen. About one day after the nuclear test in North Korea Oct. 9, 2006, there was a strong quake in Japan. Japan gets frequent quakes, but on Oct. 15th there was also a strong quake in Hawaii. Shortly after the future global nuclear war, there will be a huge global earthquake:

No earthquake like it has ever occurred since the human race has been on earth, so tremendous was the quake. (Rev. 16:18)

Also notice the word "before" in verse 10. This could mean, "preceding," but most likely means *"in the presence of"* which **would mean the earthquakes and sky turning dark, take place near** the same time as the nuclear war.

> The LORD thunders at the head of his army; his forces are beyond number, and mighty are those who obey his command. The <u>day of the LORD</u> is great; it is dreadful. Who can endure it? . . . 31 The sun will be turned to darkness and the moon to blood before the coming of the great and dreadful day of the LORD. (Joel 2:11, 31)

Notice also that, *"the sun and moon are darkened, and the stars no longer shine."* This nuclear war will bring dark clouds that will likely cover the entire globe. The above verses indicate that the nuclear war will take place at the end of the Great Tribulation and will serve as part of God's judgment upon the world.

The prophet Jeremiah also records the words of God speaking about World War 3 and the final battle of Armageddon:

> 11 At that time this people and Jerusalem will be told, "A scorching wind from the barren heights in the desert blows toward my people, but not to winnow or cleanse; 12 <u>a wind too strong</u> for that comes from me. Now I pronounce my judgments against them." 13 Look! He advances like the clouds, his chariots come like a whirlwind, his <u>horses are swifter than eagles</u>. Woe to us! We are ruined! . . . 20 Disaster follows disaster; the whole land lies in ruins. In an instant my tents are destroyed, my shelter in a moment. (Jer. 4:11-13, 20)

A squadron of planes *"advances like the clouds."* Helicopters are probably the chariots that are *"like a whirlwind"* because the blades spin around and create a strong circular wind. The horses that are *"swifter than eagles"* are missiles and rockets. And the destructive force of an explosion is released in less than a second,

"In an instant my tents are destroyed, my shelter in a moment."
These prophecies are conclusive, nuclear war is coming.

Notice the statement, *"a wind too strong;"* nuclear explosions create powerful winds that sweep across the countryside and destroy like a tornado. But it may refer to a super-storm, which will not be explained here, but must wait for another book.

The prophet Isaiah said:

> But your enemies will become like <u>fine dust</u>, the ruthless hordes like <u>blown chaff</u>. Suddenly, in an instant, 6 the Lord Almighty will come with thunder and earthquake and <u>great noise</u>, with windstorm and <u>tempest</u> and <u>flames of a devouring fire</u>. (Isaiah 29:5-6)

This likely describes nuclear war. The literal translation of *"the Lord Almighty"* is *"the Lord of Armies"* which is the way the GW translation reads. Just one hydrogen bomb, also called thermonuclear, is 1,000 times more powerful than the bomb that destroyed Hiroshima. We have bombs today that are 4,000 times more powerful than the one at Hiroshima! One American submarine can carry 24 nuclear missiles, each with 14 independently targeted warheads totaling enough explosive power to equal 24,000 Hiroshimas. Eight nations are known to have nuclear weapons: the United States, Russia, England, France, Pakistan, India, North Korea, and China, but several others are believed to have them, including Brazil and Israel. Even though Turkey does not currently have nuclear weapons, when WW3 starts, or even before, they could easily get them from Pakistan, or Russia, or Iran after Iran gets them.

The radiation from an explosion can travel for hundreds of miles in all directions, so if you do not want to die in nuclear war, and you are not one of those judged worthy of going in the Rapture or receive protection from God, then you should be far away from the high population centers of the world. And the nuclear "fallout" can fall on land hundreds or thousands of miles away. Nuclear fallout is radioactive particles of dirt and material destroyed in the blast that get taken up into the mushroom cloud and gradually falls out over a period of months. The first week is the most critical. After the first 24 hours, the radiation begins to decay and in just one week it will be 1/1000th as strong. So you must remain in a shelter for at least one week after the nuclear war.

Since nuclear explosions will not be in every city, state or nation, the real danger will be the radioactive fallout, or from the poison air. The nuclear explosions will burn up chemical plants and cities full of plastic, glue, tires, gasoline, and other toxins, creating huge clouds of toxic air that will kill people within minutes, quicker than from radioactive fallout.

(7) Ramifications

The prophecies of the missiles and rockets are of great importance, for several reasons:

(1) They can be used by Christian apologists to prove the Bible.

(2) They prove there is a spirit-world, so we are not just beings of flesh and bones; it does this because mere beings of flesh and bones could never see 2,500 years into the future, as Joel did.

(3) The prophecies also prove that there will in fact be a final war that will kill billions of people, that God will have a people which will fight in this war, and that God will fight along with them, "*The LORD thunders at the head of his army; his forces are beyond number, and mighty are those who obey his command*" (Joel 2:11). (This passage also proves the pretrib Rapture theory is false because how could God have an army after the Church is removed?

(4) It proves that the doctrine of Preterism is wrong.

(5) It also proves the doctrine of the imminent return of Christ is wrong, because no war that uses these modern missiles and rockets could ever have been fought before the 20th century.

Chapter 9
Daniel's Ten Toes

(1) Ten Toes of the Statue

Daniel had several prophetic dreams concerning the end-time; like most dreams, the message Daniel received was presented with symbolism that must be interpreted.

In Daniel chapter 2, the king of Babylon has a dream that Daniel interprets for him. He sees a huge statue that represents four great kingdoms; the head of gold represents Babylon, the chest and arms of silver represent Media-Persia that conquered Babylon, the belly and thighs of bronze represent Greece, the legs of iron represent the Roman Empire, and finally the feet and toes of baked clay represent a final kingdom that will exist at the return of Christ.

The meaning of the first four kingdoms is easily agreed upon because the text says that Babylon is the head of gold and we know which empires followed, but the ten toes are in dispute. Many Bible interpreters believe that the European Union (EU) are the ten toes because they came from the Roman Empire. But there are now over twenty-seven nations in the EU, and more could be added. At this writing, the twenty-seven EU member nations are: Germany, France, United Kingdom, Italy, Spain, Poland, Romania, Netherlands, Greece, Portugal, Belgium, Czech Republic, Hungary, Sweden, Austria, Bulgaria, Slovakia, Denmark, Finland, Ireland, Lithuania, Latvia, Slovenia, Estonia, Cyprus, Luxembourg, and Malta.

Because there are more than ten nations in the EU, some teachers are now saying the ten toes represent ten regions of the globe that will be the world government, but I have already proven that there will not be a world government or a one-world dictator. So what nations are the ten toes? An analysis of the passage reveals important details:

> 41 Just as you saw that the feet and toes were partly of baked clay and partly of iron, so this will be <u>a divided kingdom;</u> yet it will have <u>some of the strength</u> of iron in it, even as you saw iron mixed with clay. 42 As the toes were partly iron and partly clay, this kingdom will be <u>partly strong and partly brittle.</u> 43 And just as you saw the iron mixed with baked clay, so the people will be a mixture and <u>will not remain united,</u> any more than iron mixes with clay. (Daniel 2:41-43)

The time of the toes' existence on earth is not past history. The Scripture text clearly puts the ten toes here on Earth at the second coming of Christ:

> 34 "While you were watching, a rock was cut out, but not by human hands. It struck the statue on its feet of iron and clay and smashed them. . . .
>
> 44 "<u>In the time of those kings,</u> the God of heaven will set up a kingdom that will never be destroyed, nor will it be left to another people. It will crush all those kingdoms and bring them to an end, but it will itself endure forever. 45 This is the meaning of the vision of the rock cut out of a mountain, but not by human hands--a rock that <u>broke the iron, the bronze, the clay, the silver and the gold to pieces.</u> The great God has shown the king what will take place in the future. The dream is true and the interpretation is trustworthy." (Daniel 2:34, 44-45)

It says in the days *"of those kings,"* which means that while the ten toes are in power, Christ will return and set up his kingdom. It says the ten toes will have *"a divided kingdom,"* which means it is an association of separate nations like the European Union.

But how do we account for the fact that there are ten toes but twenty-seven nations? The elements of the statue should not be taken so literally. How many people do you know with twenty-seven toes? The statue is not going to show twenty-seven toes, but only ten. An example from the other parts of the statue is that Greece split into four empires, but it is not seen in the statue. And the Media-Persian empire did not split into two, but it shows two arms. Also, Rome did not start out as two empires, but it is seen as the two legs, though later it divided into east and west, and it ended as one empire after the western half fell. Did one of the legs get cut off the statue? No. So you see, you cannot force the elements of the statue into such extreme detail that is not in the text, it is only giving us partial information. The statue having ten toes merely means that there will be many separate nations joined together in an alliance.

However, it will never rule the world. Why? Because it never says anywhere that it will! Bible commentators have been making the toes to be the same as the ten horns of the forth beast in Daniel 7, but that is wrong as we will see in the next chapter, but even the ten horns on the that beast is never said to rule the world.

Notice that Daniel says the old Roman Empire was made of iron. Rome did not rule the whole world, but only western and southeastern Europe, North Africa, and part of the Middle East. Rome often had to use force to put down rebellions, and the ten toes will only have "*some of the strength of iron*," which means that the ten toes will not even be as strong as Rome, which did not have modern weapons. So if the ten toes will not even be as strong as the Roman Empire, then it certainly will not rule the entire world.

Notice also that the text does not say that one toe is iron and one toe is clay. It says that all the toes are a mixture of iron and clay; "*the iron mixed with baked clay,*" each toe is a mixture. Therefore, I believe the iron and clay represent cultural aspects of those nations which will keep them from becoming fully mixed together and united. Daniel 2 says:

> "And just as you saw the iron mixed with baked clay, so the people will be a mixture and will not remain united, any more than iron mixes with clay." (Daniel 2:42-43)

This passage tells us that the EU will never be totally united, but will continue to be a divided kingdom. This lack of total union is depicted in the iron and baked clay because iron and baked clay cannot be melted or mixed together to form one substance.

Now consider the baked clay; baked clay is pottery that breaks very easily, which is why the toes are *"partly brittle"* and represents weakness. As a result of being brittle, it *"will not remain united,"* which means some nations will leave the EU as Norway has already done, and other things will happen, such as civil wars.

Notice the statement, *"the people will be a mixture."* Even though the nations of the EU speak many different languages, because they have spent so much time living near each other, their cultural differences have become smaller. The people of modern Europe travel between the nations with ease, they view each other's TV shows, listen to each other's music, read each other's magazines and newspapers, and even intermarry. They trade with each other, use the same money, the Euro, are under the same political umbrella (EU), and therefore have almost become one nation; given another hundred years they could become one nation.

So what does it mean that the people will be a mixture and not remain united? Describing the people as iron and clay that does not mix does not seem to fit modern Europe, *until events of the last thirty years.* In recent years something new and totally foreign has entered Europe, something that is not mixing with everything I have just mentioned above. That something is vast numbers of Muslims that have entered the EU nations.

We can get more information from this passage by looking at the King James Version:

> 43 And whereas thou sawest iron mixed with miry clay, they shall mingle themselves with the <u>seed of men</u>: but they shall not cleave [mix] one to another, even as iron is not mixed with clay. (Daniel 2:43) (KJV)

The mixture is not between one nation and another nation, but is in the *"seed of men,"* the people themselves. Some modern translations say that the people are intermarrying, but that is not what it literally says. *Barnes Notes* on this verse states:

> Various explanations have been given of this verse, and it certainly
> is not of easy interpretation. The phrase "seed of men," would
> properly denote something different from the original stock that
> was represented by iron; some foreign admixture that would be so
> unlike that, and that would so little amalgamate with it, as to be
> properly represented by clay as compared with iron. . . . The word
> rendered "men" (אנשא ănâshâ') is employed in Hebrew and in
> Chaldee to denote men of an inferior class - the lower orders, the
> common herd - in contradistinction from the more elevated and
> noble classes, represented by the word איש (îysh). See Isa. 2:9; Isa.
> 5:15; Pro. 8:4.
>   The word here used . . . would properly denote feebleness or
> inferiority, and would be aptly represented by clay as contrasted
> with iron. The expression "seed of men," as here used, would
> therefore denote some intermingling of an inferior race with the
> original stock; some union or alliance under the one sovereignty,
> which would greatly weaken it as a whole, though the original
> strength still was great. The language would represent a race of
> mighty and powerful men, constituting the stamina - the bone and
> the sinew of the empire - mixed up with another race or other races,
> with whom, though they were associated in the government, they
> could never be blended; could never assimilate. This foreign ad-
> mixture in the empire would be a constant source of weakness, and
> would constantly tend to division and faction, for such elements
> could never harmonize.

The above perfectly describes Muslims living in Europe. Europe's Muslim population is not blending with Europeans; they are
not becoming European because they live by and enforce Islamic
law within their own sections of town. This is how the people are a
mixture that cannot truly blend or unite, like oil and water. Even
Sayyid Qutb, the Islamic ideologue, stated this same thing:

> "The chasm between Islam and Jahiliyyah [the unbelievers] is
> great, and a bridge is not to be built across it so that the people on
> the two sides may mix with each other, but only so that the Jahi-
> liyyah may come over to Islam." (*Milestones*)

Large-scale immigration of Muslims to Europe and North America is part of the Islamic plan for global conquest. The Muslims plan to grow in numbers and power until they are able to overthrow their host governments. The birth rates of Europeans is so low that they cannot maintain their populations, so they are importing millions of Muslim immigrants who are reproducing at high rates. In only 30 years England went from having 82,000 Muslims to having 2.5 million with thousands of mosques. The Netherlands will be 50% Muslim in 2025. Throughout Europe, Muslims are expected to be 50% of the population by 2050.

The principle reason France would not support the U.S. invasion of Iraq is because of its large Muslim population, about six million, or 10% of the total population. The Muslim birthrate in Europe is three times higher than non-Muslim.

> If current trends continue, the Muslim population of Europe will nearly double by 2015, while the non-Muslim population will shrink by 3.5 percent. (*Europe's Muslim Street*, March 2003, Omer Taspinar, The Brookings Institution; www.brookings.edu/views/op -ed/fellows/taspinar 20030301.htm)

Muslims do not need to be 51% to take over. They are already intimidating European governments into prosecuting people who criticize Islam or who warn people about Islamic fascism. In early 2009, the Dutch government ordered the criminal prosecution of Geert Wilders, who produced the film, *Fitna,* which exposes Islamic fascism. In England, a member of the House of Lords arranged for Geert Wilders to come and speak to a group of the Lords, but when a Muslim member, Lord Ahmed (originally from Pakistan), heard about it, he threatened to mobilize 10,000 Muslims to prevent Wilders from entering the House of Lords and threatened to sue his colleague who organized the event. When Wilders arrived he was deported by the British government because they feared the Muslims would riot.

In 2012, Muslims in Europe were able to cancel some Christmas pageants and the display of Christmas lights. This is just the beginning. Over the past 1,400 years, thousands of churches all over the Middle East and North Africa have been converted into mosques because of Islamic conquest, but in Europe thousands of churches are now being converted into mosques because of the decline of Christianity and the growth of Islam. An old prophecy states that the French will not wake up until Notre Dame is converted into a mosque (*Europe Turns Churches into Mosques*, October 20, 2012, www.israelnationalnews.com/articles/article.aspx/ 12333).

In the Netherlands, there are still approximately 4,400 churches, but, "*Each week, two close their doors forever. A synagogue in The Hague was turned into the al Aqsa Mosque*" (Ibid).

In England, 10,000 churches have been closed since 1960. By 2020, another 4,000 churches will close while there will be, it is predicted, 1,700 new mosques, many of which will occupy former churches (Ibid).

St. Mark's Cathedral is now a mosque called *New Peckam Mosque*. Even Germany is blind to the poison it has allowed to enter its cities.

(2) Arabs and the Ten Toes

It has been pointed out by a handful of prophecy teachers that the original Aramaic word for "mix" in Daniel 2 is actually, "arab" (6151) ערב. These teachers believe it means the ten toes are Islamic nations, the same as the ten horns of Revelation. But Islamic nations do not have big problems with mixture of the races and cultures; there is no oil and water situation. Islamic nations only have minority populations of Christians today, but by 2036, Europe is projected to be 25-40% Muslim.

Most Islamic nations have the same language, the same religion, and the same culture, because Islam dominates in the Arab world. Even though there are two divisions in Islam, the vast majority are Sunni, with only a small number of Shia (Shite). And they often work together to defeat a common enemy, the Christians and Jews. So the ten toes cannot represent Islamic nations or Islam. Although Arabic nations have some differences, those differences are not significant compared to Islam in the EU.

So why does it use the word "arab"? This word is telling us who the people are who will come into the mix and cause the oil and water, iron and clay, situation in Europe. What makes the union so brittle is the sociological / religious differences.

The issue is not a union of nations, or a union between nations, but the cohesion of people inside of those nations, which is why it uses the phrase, *"seed of men."* It is referring to people rather than governments. (Some modern translations translate *"seed of men"* in different ways, such as marriages, but they are trying to interpret the verse rather than translate the actual words. You cannot do that for prophetic verses.)

Notice that we are told that the iron and clay will not remain united; but it also tells us that iron and clay will be a mixture of different cultures, which means it will never become fully united. Yet we are expected to believe that this mixture will become so strong it will rule the entire globe! Since what little mixture there is will not last, there will likely be riots and warfare between the Muslims and their host countries, perhaps full civil war.

The information in this chapter is significant proof against the popular teaching that says the Antichrist and the EU will rule the world as the Revived Roman Empire. Nowhere does it ever say that these ten toes will rule the world or even conquer a single nation; it is not in the text! It is an extreme misreading to make such statements.

(3) Double Fulfillment

The ten toes appear to have only one fulfillment, but the rest of the statue has a double fulfillment because it says that when Messiah comes he will destroy not only the ten toes but also the other three kingdoms:

> 34 "While you were watching, a rock was cut out, but not by human hands. It struck the statue on its feet of iron and clay and smashed them.
>
> 35 Then the iron, the clay, the bronze, the silver and the gold were broken to pieces at the same time and became like chaff on a threshing floor in the summer. The wind swept them away without

leaving a trace. But the rock that struck the statue became a huge mountain and filled the whole earth." (Daniel 2:34-35)

So this means there must be four nations on Earth today that are the gold, silver, bronze, and iron and may represent the original nations, which are today Iraq, Iran, Greece, and Italy. However, I doubt that strongly because Iraq is not going to become a "gold" nation. Whoever these nations are, they will cease to exist after the global destruction, but will likely have a few survivors.

Jesus is seen symbolically as the rock that will smash these nations and set up his own Kingdom that will spread across the globe. However, it says the rock will be cut from a mountain, but not by human hands. Jesus is not a piece of rock from a mountain, so why did it say that? It is using figurative, symbolic language to describe how Jesus will bring about the destruction of those nations, which is with an asteroid impact.

If it merely called him a rock, then it would refer to his strength and stability, but it specifically says a rock cut from a mountain. A rock cut from a mountain, but not by humans, can only refer to a large asteroid. We know that Christ will come with judgment upon the whole world, and we just learned that a rock will smash the statue. The imagery of a rock smashing nations must refer to an asteroid impact, not a missile or any other man-made object, because human hands have no part in this rock. This destruction will take place in addition to, and after, the nuclear war.

Chapter 10
Daniel's Four Beasts

(1) Four Great Nations Today

Daniel 7 records a vision of four beasts which we will examine in detail; *"Four great beasts, each different from the others, came up out of the sea"* (Daniel 7:3). They represent four nations. The first beast was like a lion with two eagle's wings, the second beast like a bear, and the third one like a leopard with four heads and four wings. The fourth beast is never actually described, except that it has large iron teeth and ten horns.

The standard interpretation says these four beasts represent Babylon, Media-Persia, Greece, and Rome, and the ten horns that come from the fourth beast are supposed to be the Revived Roman Empire. But the text never makes mentions Babylon or Nebuchadnezzar or makes any reference to the nations in Daniel's vision of a great statue. The statue dream clearly said the head was Babylon and the other kingdoms will come after Babylon, but here in Daniel 7 it merely says that four beasts come up out of the sea, so there is no reason to force these beasts into the that identification.

The correct interpretation relates to recent history and the end-time years, because Daniel plainly says that all four beasts will exist on Earth at the return of Christ, and the first three will live beyond that; but the fourth beast will be killed:

> ". . . I kept looking until the beast was slain and its body destroyed and thrown into the blazing fire. (The other beasts had been stripped of their authority, but were <u>allowed to live for a period of time</u>.)" (Daniel 7:11-12)

The New King James says:

"... As for the rest of the beasts, <u>they had their dominion taken away, yet their lives were prolonged for a season and a time</u>." (Daniel 7:11-12)

All of these nations will be in power at the return of Christ, which proves conclusively that there will not be a one-world government ruled by a dictator during the GT. At the end of the Great Tribulation, the body of the fourth beast will be thrown into the blazing fire; this could refer to nuclear destruction or to an asteroid impact. The other beasts are allowed to live for more than a year (a season and a time); therefore they are not killed. If they are not killed but are allowed to keep living, then it means they will exist here on Earth at the same time as the fourth beast.

Four beasts come to power, the fourth one is destroyed but the other three are not, <u>they are still alive</u>; therefore, <u>all four must exist at the same time in the last days</u>. But the three beasts will be stripped of their authority and power during the trouble of the Great Tribulation, World War 3, and Wrath of God. This means they will suffer loss of their power and strength because of the destruction they receive, but will still be alive. Therefore, they will not be totally destroyed, but will have survivors and at least some governmental functions.

(2) Lion and Eagle: British Empire & United States

Since Daniel 7 shows that the four nations must be on Earth today, as you read the following verses, take careful note of all the symbolism and think about what nation it could represent:

"The first was like a lion, and it had two wings of an eagle. I watched until its wings were torn off and it was lifted from the ground so that it stood on two feet like a man, and the heart of a man was given to it." (Dan. 7:4)

The lion is the symbol of Britain, and here it represents the British Empire. When the wings of an eagle are torn from the lion's back is when the American colonies gained their independence in the Revolutionary War, so the eagle's wings represent the United States. The word "torn" is significant because the separation did not happen through peaceful negotiation, but through war.

(When I first figured out this interpretation I thought it was totally my own, but a few years later I remembered that a fellow had come to my church when I was about 11 years old and spoke about the lion being England and the eagle being the U.S. But I had forgotten it. So whether I figured it out for myself anew, or pulled it out of my memory, I will never know. This is the only part that may go to someone else. I do not remember the man's name, but I think he had red hair and lived in Texas.)

The British Empire once ruled a large part of the world. It was said that the sun never set on the British Empire because it was so large the sun was always shining on part of it. Britain invaded many nations to exploit the people and natural resources. Among the nations it once ruled or still rules are: South Africa, Pakistan, India, Burma, Ceylon, Dominican Republic, Uganda, Kenya, Sudan, Rhodesia (Zimbabwe), Swaziland, Nigeria, Singapore, Hong Kong, Fiji, Honduras, Bermuda, Barbados, Bahamas, Grenada, Jamaica, Canada, Australia, New Zealand, and others.

In the Opium War of 1839-1842, England fought with China to force it to allow England to sell opium freely in China. This is how England acquired Hong Kong. A present-day equivalent of this war would be if Columbia fought a war with Brazil to force them to legalize the unlimited importation of cocaine. No wonder the Bible portrays Great Britain as a beast.

However, the verse also says, "*it was lifted from the ground . . . and the heart of a man was given to it.*" This passage tells us that England will stop being a beast, and so it has. Britain remained a beast well into the 20th-century when it stopped invading nations and allowed most countries in its empire to have independence. It is now a modern civilized nation, so far as unprovoked military aggression for profit is concerned.

(3) Bear: Russia

"And there before me was a second beast, which looked like a bear. It was raised up on one of its sides, and it had three ribs in its mouth between its teeth. It was told, "Get up and eat your fill of flesh!" (7:5)

This bear is Russia that became the Soviet Union in the Bol-shevik Revolution of 1917. It is impossible to say with certainty what the three ribs represent; three wars, or maybe three regions that Russia conquered. Russia has conquered many peoples and land as it enlarged itself in all directions.

Russia became part of the U.S.S.R., but the U.S.S.R. no longer exists. Russia was the bear before it became the Soviet bear, and the fighting in Chechnya in 1994-96 to keep control over land it acquired when it was a monarchy is evidence that Russia is still the bear, and will remain so.

We should keep in mind that one verse of Scripture cannot possibly detail the entire history of a nation. We are only given enough information to be able to identify who these beasts are.

Notice also that the bear came up after the lion, and Russia be-came powerful after Britain.

(4) Leopard: Saudi Arabia

"After that, I looked, and there before me was another beast, one that looked like a leopard. And on its back it had four wings like those of a bird. This beast had four heads, and it was given authori-ty to rule." (7:6)

The identity of this beast is much harder to ascertain, so I am not 100% certain of my analysis, but it is the best I can do. This beast is Saudi Arabia. How could this be? Notice that it does not say that this beast will eat much flesh like the bear, but merely that the beast has power to rule-- to rule its own land.

The leopard was once common in Africa, Asia, and the Middle East. It is quick, fierce, likes to hunt at night, and takes its victims by surprise. The Saud dynasty began in the fifteenth-century Ara-bia but was unimportant until the mid 18th-century when Muhammad ibn Saud joined forces with Muhammad ibn-Abdul Wahhab, who preached a strict form of Islam known as Wahhabi. Together they spread Wahhabi with the sword. By 1805, the Saudis and Wahhabis controlled most of Arabia, but foreign invaders and tribal disputes shrank the holdings to the central Najd region.

In 1867, family feuds weakened the Saud's hold on the Najd, resulting in civil war among the tribes. When Abdul Aziz ibn Saud was born in 1880, his father held only the city of Riyadh. Then in 1891, the Saud family was forced to flee into exile. In 1901, ibn-Saud returned and easily captured Riyahd in a surprise night attack. His father then formally proclaimed him Governor of *Najd*, and leader of the Wahhabi. With the help of the Wahhabi, he spent the next several years fighting for control of Arabia. In 1913, he proceeded to take the eastern region of Hasa:

> Resorting to his favorite surprise tactics, he marched on Hofuf with seven hundred picked camel cavalrymen who crossed the moat, scaled the wall, killed the sentries, stormed the main fort and had the Governor captured- all within six hours. (*Saudi Arabia*, by K.S. Twitchell, Princeton U. Press, 1947, p. 96)

In 1921, after taking the region of Hail, he was proclaimed Sultan. After many victories against tribal uprisings, he captured the western region of Hijaz in 1925. This region had recently been freed from the Turks by King Husain, with help from Colonel T.E. Laurence of Britain, "*Laurence of Arabia*," and includes the cities of Mecca and Medina. In 1926, the region of Asir was annexed into Najd. At an assembly presided over by his father, ibn-Saud was asked to be King. Then in 1932, the four regions of Najd, Hijaz, Hasa, and Asir, became the Kingdom of Saudi Arabia.

So the four wings on the body of the leopard are the four regions that became modern Saudi Arabia. The country is also the place where Islam began, so the four heads represents the four men who helped establish Islam after Muhammad, the four Rightly Guided Caliphs, which were the first four caliphs. Without Islam, Saudi Arabia would not exist; it would be a totally different nation, having a different character, laws, boundaries, etc.

So the leopard signifies Saudi Arabia, the modern home of Islam; the four wings are the four regions, and the four heads are the first four Caliphs. You can see from the history of Arabia how the symbolism of the leopard signifies the character of the Saudis and Wahhabis. About the leopard in this verse, *Barnes Notes* says:

> The proper idea in this representation, when used as a symbol, would be of a nation or kingdom that would have more nobleness than the one represented by the bear, but a less decisive headship over others than that represented by the lion; a nation that, was addicted to conquest, or that preyed upon others; <u>a nation rapid in its movements, and springing upon others unawares, and perhaps in its spots denoting a nation or people made up, not of homogeneous elements, but of various different people.</u>

The different people being the different tribes. Even though modern Saudi Arabia does not send armies to conquer and prey on others, it is the home of the religion that has and does and will continue to conquer and oppress others. But Saudi Arabia is spending billions to finance the spread of terrorism and oppression worldwide. Now we move on to the fourth beast which is supposedly the Roman Empire and the ten horns coming from that region.

(5) Ten Horned Beast: Commonwealth of Independent States

> "After that, in my vision at night I looked, and there before me was a fourth beast--terrifying and frightening and very powerful. It had large iron teeth; it crushed and devoured its victims and trampled underfoot whatever was left. It was different from all the former beasts, and it had ten horns. . . .
>
> 23 "He gave me this explanation: 'The fourth beast is a fourth kingdom that will appear on earth. <u>It will be different from all the other kingdoms</u> and will devour the whole earth, trampling it down and crushing it. 24 The ten horns are ten kings who will come from this kingdom." (Dan. 7:7, 24)

Many people teach that the fourth beast was the Roman Empire, so then the ten horns will be ten modern nations that will come from the Roman Empire, and that the ten horns will rule the world with the Antichrist. But the verses don't say that the ten horns will rule the world, but <u>only the fourth beast *from* which the horns come</u>! This is not splitting hairs. Let me say that again to let it sink in to your brain. Only the fourth beast is said to rule the world, not the ten horns that come from it. So whoever the ten horns are, they will never rule the world.

But not even Rome actually ruled the world. No nation or empire has ever ruled the whole planet, Rome did not even rule the known world. Rome traded with far away places like India, so they knew that they did not rule the known world, yet they claimed that "all roads lead to Rome," because they ruled their part of world; meaning that they ruled everything within a reasonable distance of Rome.

However, this fourth beast, in actual fact, does not refer to the Roman Empire, because as we have seen, all these beasts represent nations that exist today and since the other three did not represent Babylon, Media-Persia, or Greece, then this final one does *not* represent Rome!

It is worth noting again that in this chapter each of the nations shown have come upon the world scene after the other, with some overlapping; England came upon the world scene hundreds of years before Russia, and then Saudi Arabia came up last as a whole nation. Next is the beast with ten horns that was born while Arabia was in the process of becoming the Kingdom of Saudi Arabia, and continued to grow in power, trampling down many other nations.

Notice that the fourth beast is different from the other beasts; it is different because it is the beast of Communism! The Communist Manifesto was written by Karl Marx and Friedrich Engels in December 1847 in London. In 1917, Russia became the second country to become Communist, when it became the U.S.S.R. (the 1st was Portugal, in 1910, but it did not remain Communist very long).

The U.S.S.R. spent 70 years trampling over many other nations, until it dissolved itself and left Communism in 1991; then ten of the fifteen U.S.S.R. nations formed the *Commonwealth of Independent States* (CIS). They are: Armenia, Kazakhstan, Belarus, Kyrgyzstan, Moldova, Russia, Tajikistan, Turkmenistan, Ukraine, and Uzbekistan. They are the ten horns that came "from" the beast of Communism.

You might suppose that if these ten horns are the Commonwealth, then the beast would have to be the U.S.S.R., but additional information is given to us later in Daniel 7:

> I kept looking until <u>the beast was slain and its body destroyed and thrown into the blazing fire</u>. 12 (The other beasts had been stripped of their authority, but were allowed to live for a period of time.) (Daniel 7:11-12)

If the body of the beast is the U.S.S.R., how can the body of the beast be destroyed at the coming of Christ if it no longer exists after the ten horns come from it? The ten horns <u>are not *on* the beast</u>, they <u>come *from* it</u>, which means they are now separate from the beast. The wording requires that the body of the beast continue to exist even after the ten horns come from the beast.

Since the beast continues to exist after the ten horns come from it, and it is not slain until the coming of Christ, then this beast represents Communism that will be destroyed in WW3 and the Wrath of God. The ten horns did not only leave the U.S.S.R., they also left Communism. How could the body of the beast be the old Roman Empire? Has it lasted more than 2,000 years? No.

Nowhere does it say that the ten horns are thrown into the fire, but only the body of the beast from which the horns come. It may be argued that the ten horns must also be in the fire since they are attached to the beast, but if they come from the beast and the beast is Communism, and they are no longer Communist countries, then it is not required that they also be in the fire. And since Russia is one of the ten horns and was the main country of the U.S.S.R., if the body of the beast were the U.S.S.R., then Russia would surely be destroyed. But it clearly states that the other three beasts previously mentioned, are not killed, and Russia is one of those beasts.

Only Communism and the *Commonwealth of Independent*

States fit the description given us here in Daniel. But where are the other five nations that were part of the U.S.S.R. that did not become part of the *Commonwealth of Independent States*? They are not mentioned because only ten of the fifteen nations formed an alliance together.

However, since the original formation of the CIS, two of the other five nations have joined; they are Georgia and Azerbaijan. The addition of two nations does not void the above interpretation because only ten came up together. The symbolism is not specific enough to detail every event that will take place during the existence of the CIS. But beyond that, the wording of verse 8 actually infers that other horns will come up besides the first ten:

> "While I was thinking about the horns, there before me was another horn, a little one, which came up among them; and three of the first horns were uprooted before it. This horn had the eyes of a man and a mouth that spoke boastfully." (Daniel 7:8)

I have often wondered about the wording of this passage; why did it say *"three of the first horns,"* why not merely say that it uprooted three of the horns? It indicates that other horns may join the ten, and that when the little horn comes to power it will uproot three of the original ten.

We cannot suppose that the only event that will happen among the ten horns is for a little horn to uproot three. Even though ten horns, followed by three being uprooted, are all that are seen in this vision, there could be many changes as the years go by. It was not possible to detail an extended history; many other events will surely happen.

Since Communism is thrown into the blazing fire, does this mean that China will be totally destroyed? No, it means that the governments and people who are Communists will no longer exist. There are over 100 million Christians in China, and the Christians there who do not go in the Rapture will survive the Wrath of God to become the rulers of that nation. Likewise, the rulers of North Korea will be destroyed, and the south will likely rule the north thereafter because there are many Christians there.

(6) The Little Horn

I have already established that the ten horns of the fourth beast have an alliance as the *Commonwealth of Independent States* (CIS). In Daniel's vision he sees another horn come up among the ten:

> 8 "While I was thinking about the horns, there before me was another horn, a little one, which came up among them; and three of the first horns were uprooted before it. This horn had eyes like the eyes of a human being and a mouth that spoke boastfully. . . ..
>
> 23 "He gave me this explanation: 'The fourth beast is a fourth kingdom that will appear on earth. It will be different from all the other kingdoms and will devour the whole earth, trampling it down and crushing it. 24 The ten horns are ten kings who will <u>come from this kingdom</u>. After them another king will arise, different from the earlier ones; <u>he will subdue three kings</u>. 25 He will speak against the Most High and oppress his holy people and try to change the set times and the laws. <u>The holy people will be delivered into his hands</u> for a time, times and half a time. (7:8, 23-26)

It is impossible to know all the details until they begin to happen, but the most likely interpretation is that the little horn, which is *"different from the earlier ones"* (7:24), also refers to an ideology the way the fourth beast was different because it was Communism. The verse says that three of the horns will be uprooted (7:8); then in verse 24 it says the little horn will "subdue" the three horns.

Therefore, the little horn most likely represents radical Islam that will cause internal revolution in three nations of the CIS. The three horns will then likely become part of the Islamic empire that will form. The mouth and eyes on the horn likely represent the final Antichrist, though it could represent Muhammad because he founded Islam.

When you look at the original ten nations that became the CIS, you will notice that several of them are predominately Muslim, such as Tajikistan (80% Muslim), Turkmenistan (87%), Uzbekistan (88%), and Azerbaijan (95%). In 1998, Kazakhstan (47%) was accused of selling nuclear weapons to Iran that were left over from the U.S.S.R. *Newsweek* magazine said in 1996 that Tajikistan was already *"teetering, as 40,000 Russian troops try to shore up a shaky secular government"* (Powell, "A Religious War?", 14 October 1996, p. 52).

One mullah said, *"We will take Kazakstan, then Uzbekistan and then,"* he roared, *"we will take Moscow!"* (Clifton, "The Islamic Nightmare", *Newsweek*, 14 October 1996, p. 51). That is a very boastful statement, which points us to Rev. 13, and to the little horn.

The *"time, times and half a time"* refers to 3.5 years (time=one year, times= two years), and refers to the 42-month rule of the beast of Revelation. This is more evidence that the three horns will become part of the coming Islamic empire, but not willingly. They either have civil war or will be invaded, thereby uprooting them from the CIS. Daniel says:

> . . . this horn was <u>waging war against the holy people</u> and defeating them, 22 until the Ancient of Days came and pronounced judgment in favor of the holy people of the Most High, and the time came when they possessed the kingdom. (Daniel 7:21-22)

The little horn will wage war against the Christians, but also Jews. Many Christians in the nations that get taken over by the next Islamic empire will probably be martyred or imprisoned. Islamic countries have always persecuted and killed Christians and Jews, so we should not be surprised when the persecution increases with the arrival of revived Islamic empire; which empire is now in the early stages of developing, as Muslim nations throw off their dictators and open the door to radical groups.

It is important to notice that it says the little horn will wage war against Christians; that is also what Revelation 13 says the beast will do. Notice that nothing is said here about the little horn rising to power by bringing world peace. It says nothing of world peace or world government.

Also, these ten horns are not the same as the ten horns in Revelation, because the text clearly states that the ten in Rev. are in full agreement. Rev. 17 says this about the ten horns:

> 12 "The ten horns you saw are ten kings who have not yet re-
> ceived a kingdom . . . 13 They <u>have one purpose</u> and will <u>give
> their power and authority to the beast</u>. 14 They will make war
> against the Lamb, . . . 17 For God has put it into their hearts to
> accomplish his purpose by <u>agreeing to give the beast their
> power to rule</u> . . . (Rev. 17:12-14, 17)

Notice that the ten horns all "agree" to give the beast their
power to rule. Which means they join together to form an empire,
thus becoming the final head of the beast.

The text does not say that their purpose is to give their power
and authority to the beast, but that they have the same purpose; it
says "they *have <u>one purpose</u>* AND *will give their power and authority . . .*" (NIV). The NKJV says, *"These are of one mind."*
Their one purpose is to make Islam the dominant world political
and religious power, and to kill all Christians and Jews who do not
convert.

The ten horns mentioned in Daniel 7 are not in agreement or
three would not be uprooted by the little horn. Therefore, the horns
in Daniel are different from those in Rev. 12. Revelation repeatedly mentions ten horns and makes no mention of three that are not
in agreement or are uprooted; all ten are in full agreement. No information is missing from Rev.

(7) Day of Judgment

Daniel 7 also confirms details of the global judgment from
God, after-which Christians will rule the world:

> 9 "As I looked, "thrones were set in place, and the Ancient of Days
> took his seat. His clothing was as white as snow; the hair of his
> head was white like wool. His throne was <u>flaming with fire</u>, and its
> wheels were all ablaze. 10 <u>A river of fire was flowing</u>, coming out
> from before him. Thousands upon thousands attended him; ten
> thousand times ten thousand stood before him. The court was seat-
> ed, and the books were opened. 11 "Then I continued to watch be-
> cause of the boastful words the horn was speaking. . .
> 13 "In my vision at night I looked, and there before me was

one like a son of man, <u>coming with the clouds of heaven</u>. He approached the Ancient of Days and was led into his presence. 14 He was given authority, glory and sovereign power; all nations and peoples of every language worshiped him. His dominion is an everlasting dominion that will not pass away, and his kingdom is one that will never be destroyed. 15 "I, Daniel, was troubled in spirit, and the visions that passed through my mind disturbed me. 16 I approached one of those standing there and asked him the meaning of all this. "So he told me and gave me the interpretation of these things: 17 'The four great beasts are four kings that will rise from the earth. 18 But <u>the holy people of the Most High</u> will receive the kingdom and will possess it forever—yes, for ever and ever.'" (Daniel 7:9-18)

The flaming fire and river of fire represent the type of judgment that will come upon the world, when fire rains down from heaven. Also, notice that the Son of Man comes on the clouds; the world will be covered with clouds at the end of the Great Tribulation because of all the fires, and the nuclear bombs and missiles. Clearly, Daniel was a true prophet. But coming with the clouds also signifies that Christ's coming will be first seen in the sky.

Notice that God will pronounce judgment upon all nations, including the four great beasts, which tells us that all four beasts will exist on Earth as separate nations at the time of the Day of Judgment, not just the fourth beast or the ten horns. No world-government shown here!

Also, these four beasts cannot be the four kingdoms of the statue in Daniel 2 because the text says the kingdoms of the statue will be destroyed by the coming of Christ, but the first three beasts are allowed to live, though they will most certainly be badly wounded. The only survivors will be Christians, so they will of course gain rulership of all nations by the authority of Christ.

Chapter 11
The End Arrives

(1) Mystery Accomplished

Next, Revelation 10 continues from Rev. 9:

> 1 Then I saw another mighty angel coming down from heaven. He was robed in a cloud, with a rainbow above his head; his face was like the sun, and his legs were like fiery pillars. 2 He was holding a little scroll, which lay open in his hand. He planted his right foot on the sea and his left foot on the land, 3 and he gave a loud shout like the roar of a lion. When he shouted, the voices of the seven thunders spoke. 4 And when the seven thunders spoke, I was about to write; but I heard a voice from heaven say, "Seal up what the seven thunders have said and do not write it down."
>
> 5 Then the angel I had seen standing on the sea and on the land raised his right hand to heaven. 6 And he swore by him who lives for ever and ever, who created the heavens and all that is in them, the earth and all that is in it, and the sea and all that is in it, and said, "There will be no more delay! 7 But in the days when the seventh angel is about to sound his trumpet, the mystery of God will be accomplished, just as he announced to his servants the prophets." (Rev. 10:1-7)

Here we learn that the mystery of God is completed just before the 7th Trumpet; in other words, the 7th Trumpet signals the completion of the mystery of God. The *Zondervan Ency.* defines mystery as, *"The counsel of God, unknown to man except by revelation, especially concerning His saving works and ultimate purposes in history"* (Vol. 4, p. 327).

Paul said:

9 And he made known to us the mystery of his will according to his good pleasure, which he purposed in Christ, 10 to be put into effect when the times will have reached their fulfillment--to bring all things in heaven and on earth together . . . (Ephesians 1:9-10)

Homer Hailey, in *Revelation: An Introduction and Commentary*, says:

> In the New Testament the word mystery describes the purpose and plan of God for human redemption. . . . The word does not imply the idea of "the mysterious," that which cannot be understood by man, but refers to that which can be understood only when the meaning is revealed to the initiated by the Holy Spirit through the apostles and prophets. (p. 114-115)

The 7th Trumpet signals the completion of God's plan to bring his Kingdom to Earth, which brings with it the Day of Judgment for the world and the rule of Christ on Earth. Though God's Wrath has already been visiting Earth in a limited way, it is not until the 7th Trumpet that his total Wrath will come upon the world. But the 7th Trumpet is not sounded here in Rev. 10; the angel is only *about to sound*. It will actually sound in the second half of Rev. 11. The *New English Bible* says:

> "There shall be no more delay; but when the time comes for the seventh angel to sound his trumpet, the hidden purpose of God will have been fulfilled, as he promised . . ." (NEB)

Revelation 10 continues:

> Then the voice that I had heard from heaven spoke to me once more: "Go, take the scroll that lies open in the hand of the angel who is standing on the sea and on the land." 9 So I went to the angel and asked him to give me the little scroll. He said to me, "Take it and eat it. It will turn your stomach sour, but in your mouth it will be as sweet as honey." 10 I took the little scroll from the angel's hand and ate it. It tasted as sweet as honey in my mouth, but when I had eaten it, my stomach turned sour. 11 Then I was told, "You must

prophesy again about many peoples, nations, languages and kings." (Rev. 10:8-11)

The little scroll is God's plan to bring in his Kingdom. The events in the scroll, or book, are being completed here in Revelation. Many Christians will become end time prophets and proclaim the coming of events described in Rev. and many other events not detailed in Revelation or Daniel. All genuine end time prophets will be persecuted in every way possible. Every kind of evil will be said about these end time prophets, and every backstabbing act will be done to them, even by other Christians who do not agree with what they are doing and saying. Some of them will be put in prison by false charges, some will be killed.

(2) Measuring the Temple

The first half of Revelation 11 will take place during the GT and will bring us up to the 7th Trumpet, where Revelation 10 left off.

> I was given a reed like a measuring rod and was told, "Go and measure the temple of God and the altar, and count the worshipers there. 2 But exclude the outer court; do not measure it, because it has been given to the Gentiles. They will trample on the holy city for 42 months." (Rev. 11:1-2)

The first response to this passage is the expectation that the Jewish Temple will be rebuilt, but this is symbolism like the seven candles mentioned in chapter one. As such, it does not refer to a literal temple. *Barnes Notes on the New Testament* says:

> Of course, this could not be understood of the literal temple - whether standing or not - for the exact measure of that was sufficiently well known. The word, then, must be used of something which the temple would denote or represent, and this would properly be the church, considered as the abode of God on the earth.

The literal Greek does not say anything about counting the worshipers, as some translations have it, but merely to measure the worshipers.

> And a reed like a staff was given to me, and the angel stood, saying, Rise and <u>measure the temple of God</u> and the altar, <u>and those worshiping</u> in it. (Rev 11:1) (LIT)

The measuring of the temple, the altar, and the worshipers refers to God judging the hearts, works, and purity of devotion of individual believers at the start of the GT to determine who will go in the Rapture. Those found worthy will be numbered among the 144,000. The fact that the outer court and the holy city are not measured means that they are not yet judged. The non-Christian Gentile world will be judged during the tribulation and especially at the end of the tribulation, but not at the start of the tribulation. Christians are judged first (1 Peter 4:17), whether Jew or Gentile.

Every occurrence of the word "temple" in Revelation is the Greek word "naos" (3485), and refers to the Holy Place inside the Temple, and is used of *"the mystical Body of Christ . . . of a local church . . . of the present body of individual believers"* (VED). The physical Temple building is referred to by the Greek "hieron."

So this temple is the inner temple, and refers to all Christians, because Christians are now the temple of God. Peter said that we *"like living stones, are being built into a spiritual house to be a holy priesthood, offering spiritual sacrifices acceptable to God through Jesus Christ"* (1 Peter 2:5). Some people believe the passage in Revelation refers to a literal tribulation Temple, but the Temple never had a place for "worshipers." Only priests entered the Temple; when the Bible speaks of Jesus and the Apostles going to the Temple, it refers to the outer courts where they did not "worship" but spoke to others.

Notice that the Temple is <u>not</u> trampled on by Gentiles, but only the outer court and the Holy City; which means that the literal Temple will not be rebuilt and then desolated by the Antichrist, as taught by believers in a 7-year tribulation. This is a very important point which they have failed to notice.

The *Zondervan NIV Bible Commentary* says:

> Just as the Jews referred to all other people outside the covenant as "Gentiles," so there gradually developed a similar Christian usage of the term that saw all peoples who were outside of Christ as eth-nos [Gentiles], including unbelieving Jews. (Vol. 2, p. 1176)

Since Christians are the Temple, which is spiritual Israel, they are not part of the Gentiles mentioned here. The Gentiles here are non-believers. Notice that the Gentiles trample on both the outer court and the holy city, but not the Temple. The Gentiles are now in charge of the governments of this world, but they cannot trample the hearts of Christians.

> * The Temple = the hearts of Christians throughout the world.
> * Measure the temple, altar, and worshipers = Judging individual Christians to determine who is worthy to take part in the Rapture; same as the numbering of the 144,000.
> * The outer court = non-believers.
> * The Holy City = the outward physical world. Just as God considers the whole planet to be his kingdom in Matthew 13, here it is the Holy City.
> * Trample for 42 months = the final 42 months of non-believing Gentile rule over this world, before Christians take over. Corresponds to the 42 months of the beast (Rev.13).

There might be a physical parallel to the above scenario. Jesus said, *"Jerusalem will be trampled on by the Gentiles until the times of the Gentiles are fulfilled"* (Luke 21:24). The Jews took control of most of Jerusalem in 1967, but not the Temple Mount, where a Muslim temple now stands. So the most important plot of land is still controlled by Gentiles. Which means that, if Rev. 11 has any application to the Temple Mount and a literal Temple, the Gentiles will continue to control the Temple Mount to the very end of the Gospel Age and the return of Christ and there will be no tribulation Temple. The times of the Gentiles are not fulfilled until Christ returns and ends the Gentile rule over this world.

Someone might say, wasn't the Church already seen in the 12-

tribes and the sealing of the 144,000? Yes, but the main point there was the choosing of the Firstfruits, which is confirmed in this passage by the measuring of the Temple. But this passage gives us more information, including that Gentile control over the Temple Mount will continue to the return of Christ, and that there will not be a tribulation Temple. Revelation 11 continues:

(3) The Two Witnesses

3 And I will give power to my two witnesses, and they will prophesy for 1,260 days, clothed in sackcloth." 4 These are the two olive trees and the two lampstands that stand before the Lord of the earth. 5 If anyone tries to harm them, fire comes from their mouths and devours their enemies. This is how anyone who wants to harm them must die. 6 These men have power to shut up the sky so that it will not rain during the time they are prophesying; and they have power to turn the waters into blood and to strike the earth with every kind of plague as often as they want.

7 Now when they have finished their testimony, the beast that comes up from the Abyss will attack them, and overpower and kill them. 8 Their bodies will lie in the street of the great city, which is figuratively called Sodom and Egypt, where also their Lord was crucified. 9 For three and a half days men from every people, tribe, language and nation will gaze on their bodies and refuse them burial. (Rev. 11:3-9)

It does *not* say the witnesses prophesy on the streets of Jerusalem. They prophesy *"before the Lord of the earth."* They will prophesy before many people, tribes, and nations, so they prophesy worldwide; but they are *not* two individual people, it is symbolism.

The two witnesses are described as two olive trees and two lampstands. God would not have put this symbolism here unless he wants us to discover the meaning of the olive trees and lampstands. They are also mentioned in Zechariah 4. Most Bible commentaries believe that the two lambstands and two olive trees in Zech. 4 represent Zerubbabel and Joshua, which speaks of anointing oil and light. These two men were actively building the Temple of God. So if the two witnesses are symbolically Zerubbabel and Joshua, then the two witnesses are building the Temple of God today, so this points us to the global Church.

In the Old Testament, God used teams, such as Moses and Aaron, Joshua and Caleb, Elijah and Elisha, and Zerubbabel and Joshua. And Jesus originally sent his disciples out in twos, and later he said, *"you will be my witnesses . . . to the ends of the earth"* (Acts 1:8). So all Christians are the two witnesses that symbolize the spreading of the Gospel. When the two witnesses are killed, it signifies the end of the Gospel Age.

Literal fire will *not* come from the mouths of those preaching and witnessing for Christ. The fire symbolizes the Word of God that includes words of judgment, and the next judgment will be with fire. Therefore, anyone or any government that persecutes Christians will receive the plagues and the fire of God's Wrath in the coming time of global destruction.

Since all true Christians are the two witnesses, it's possible that some Christians will be moved by the Holy Spirit to prophesy the coming of a plague or the destruction of a city during the Great Tribulation, and it will happen shortly thereafter.

How could two literal people, which is the common interpretation, be immortal for 3.5 years, then suddenly they are able to be killed? The literal view does not make good sense. Though many Christians die for their faith, that does not stop the spread of the Gospel. You cannot stop the spread of the Gospel until the end of the Gospel Age. It says that no one can kill them until they have *"finished their testimony."*

The Greek for "finished" is teleo (5055) and means, *"To make an end or accomplish, to complete something, not merely to end it, but to bring it to perfection or its destined goal, to carry it through"* (CWD). The same word is used to record what Jesus said on the cross, *"it is finished"* (John 19:30), referring to the completion of his ministry on Earth. When the two witnesses are killed, the Gospel Age is not merely ended, but the task of taking the Gospel to the world will be fully completed. The preaching of the Gospel cannot be stopped until the task is completed. The death of the two witnesses signifies the end of the Gospel Age. But how will the beast bring an end to the Gospel Age?

The Greek for "gaze" is blepo (991) and means *"to have sight, is used of bodily vision"* (VED). It denotes the physical act of looking and suggests that people will be physically able to see the witnesses lying dead. So this refers to a globally coordinated terrorist attack upon Christians. They will be attacked and killed in one day and their dead bodies will be left lying on the streets.

> Why do the nations conspire and the peoples plot in vain? The kings of the earth take their stand and the rulers gather together against the LORD and against his Anointed One. (Psalm 2:1-2)

Muslims will kill Gentile and Jewish Christians, then drag their bodies into the street, and raise their arms in victory and shout, *"Allah Akbar, Allah Akbar."* Muslims will not be able to get their hands on Christians in every single city or town in the world, but it will occur in every city where Muslims live.

What about Enoch and Elijah? Many people believe that we must all die, so Enoch and Elijah must come back so they can die a natural death since neither of them died but were taken to heaven. Yet these same Christians believe they themselves will go in the Rapture and thus never die!

Notice that verse 7 says the beast, *"will attack them, and overpower and kill them."* But it literally says, *"will make war with them"* (LIT). This refers to literal warfare. You do not need millions of armed soldiers to kill two prophets, but you will need that many to carry out a global attack. It does not matter whether they are wearing military uniforms and carrying AK47s or wearing jeans and carrying clubs, they will be an army.

If the two witnesses are the global Church, wouldn't that mean that all Christians will go in the Rapture? All Christians who are right with God at the time of the pretrib judgment will go (see c.4).

(4) The Great Festival

After the attack, the followers of the beast will send gifts to each other.

> The inhabitants of the earth will gloat over them and will celebrate

by sending each other gifts, because these two prophets had tormented those who live on the earth. (Rev. 11:10)

Every year at the end of the Islamic Pilgrimage, the Hajj, Muslims have the Great Festival, or Feast of Sacrifice (Eid-al-Adha). They make a sacrifice to Allah by killing a goat, sheep, or camel, and *"strewing the entrails over the earth"* (Payne, p. 5). Part of the sacrifice is eaten and the rest is given to the poor, and Muslims exchange presents and wear new clothes. This festival is celebrated by Muslims all over the world. Therefore, this slaughter of Christians will become another festival and they will celebrate it by giving gifts to each other just like at the Great Festival.

But how can the beast accomplish the global slaughter of Christians unless it rules the world? There are already Muslims in almost every nation, and they will work together on this coordinated terrorist attack. On a particular day, the Muslims among the world's nations will attack and kill every Christian they can get their hands on. Even dragging their bodies into the streets could be part of the plan.

The concept of a city-wide or nationwide mob attack by one group upon another group goes back thousands of years. The book of Esther describes a plan by Haman to kill all the Jews in the Persian empire *"on a single day . . . and to plunder their goods"* (3:13). But this proposed mob attack was counteracted by another decree that said the Jews could defend themselves and kill and plunder those who attack them. This is commemorated each year at the festival of Purim.

There is actually historical evidence that Muslims have engaged in this sort of organized mob violence and are still doing so today. In the 19th century, an incident occurred in Nazareth:

When the ruling pasha came to investigate, he noticed that the Christians and Muslims of Nazareth were all wearing the same style and color of head coverings. This was very unusual for a region where Christians and Jews were required to differentiate themselves in their attire from the Muslims. The Pasha ordered Christians to stop wearing black headdresses, then ordered the

Muslims to attack and kill Christians. The Muslims protested with the argument that a man does not kill his milking cow. The Pasha rescinded his order and instead ordered the Muslims to rob the Christians . . . (*Beyond the Bascilica: Christians and Muslims in Nazareth*, by Chad F. Emmett, 1995, U. of Chicago Press) (p. 24)

The Muslim population was ordered to do the killing, not the soldiers, and they did not object to the order on moral grounds but only because they were making money from Christian pilgrims who came to visit the Christian holy sites, and from heavily taxing the Christian residences.

The *New Foxe's Book of Martyrs* gives several examples of Muslim mob violence upon Christians. In 1996, on Sunday, June 9, several mobs totaling about 5,000 Muslims attacked ten churches *"simultaneously in and around the city of Surabaya in southern Indonesia"* (p.358). The Muslims beat, robbed, and killed Christians and looted and destroyed churches. Here are other examples of organized Muslim violence:

[Nigeria, 1995] In the town of Potiskum, a Christian believer, Azubuike, was stoned and macheted almost to death by Muslims. Another Christian was beheaded. His head was then placed on a stick and carried around the town by a Muslim who repeatedly shouted, "Allah Akbar! Allah Akbar!" (God is great!) This happened when about 5000 Muslims, mostly young Quranic students, invaded Potiskum with the same shouts.

The Muslims burned nine churches to the ground, and killed several Christians, among them Pastor Yahaya Tsalibi and Brother Ezra Turaki. Another 165 Christians were injured, and Bibles, books, cars, trucks, and equipment belong[ing] to Christians and the churches were set on fire. (p. 355-356)

These acts of violence were not committed by terrorists but devout Muslims, and happens in many different Islamic nations. *"On August 17, 2005, there were five hundred synchronized terror bombings across Bangladesh"* (*Because They Hate*, p. 128), carried out by Muslims.

(5) Other Prophecies

There will likely be many thousands of Christians out on the streets preaching the Gospel and warning people of the coming global destruction, which will anger Muslims even more, and will make easy targets for this global attack. This attack will not be upon Protestants only, but will include Catholics. A Catholic prophecy from the 14th century says:

> Towards the end of the world, tyrants and hostile mobs will rob the Church and the clergy of all their possessions and will afflict and martyr them. (Bro. John of the Cleft Rock) (Dupont, *Catholic Prophecy*, p. 49)

In the context of the Last Days, the prophet Ezra speaks of a great uprising against God's elect, Christians, in 2 Ezra:

> For in many places and in neighboring cities there shall be a great insurrection against those who fear the Lord. 71: They shall be like mad men, sparing no one, but plundering and destroying those who continue to fear the Lord. 72: For they shall destroy and plunder their goods, and drive them out of their houses. 73: Then the tested quality of my elect shall be manifest, as gold that is tested by fire. (2 Ezra 16:70-73)(RSV) (Apocrypha)

It is referring to this very same event, the global terrorist attack upon Christians that will signal the end of the Gospel Age, which means the Rapture and Wrath of God upon the world will soon follow.

The Nursing Nun of Belay, 1800-1850, gave a prophecy similar to what we have been discussing in this chapter:

> Once again the madmen seem to gain the upper hand! They laugh God to scorn. Now, the churches are closed; the pastors run away; the Holy Sacrifice [Mass] ceases. . . . There was also a great battle, the like of which has never been seen before. Blood was flowing like water after a heavy rain. The wicked were trying to slaughter all the servants of the Religion of Jesus Christ. After they had killed a large number, they raised a cry of victory, but suddenly the

just received help from above. (Birch, *Trial, Tribulation, & Triumph*, p. 234)

The above prophecy seems to show the global attack on Christians, and then the Wrath of God will kill those who are killing Christians. Fr. Nectou (18th century) foresaw the Great Tribulation, the civil wars in Europe, and the destruction of the Satan's followers:

The confusion will be so general that men will not be able to think aright, as if God had withheld His Providence from mankind, and that, during the worst crisis, the best that can be done would be to remain where God has placed us, and persevere in fervent prayers.... At that time there will be such a terrible crisis that people will believe that the end of the world has come. Blood will flow in many large cities. The very <u>elements will be convulsed</u>. It will be like a little General Judgment.

A great multitude of people will lose their lives in those calamitous times, but the wicked will not prevail. They will indeed <u>attempt to destroy the whole Church</u>, but not enough time will be allowed them, because the frightful crisis will be of short duration. When all is considered lost, all will be found safe. . . . England in her turn will experience a more frightful revolution than that of France. It will continue long enough for France to recover her strength; then she will help England to restore peace and order.

During this revolution, which will very likely be general and not confined to France. <u>Paris will be destroyed</u> so completely that twenty years afterwards fathers walking over its ruins with their children will be asked by them what kind of place that was; to whom they will answer: "<u>My child, this was a great city which God has destroyed on account of her crimes.</u>"

Yes. Paris will certainly be destroyed: but, before this happens, such signs and portents will be seen, that all good people will be induced to flee away from it. After these most frightful events, order will be restored everywhere. Justice will reign throughout the whole world . . . (Yves Dupont, *Catholic Prophecy*, page 47-48).

The *elements* being "convulsed" puts this prophecy nowhere but in the Great Tribulation and Wrath of God. So, World War 3 will include Muslims in Europe trying to take control of the EU nations. The civil war in France is doubtless between the imported Muslims and the native French.

Next is a prophecy by Sister Rose Columba of Taggia who died in 1847:

> There shall be great confusion of people against people, and nations against nations, with clashing of arms and beating of drums. The Russians and Prussians shall come to make war in Italy. They shall profane many churches, and turn them into stables for their horses. Some bishops shall fall from the faith, but many more will remain steadfast, and shall suffer much for the Church. (*The Christian Trumpet*, 1873; quoted in Dupont, *Catholic Prophecy*, p. 74)

Why so many Catholic prophecies? Because the Catholic Church has never recognized a secession of the prophetic gift. There have been prophecies throughout Church history. But the first Protestants rejected the gift and so there is *little* evidence for it among Protestantism until the arrival of Pentecostalism. However, there are a few isolated instances. Many Protestant churches still reject any prophecy not found in the Bible.

(6) Second Woe

The 1,260 days that the two witnesses prophesy represents the last 3.5 years of the Gospel Age, which is different from the 42 months the beast will rule. The beast will kill the two witnesses, so the beast will continue to exist beyond the end of the 1,260 days until it is destroyed in the Wrath of God.

Rev. 11 continues:

> 11 But after the three and a half days a breath of life from God entered them, and they stood on their feet, and terror struck those who saw them. 12 Then they heard a loud voice from heaven saying to them, "Come up here." And they went up to heaven in a cloud, while their enemies looked on. (Revelation 11:10-12)

The Rapture will take place 3 1/2 days after the global slaughter of Christians and just moments before the blowing of the 7th

Trumpet, not at the 7th Trumpet. This is why Rev. 10 tells us that the mystery of God is accomplished as the 7th angel "*is about*" to blow his Trumpet. This is because the 7th Trumpet cannot blow until the Rapture takes place, because the 7th Trumpet signals the arrival of the Day of the Lord and God's Kingdom. Rev. 11:

> 13 At that very hour there was a severe earthquake and a tenth of the city collapsed. Seven thousand people were killed in the earthquake, and the survivors were terrified and gave glory to the God of heaven. 14 The second woe has passed; the third woe is coming soon. (Rev. 11:13-14)

Whether this refers to a literal hour or not remains to be seen, but within a short space of time after the Rapture, God sends an earthquake. Since the 144,000 represents the total number that will be in the Rapture, the 7,000 killed in the earthquake probably represents the total number who will actually be killed, 7 being the number of completeness. And since the two witnesses are not just two people who will be prophesying in Jerusalem but are spread out worldwide, the earthquake could also be worldwide. It will be a warning to the world as we get closer to the full Wrath of God.

In Rev. 8 three woes were pronounced on the people of Earth. The first woe took place under the 5th Trumpet; the second woe was the worldwide terrorist attack and/or earthquake, which took place under the 6th Trumpet. The third woe is never mentioned but is likely the nuclear war that takes place under the 7th Trumpet, because its aftereffects will be enormous.

(7) Seventh Trumpet: God's Wrath and Kingdom
The 7th Trumpet does not signal the end of World War 3, just the start of the total Wrath of God. It also signals the coming of the Kingdom of God on Earth. Read these verses carefully:

> 15 The seventh angel sounded his trumpet, and there were loud voices in heaven, which said: "The kingdom of the world has become the kingdom of our Lord and of his Christ, and he will reign for ever and ever." 16 And the twenty-four elders, who were seated

on their thrones before God, fell on their faces and worshiped God, 17 saying: "We give thanks to you, Lord God Almighty, the One who is and who was, because you have taken your great power and have begun to reign. 18 The nations were angry; and your wrath has come. <u>The time has come for judging the dead, and for rewarding your servants the prophets and your saints and those who reverence your name, both small and great-- and for destroying those who destroy the earth.</u>" 19 Then God's temple in heaven was opened, and within his temple was seen the ark of his covenant. And there came flashes of lightning, rumblings, peals of thunder, an earthquake and a great hailstorm. (Rev. 11:15-19)

This clearly describes the full arrival of Judgment Day that will last longer than just one day. It will bring rewards for Christians and suffering and death for those who reject Christ. In Rev. 4:8, God is referred to as he *"who is, who was, and who is to come."* But here, the *"to come"* is left out, and in its place it says *"you have begun to reign."* The Kingdom of God is no longer "to come" because it now has come. Even though the Kingdom of God is here now, it contains many weeds, which are unsaved people. The 7th Trumpet signals the removal of the weeds in the Wrath of God and thus the Kingdom of God will come fully upon the entire world, and in every area of life, even animal and plant life.

It is during this time that the Earth itself will be in the greatest turmoil and upheaval in recorded history with earthquakes, floods, hail, rain, and major storms. In verse 19, God's Temple is opened in heaven and there is an earthquake and a great hailstorm which doubtless signify the same events that are mentioned in Revelation 16 at the conclusion of the Wrath of God:

17 The seventh angel poured out his bowl into the air, and out of the temple came a loud voice from the throne, saying, "It is done!" 18 Then there came flashes of lightning, rumblings, peals of thunder and a severe earthquake.... From the sky huge hailstones, each weighing about a hundred pounds, fell on people.... (Rev.16:17-18, 21)

All the events of the seven Bowls of Wrath mentioned in Rev. 16 take place after the blowing of this 7th Trumpet.

Chapter 12
2 Thessalonians 2

(1) Apostasy and Antichrist Must Come First

Even though I do not cover the beast and false prophet in this book, I will include a discussion of 2 Thess. 2, because it includes information on the Rapture.

2 Thessalonians 2 is amazingly misunderstood. It supposedly refers to a future Antichrist who will lead many people into worshiping him as God, but, in fact the man of sin has already come and his name was Muhammad. The apostasy also has already happened, because it was to happen along with the rise of the man of sin. It was in the distant future at the time Paul wrote 2 Thessalonians, but was fulfilled in the 5th century. Read these verses to refresh your memory, and pay special attention to the underlined parts:

1 Concerning the coming of our Lord Jesus Christ and our being gathered to him, we ask you, brothers, 2 not to become easily unsettled or alarmed by some prophecy, report or letter supposed to have come from us, saying that the day of the Lord has already come.

3 Don't let anyone deceive you in any way, for <u>that day will not come until the rebellion occurs and the man of lawlessness is revealed</u>, the man doomed to destruction.

4 He will <u>oppose and will exalt himself</u> over everything that is called God or is worshiped, so that he sets himself up in God's temple, proclaiming himself to be God.

5 Don't you remember that when I was with you I used to tell you these things?

6 And now you know what is holding him back, so that he may be revealed at the proper time.

7 For the secret power of lawlessness is already at work; but the one who now holds it back will continue to do so till he is taken out of the way. 8 And then the lawless one will be revealed, whom the Lord Jesus will overthrow with the breath of his mouth and destroy by the splendor of his coming.

9 The coming of the lawless one will be in accordance with the work of Satan displayed in all kinds of counterfeit miracles, signs and wonders,

10 and in every sort of evil that deceives those who are perishing. They perish because they refused to love the truth and so be saved.

11 For this reason God sends them a powerful delusion so that they will believe the lie

12 and so that all will be condemned who have not believed the truth but have delighted in wickedness.

(It is odd that this chapter is used to support all the three major Rapture doctrines; the pretrib, posttrib, and prewrath. Someone is not reading it correctly.)

The following events take place before The Day of Christ can come:

1. The apostasy must come
2. A false prophet appears
3. He exalts himself
4. He declares himself God

The pretribulation Rapture theory says the Rapture will take place at the start of a seven-year tribulation, because the entire GT is supposed to be the Day of the Lord. But the Day of the Lord is the time of God's full unrestrained Wrath upon the world, not the GT. Paul clearly says the apostasy and the Man of sin both come *before* the Day of the Lord. The apostasy is supposedly done by people who convert to Christianity after the Rapture, but get deceived by the Antichrist. Though some people believe the apostasy is taking place now because of all the false gospels being preached, I believe that the apostasy is a total turning away from Christianity. The ESV says:

> For that day will not come, unless the rebellion comes first, and the man of lawlessness is revealed, the son of destruction.

So the apostasy and man of sin come before the Day of the Lord and the Rapture (our being gathered to Him), but it does not say they will come right before the Day of the Lord; it could happen many years before, as it did. *Robert's Word Pictures* says:

> It is not clear whether Paul means revolt of the Jews from God, of Gentiles from God, of Christians from God, or of the apostasy that includes all classes within and without the body of Christians. But it is to be first (prōton) before Christ comes again.

Most of the modern translations have "rebellion" for "apostasia" (646); the KJV says, *"falling away."* Notice carefully this wording, *"the falling away."* The word "the" is a definite article which is in the original text (Earle, *Word Meanings of the New Testament* p. 375). This means it does not refer to this or that small group of Christians falling from the true faith, but to a specific, significant, prophesied falling away that the Thessalonians already knew was coming:

> The noun [apostasia] occurs only here and in Acts 21:21. In the latter passage it is translated "to forsake." Abbott-Smith defines the term as follows: "defection, apostasy, revolt." (Ibid, p. 375)

You cannot fall away from somewhere you were never at; therefore, this can only refer to a major apostasy of Christians. The apostasy, or falling away, is not the Antichrist deceiving the whole world after the Rapture; no, it is only people who have the truth who can fall from it. You cannot fall away unless you had the truth to begin with. So how can there be a great apostasy from Christianity after the Church has been removed? (This is what the pretribulation Rapture theory believes.) Oh, the false Christians who did not make the Rapture are going to apostatize? How can someone who is *not* a true believer fall from the faith? With the Church in heaven (according to the pretrib theory) it must refer to the false Christians who decide to become real Christians after the Rapture, then become followers of Antichrist! That is convoluted nonsense. That is not *the apostasy*. There is a bigger apostasy that fits this much better.

It refers to the millions of Christians who apostatized to the religion of the beast over the past 1,400 years by gradually converting to Islam. All the Middle East was ruled by the Eastern Roman Empire, which had converted to Christianity, so it is safe to say that 90% of the entire population was Christian before the Muslims invaded, along with some Jews. After the invasions, many Christians were forced to convert, others converted because of economic or social pressures.

Looking again at the pretrib theory, in addition to those who are supposed to apostatize, there are many who will be persecuted for holding to their faith during the Great Tribulation. Where are all these Christians coming from during the Great Trib, after the Church is supposedly removed? Just another point about the pretrib theory that does not make good sense.

(2) Will Exalt Himself

Notice that verse 4 is very similar to a passage in Daniel 11; that refers to the coming of Muhammad and Allah (Dan. 11 will be covered in the next book). Here are both verses so you can see the similarity:

4 He will oppose and will <u>exalt himself over everything that is called God</u> or is worshiped . . . (2 Thess. 2:4)

He will exalt and magnify himself above every god . . . (Dan. 11:35)

Islam declares that there is no other God but Allah, and it is even part of their official statement of faith, *"There is no God but Allah, and Muhammad is his messenger."* But Christians know that there is no God but Yahweh, and Jesus is the Son of Yahweh.

You may have heard Muslims say, *"God is Great,"* in English, but in Arabic, it is really, *"God is Greatest."* Or, more correct, *"Allah is Greatest."* The Islamic yell, *Allah u Akbar*, means *"Allah is Greatest* [of all]." According to several websites, including www.islamic-dictionary.com, it should be "greatest" not "great." Therefore, when they are yelling *Allah u Akbar*, they are declaring that Allah is greater than all other gods, or all that is called god, which is exactly what Daniel and Paul were saying. So, *Allah u Akbar* means, *"Allah is above any and all gods."* (The web site, wikiislam.net/wiki/Allahu_Akbar, gives a detailed article which proves this view, with much evidence.)

Many Muslims claim that Allah is the same god as the Christians and Jews worship, but Muslims have demanded that Christians not use the word *Allah* for God, that it is only for Muslims. In Malaysia, the government confiscated 20,000 bibles in 2009 because it used the word "Allah" for God. In the Malay language there is no word for "God," so they are using "Allah." The conflict over this has resulted in protests and violence against Christians. When Islamic prayers and statements of faith are said, Muslims must say "Allah," not God.

(3) Important Word Meanings

For a complete understanding of 2 Thess. 2 we will examine what some of the words mean in Greek. Most translations use a word in verse 7 that is similar or the same as the one they use in verse 3, such as "sin" or "lawlessness," but in the Greek they are different words. The LIT says, *"man of sin is revealed, the son of perdition . . . For the mystery of lawlessness already is . . ."*

The Greek for "sin" in verse 3 is *hamartia* (266), and refers to *"An offense in relation to God with emphasis on guilt. (I) Aberration from the truth, error"* (CWD). This easily fits the coming of another religion that many Christians will join over the centuries.

The man of lawlessness comes from what is spiritually dead, which is why he is called, *"son of perdition."* Islam came from paganism, and Muhammad was a pagan before he followed the spirit that claimed to be God. Historical evidence shows that Allah was the chief deity in Mecca before the coming of Islam and was the god of Muhammad's tribe (www.faithfreedom.org/Articles/skm30804.htm), and was only one of 360 gods in the Kaaba.

The Greek for "perdition" is *apoleia* (from apollumi), and literally means *"to destroy fully"* (CWD). It can refer to either physical or spiritual destruction and ruin. Notice the closeness in spelling and meaning to *apollyon* (Rev. 9:11), the king of the locusts that will come out of the Abyss, and means *"the Destroyer."* This is because *apollyon* also comes from *apollumi*. So *son of perdition* or "destroyer" points us directly to Islam, because Allah is the Destroyer, as we learned in a previous chapter.

Although this passage in 2 Thess. could refer to the next global leader of Islam, the final Antichrist, it most likely refers to Muhammad and Islam, which Muhammad started. The literal translation of 2 Thess. 2:4 says:

> the one opposing and exalting himself over everything being called God, or object of worship, so as for him "to sit in the temple of God" as God, setting forth himself, that he is God. (LIT)

The phrase, *"temple of God"* is used twice in Matthew to refer to the Temple in Jerusalem, but in 1 and 2 Corinthians it is used three times referring to the Church. Since Paul knew what was going to happen in the future to Christianity, this passage most likely refers to the Church. Most people who teach on this passage believe that it refers to the Antichrist sitting in a rebuilt Jewish Temple in Jerusalem. However, during the course of the Islamic invasions, the Muslims converted a large number of churches into mosques, including the greatest church of the age, the Hagia Sofia (Church of the Holy Wisdom) in Constantinople, so that Allah was literally worshiped in churches as God.

Even though this passage describes Muhammad and Islam, the part about claiming to be God will most literally be fulfilled by the Islamic Jesus. (Islam will have a political leader called the Mahdi, but it will also have a false Jesus, because Islam teaches that Jesus was not actually crucified on a cross and will return and force all Christians to convert to Islam, thus destroying Christianity. More on this in Book Two.) The man who will claim to be the returned Jesus will not actually say the words, "I am God," but Jesus is God, so by claiming to be Jesus he will claim to be God.

Many of the 7th and 8th century Christians believed that the Bible's prophecies, including this chapter, refer to Muhammad, Allah, and Islam (there is a whole chapter about what the 7th and 8th century Christians believed about Islam in the next book). 2 Thessalonians continues with verse 6:

And now you know what is holding him back, so that he may be revealed at the proper time.

About this verse, the New King James Study Bible says:

There are a variety of other interpretations for this verse and the identity of the restrainer. The Roman state, the emperor of Rome, Paul's missionary work, the Jewish state, or the principle of law and government embodied in the state have all been proposed as the restrainer of lawlessness. (NKJV Study Bible)

The pretrib theory teaches that the Holy Spirit and the Church is holding back the coming of the Antichrist, and only after the Holy Spirit and the Church are removed at the Rapture can the Antichrist arise. This is total nonsense; it is likely that Paul knew that pagan Rome would convert to Christianity before this new religion, Islam, would rise, and so the only thing holding back the coming of this new religion was the fall of pagan Rome.

Satan attacked Christianity and tried to destroy it through pagan Rome, but Rome was eventually converted, so Satan had to bring in another way to attack Christianity, which was why Satan raised up Islam. Paul was not going to say in a letter that pagan

Rome would fall or convert to Christianity before the man of sin would arise, because that could get him killed. So that explains why he did not state it clearly.

What's more, Paul said the mystery of sin was already at work; how could the false religion of a future Antichrist already be at work in Paul's day? The most likely meaning is that it refers to the belief in Allah that already existed in Arabia at that time. Arabia was literally next door to Israel, and Saul (Paul) traveled widely as a persecutor of Christians before he was struck down on the road to Damascus. Plus, Arabic traders traveled to Israel to sell their wares, so it is a near certainty that Paul knew about the existence of Allah.

And the way the Holy Spirit worked among the Apostles, it is probable that the Holy Spirit revealed to Paul that the religion of Allah would spread by force, and attack Christianity. Therefore, Paul was most likely knowingly speaking of Allah's future religion in 2 Thess. 2.

The Apostles took the Gospel to many areas outside of Israel. Apostle Thomas started a church in India, and Joseph of Arimathaea went to the British Isles; others went to Persia, Syria, Ethiopia, etc. Therefore, it is more than probable that one of the Apostles took the Gospel to Arabia; in fact, Paul went to Arabia after his conversion:

> . . . nor did I go up to Jerusalem to see those who were apostles before I was, but I went immediately into Arabia and later returned to Damascus. (Gal 1:17)

In the first century, Arabia extended north to include part of present-day Jordan. Paul indicates here in 2 Thess. that the people of the lawless one heard the Gospel, but completely refused it:

> 9 The coming of the lawless one will be in accordance with the work of Satan displayed in all kinds of counterfeit miracles, signs and wonders, 10 and in every sort of evil that deceives those who are perishing. They perish because they refused to love the truth and so be saved.

11 <u>For this reason</u> God sends them a powerful delusion so that they will believe the lie 12 and so that all will be condemned <u>who have not believed the truth but have delighted in wickedness</u>. (2 Thess. 2:9-10)

They refused the Gospel, so God allowed Satan to deceive them with a false religion that would lead them into hell. The coming of this lawless person includes lying miracles designed to deceive those who are perishing; the Quran itself is called a miracle by Muslims because Muhammad was supposedly illiterate. Also, many supposed miracles were attributed to Muhammad, which the unlearned tribes easily believed (more in the next book).

(4) Only One Coming of Christ

Notice that there are *not* two comings of Christ in 2 Thess., at the Rapture and at the Day of Judgment, but only one. Read this carefully:

Concerning the <u>coming of our Lord Jesus Christ and our being gathered to him</u> . . . that day will not come until the rebellion occurs and the man of lawlessness is revealed . . . <u>whom the Lord Jesus will</u> <u>overthrow</u> with the breath of his mouth and <u>destroy by the splendor of his coming</u>.

The text clearly says that <u>Christ will destroy the lawless one when he comes at the Day of the Lord to gather us to him!</u> This means the Rapture will not happen until it is time to destroy the beast and false prophet. And as we have learned, the Rapture takes place just days before the Day of Judgment, which is when the beast and false prophet are killed. It does not have to be the exact same day as the Rapture, because the entire period from the Rapture to the end of the Wrath of God is considered the coming of Christ, which is the Day of the Lord.

So to be clear, since the Lawless one is not destroyed until the end of the GT, during the Wrath of God, then that is proof positive of when the Rapture will take place: at the end of the GT, just before the Day of the Lord.

But if this refers to Christ's return with judgment after the tribulation, could the Rapture still come seven years before? No, because Paul clearly says the gathering, which is the Rapture, will
happen at the Day of the Lord (actually the start of the Day of the
Lord). This is confirmed in 1st Thessalonians:

> For the Lord himself will come down from heaven, with a loud
> command. . . the dead in Christ will rise first. [the Rapture] . . . 5:1
> 1 Now, brothers, about times and dates we do not need to write to
> you, 2 for you know very well that the day of the Lord will come
> like a thief in the night. 3 While people are saying, "Peace and
> safety," destruction will come on them suddenly, as labor pains on
> a pregnant woman, and they will not escape. (1 Thess. 4:16; 5:1-3)

In this passage, the Rapture and resurrection take place at the
coming of Christ, which is also the start of the Day of the Lord
followed by the total destruction of the wicked. There is not a 7-
year gap between the Rapture and the destruction of the wicked, or
even a 3.5-year gap.

Does the statement, *"peace and safety"* refer to the fact that
Islam claims to be a religion of peace? But it only offers peace to
those who are under the thumb of Islam, so does this mean that
Islam will conquer much of the world just before they are destroyed by the hand of God? It may refer to the fact that they will
think that they have won because of their global attack upon
Christianity. 1 Thessalonians continues:

> 4 But you, brothers, are not in darkness, that the Day should over-
> take you as a thief. 5 . . . 6 So then, we should not sleep, as the rest
> also do, but we should watch and be sober. . . . 9 because God has
> not appointed us to wrath, but for obtaining salvation through our
> Lord Jesus Christ, . . . (1 Thess. 5:4-6, 9 (ESV)

Here Paul is saying that those who are alive will be watching
for the coming of the Day of Lord, the time of God's Wrath on the
world. And the reason we must watch is so that we can be ready,
whether that means spiritually ready for the Rapture or physically
ready so that we will live through the time of Wrath. Whether Paul

knew that some Christians will be Raptured and some will not is not clear from this passage, but it could certainly mean that.

Paul said that God has not *"appointed us to suffer wrath."* In other words, God has not declared that we must suffer in the Wrath of God along with the rest of the world, which is why he wants us to be ready so that we can obtain salvation, that is, go in the Rapture or be chosen to be protected from the Wrath.

Only one coming of Christ is also seen in 2 Thess. 1:

> God is just: He will pay back trouble to those who trouble you 7 and give relief to you who are troubled. This will happen when the <u>Lord Jesus is revealed from heaven in blazing fire</u> with his powerful angels. 8 He will punish those who do not know God and do not obey the gospel of our Lord Jesus. 9 They will be punished with everlasting destruction ... (2 Thessalonians 1:6-9)

This passage tells us that we will get relief from persecution when Christ returns with blazing fire to destroy the wicked. So this proves that we will be here right up to the time when Christ comes to destroy the Antichrist. Though it won't happen the exact same day, as explained above.

Also, in 1 Thess., it says Christ will come *"with a loud command, with the voice of the archangel and with the trumpet call of God"* (1 Thess. 4:16). This does not look like a secret Rapture to me. It does not say that only the Raptured will see or hear him. In fact, it says that the whole world will see him in Matthew 24:30, and Rev. 1:7, which has been previously taught to refer to his coming at the end of the GT, to bring judgment. But there is just one second coming of Christ, as we have seen in this chapter.

This information about only one coming of Christ without a 7-year gap is not new, it has been taught for a long time, but many people have a vested interest in the pretrib theory, so they ignore this powerful evidence.

Chapter 13
The Abomination of Desolation

(1) No Tribulation Temple

The Abomination of Desolation is not the stopping of the sacrifice or the setting up of an image in the Temple, because the Jewish Temple will never be rebuilt in this age. There is a lot of wrong teaching on this subject, but I will attempt to present a concise argument why there will not be a tribulation Temple and what the abomination actually will be.

One reason the Temple will not be rebuilt is because the Muslims control the Temple Mount and they will never let the Jews build the Temple there. To believe otherwise ignores 1400 years of history, much Scripture, and is just wishful thinking. I have already proven that the 7-year peace treaty is total nonsense. Also, a certain number of Jews will convert to Christianity before the GT as we saw in previous chapters. Plus, many Jews do not believe that the Temple should be built until the coming of Messiah.

If in fact a 7-year agreement were to occur, which would allow the Jews to rebuild their Temple, it would mean that they have less than 3.5 years to actually cut all the stones and rebuild the Temple, which would be a real rush job. But it would take longer than that to do the archeological excavation of the site before building. Seriously, do you really believe that the Jews, who care greatly for every piece of pottery relating to their history in Israel, would build on top of perhaps the greatest archeological treasures in world history? Some people are just not thinking clearly! The Temple Mount most certainly has incredible archeological treasures buried there, such as evidence of both Temples, what they looked like, how they were built, how they were destroyed, etc.

Add to this the fact that the exact length of the cubit is not known. Some people believe it was 1.5 feet, but the measure is not known for certain. Without an exact measure, how can the Temple and the articles in the Temple be made? This is another reason to do a complete archeological excavation of the site.

If God wanted the Temple rebuilt, it could have been during the rule of the Emperor Julian, who favored non-Christian religions. He commanded the Temple be rebuilt with public funds, but God stopped it. First there were very high winds that blew dirt and covered up what had been dug, then an earthquake in 363 A.D. destroyed much work and killed some of the workers. But the work continued, then explosive gases came up from crevices in the ground and burst into fire, burning some of the workers until they finally gave up. But that was not all:

> A more tangible and still more extraordinary miracle ensued; suddenly the sign of the cross appeared spontaneously on the garments of the persons engaged in the undertaking. These crosses looked like stars, and appeared the work of art. Many were hence led to confess that Christ is God, and that the rebuilding of the Temple was not pleasing to Him; others presented themselves in the church, were initiated, and besought Christ, with hymns and supplications, to pardon their transgression. (*The Jew in the medieval world: a source book, 315-1791*. By Jacob Rader Marcus, Marc Saperstein, Hebrew Union College Press, 2000, page 12)

God kept it from being built, but we are expected to believe that God is going to change his mind and allow it to be rebuilt just in time for the Antichrist to desecrate it? No, there will be no Antichrist Temple!

The claim is made that Paul and the other Apostles did not reject the Temple and that they continued to practice Judaism; therefore, the passages in the New Testament that refer to Christians being the Temple does not refer to replacement theology, which states that Christians have replaced the Jews. But Jesus did not give them detailed information about the coming changes before he went to heaven, which is why the Holy Spirit gave Peter the dream about not calling unclean what God has made clean. God revealed things to them gradually, which is why they had the argument in Acts 15 which concluded that the Gentiles do not have to keep the Law of Moses, but apparently the Jews did.

So even if they originally did not reject the Temple and its service, they certainly would have done so after the destruction of the Temple in 70 A.D., because they knew that the Old Covenant had been replaced by the New Covenant, and that the old was *soon* to stop completely, as seen in Hebrews 8:

> By calling this covenant "new," he has made the first one obsolete; and what is obsolete and aging will soon disappear. (8:13)

Perhaps they believed they should keep the outward law as long as it was being practiced, until God removed it, as he certainly did with the destruction of the Temple.

The abomination as we have come to understand it, would occur by the Antichrist stopping the sacrifice in the Temple and entering the Temple and declaring himself God. As we have seen above, God will not allow this to happen, because offering sacrifices for sin in the Temple would be a greater abomination than someone going into the Temple and sitting on a throne, because offering sacrifices would be trampling on, or attempting to void, the sacrifice of Jesus for our sins. This is why God will never again allow any offerings for sin in the Temple, or even allow the Temple to be rebuilt for the purpose of offering sacrifices.

What about the statements of Jesus and Paul that seem to refer to the literal Temple? What Paul said about it in 2 Thessalonians 2 was explained in the last chapter, the other is given below.

(2) Abomination of Desolation

So if the Temple is not going to be rebuilt, then what is the Abomination? There are a few possibilities, and I will present the most likely here.

"Abomination" is defined as *"to be filthy,"* *"to loathe,"* *"to ab-*

hor," and refers to something that is disgusting and detestable. The term *"abomination of desolation"* refers to the desecration of a holy site or something that offends the religious sensibilities of a people.

A previous abomination of desolation was when Antiochus Epiphanes erected a statue of Zeus in the Most Holy Place in the Temple and burned sacrifices on the altar to Zeus. Another abomination of desolation occurred when the Romans destroyed the city and the Temple then afterwards brought in their ensigns on the Temple Mount and offered sacrifices to them. These were certainly abominations of desolation, but the context of Matthew 24 puts it still in the future.

In the 5th century, the first Islamic empire invaded the Middle East. When Caliph Omar entered Jerusalem after its capitulation, he rode his horse to the Temple Mount, at which time the Patriarch Sophronius muttered, *"Behold the abomination of desolation, spoken of by Daniel the prophet,"* (Steve Runciman, *A History of The Crusades. Volume One: The First Crusade,* Cambridge Univ. Press, 1951, p. 3).

Some sources report Sophronius saying, *"So this is the abomination of desolation spoken of by Daniel the prophet standing in the holy place."* Some sources report that he made that statement upon Omar's arrival at the Temple Mount, some that he made it after Omar built the first wooden structure that would later become the Dome of the Rock. The seventh century bishop and historian, Sebeos, agreed with Sophronius:

> Sebeos tells of the "horror of the invasion of the Ishmaelites who conquered land and sea." He too saw in the Arab conquests the fulfillment of Daniel's prophecy. (Greek Christian and Other Accounts of the Muslim Conquests of the Near East, by Demetrios Constantelos, in *The Legacy of Jihad*, Edited by Andrew G. Bostom. p. 395)

What is certain is that the abomination will be something that can be seen "standing" on the Temple Mount, so it cannot be the death of the pope, a saint, and it is not a false doctrine. There is evidence that the Muslims are planning a new building project that will take several years to complete. Evangelist Perry Stone reports that the Mufti of Jerusalem, Ekrima Sabri, said the Palestinian Authority has drawn up plans for a large mosque on the Temple Mount (*Unleashing the Beast*, p. 118, 2003 edition).

A very large mosque would prevent the building of the Jewish Temple next to the Dome of the Rock, so such a plan is certainly possible. There have already been some excavations of the mount near the Al-Aqsa Mosque that is located in the southern corner of the Temple Mount. "*All these activities show very clearly that their plan is to make most of the Temple Mount into an area of one great mosque*" (http://christianactionforisrael.org/5thtemple.html). All of this destruction and construction is very offensive to Jewish people all over the world.

In Matthew 24 Jesus never said that abomination would be of the Temple, or in the Temple. He never said the word *Temple*, he just said it will be standing where it should not be standing:

"So when you see standing in the holy place 'the abomination that causes desolation,' spoken of through the prophet Daniel . . ." (v. 15)

Compare what Jesus said above with the KJV of Dan. 9:27b:

. . . and for the overspreading of abominations he shall make it desolate, even <u>until the consummation</u>, and that determined shall be poured upon the desolate.

Notice that the word "Temple" does not appear here either, merely that something will be made desolate. After the destruction of the Temple, it can only be the Temple Mount. The wording also suggests that the abomination will continue for an extend period of time, "*until the consummation*." Here is how the LXXE words it:

and on the temple shall be the abomination of desolations; <u>and at the end of time</u> an <u>end shall be put</u> to the desolation.

It mentions the abomination, and then it says the abomination will come to an end at the end of, or consummation of the age. So the wording of this passage suggests that the abomination will continue over a long period of time, which would make the Dome of the Rock *an* abomination of desolation. Several other translations agree with the wording of the LXXE, that the abomination will last a long time:

> And on a corner of the altar will be abominations that desolate, <u>even until the end</u>. And that which was decreed shall pour out on the desolator. (ESV)

> And in the train of these abominations shall come an author of desolation; <u>then, in the end</u>, what has been decreed concerning the desolation will be poured out. (NEB)

So, if the Dome of the Rock is the abomination spoken of the Daniel 9:27, then there will be another building constructed on the Temple Mount. Even though the Temple Mount is already in a state of desolation with the Dome of the Rock and the Al-Aqsa Mosque, there will be a future abomination of desolation because the statement of Jesus in Matthew 24 is still in the future. The statement in Daniel 12 supports the belief in another abomination,

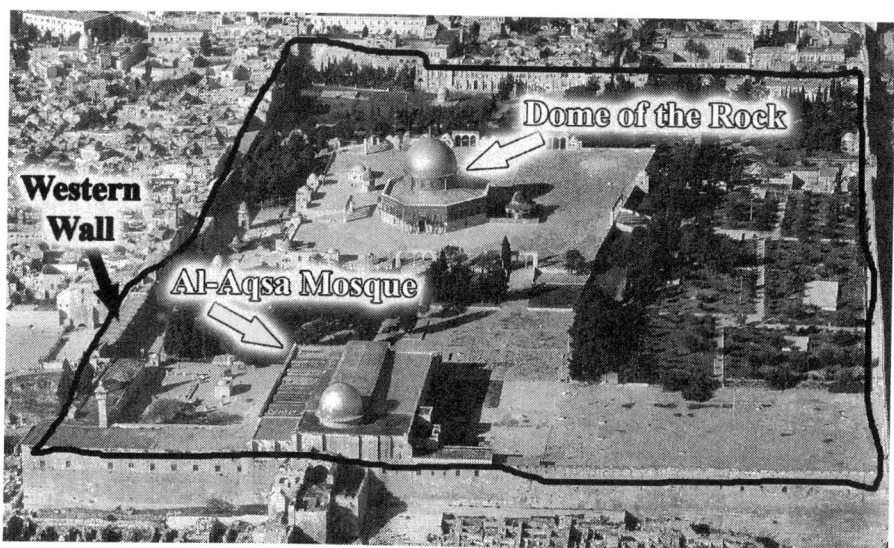

because it says the abomination will take place at the 1,290th day. So the final abomination of desolation probably will be the completion and dedication of a new structure, or when it is first opened for use as a mosque.

In the photo on the previous page, the black line shows the extent of the Temple Mount, so there is plenty of room to build another mosque; either between the Dome of the Rock and the Al-Aqsa Mosque, or east of them. The Dome of the Rock is not a mosque as some people believe, but is a shrine to the rock inside it.

The Abomination of Desolation is a sign of the end, but only for those who will not go in the Rapture. It is the main sign directly related to Jerusalem that will point to the approaching Wrath of God. Most other signs will be seen in the sky.

(3) The End of the Gospel Age

In Matthew 24, Jesus reaches the end of the age in verse 14, where he says the Gospel will be preached in the whole world *"and then the end will come."* Then he said:

> 15 "So when you see standing in the holy place 'the abomination that causes desolation,' spoken of through the prophet Daniel—let the reader understand— 16 then let those who are in Judea flee to the mountains. (Matthew 24:15-16)

The word "so" connects what was just said with what is going to be said. This means there is a connection between verses 14 and 15. In the Greek text, the word translated "so" is (oun). Thayer's Greek Dictionary says, *"then, therefore, accordingly, consequently, these things being so."* The *Complete Word Study Dictionary* gives us more detail:

> Accordingly, thereupon, then, now, certainly. Put after one or more words in a clause, and expressing either the merely external connection of two sentences, that the one follows upon the other, or also the internal relation of cause and effect, that the one follows from the other.

The best translations use the conjunction "so" or "therefore" which connects verses 14 and 15. So, we know the two sentences are connected, and if we examine them we come to realize from this connection that the abomination will mark the end of the Gospel Age: *"the end will come . . . So when you see . . . the abomination . . ."* The Gospel will be preached right up to the abomination. It also puts the Abomination of Desolation at the end of the GT, just before the full Wrath of God is poured out upon the world.

There is an important point here that is being missed. We have just learned that the abomination will mark the end of the Gospel Age; this fact by itself proves that the pretrib Rapture theory is unworkable. The pretrib theory says the Rapture will take place at the start of a 7-year tribulation, and then 3.5 years later, the abomination takes place in the newly rebuilt Temple, followed by another 3.5 years. But according to Matthew 24:14-15, the abomination takes place just before the Rapture or just after it, (it can take place a few days before or after the Rapture without it losing its designation as marking the end of the Gospel Age). Therefore, this information destroys the pretrib theory. It would come closer to a midtrib theory than pretrib, except for the fact that we already know the abomination will take place at the 1,290 day point, not the mid-point. You will understand this better the farther we get into this chapter.

You may be tempted to place the abomination at the start of the GT because of what Jesus said a few verses later; *"For then shall be great tribulation, such as was not since the beginning of the world to this time, no, nor ever shall be* [again]*"* (v.21)(KJV). This does NOT refer to the start of what Revelation says is the Great Tribulation; this statement in Mat. 24 refers to the approaching full Wrath of God upon the world, which is why Jesus immediately says that when you see the abomination then drop everything and flee to the mountains (24:16-20).

The period of time between the abomination and the statement Jesus made on the tribulation, *"Immediately after the tribulation of those days . . "* (KJV) will be a very short period because it refers to the Days of Awe after the Feast of Trumpets that lead up to the

Day of Atonement, which is also the Day of Judgment.

The Rapture will take place in conjunction with the Feast of Trumpets, which is followed by the Days of Awe leading up the Day of Atonement ten days later. It is during the Days of Awe that people are supposed to afflict their souls by thinking about and repenting of their sins in order to be ready for the Day of Judgment. It is also during this time that the people are supposed to be traveling, making their way to Jerusalem where they celebrate the feast. But of course, Christians won't actually being traveling to Jerusalem, those who don't go in the Rapture should go to a shelter that will protect them from the after affects of nuclear war and the huge natural disasters. (All this will be covered in great detail in the next book.)

The Great Tribulation as given in the book of Revelation begins before the 7 Trumpets, and includes the first 6 Trumpets, so this passage in Matthew 24 would be better understood if Jesus had said, *"the greatest of all tribulation"* will take place after the abomination. So, the very end of the GT will be the greatest tribulation because of the knowledge of the soon-coming Wrath of God.

So Jesus said, when we see the new building on the Temple Mount, then that will signal the end of the Gospel Age, and the Wrath of God upon the world will soon begin, so we are to flee.

(4) Daniel 12: Time of the End

Daniel 12 speaks of the time of the end, which is the Great Tribulation, and agrees with Matthew 24. Daniel 12 says:

> "There will be a time of distress such as has not happened from the beginning of nations until then. But at that time your people- everyone whose name is found written in the book- will be delivered. Multitudes who sleep in the dust of the earth will awake: some to everlasting life, others to shame and everlasting contempt." (12:1-2)

"At that time" tells us when people will be delivered and the dead will come back to life; the Rapture will happen during the

time of great distress, not before the great distress. Though the entire Great Tribulation is the time of distress, the greatest will be at the end of the Great Tribulation immediately after the Abomination of Desolation. This final distress is caused by the knowledge that nuclear war and the global Wrath of God will soon take place. Daniel 12:

> "Those who are wise will shine like the brightness of the heavens, and those who lead many to righteousness, like the stars for ever and ever." (Daniel 12:3)

The context of this is very important, so it refers to the large harvest of people who will be converted to Christianity during the Great Tribulation. Workers for Christ will finally get their reward at the Rapture. Daniel 12 continues:

> Then I, Daniel, looked, and there before me stood two others ... "How long will it be before these astonishing things are fulfilled?"
> The man clothed in linen, who was above the waters of the river, lifted his right hand and his left hand toward heaven, and I heard him swear by him who lives forever, saying, "It will be for a time, times and half a time. When the power of the holy people has been finally broken, all these things will be completed." (12:5-7)

Normally you would suppose that the *"holy people"* refers to righteous Jews here in the Old Testament, but this is a prophecy of the end of the age in which even the Jews have converted 30 days before the abomination of desolation. So when *"the power of the holy people has been finally broken"* is when the two witnesses are killed and the Gospel Age comes to an end.

But before the end comes, God will use the time of testing, which is the Great Tribulation, to get his people ready for the Day of Judgment:

> He replied, "Go your way, Daniel, because the words are closed up and sealed until the time of the end. Many will be purified, made spotless and refined, but the wicked will continue to be wicked. (Dan. 12:9-10)

This tells us that the understanding of Daniel, and other apocalyptic writings, will not be known until we reach or near the Great Tribulation, which is the time we are in now. The smartest man in the world could not have written this book 100 years ago, because he would need to know about missiles and nuclear war, the end of the Ottoman Empire, and much more.

Whenever gold ore is refined, the ore is heated until it becomes boiling liquid, which allows the impurities in the ore to come to the surface where they can be scooped off. The refining is necessary because Christians today are so much like non-Christians that it is difficult to tell one from the other. It is not in our appearance, as much as how we behave, which reflects what is in our hearts.

> "Some of the wise will stumble, so that they may be <u>refined, purified and made spotless</u> until the time of the end, for it will still come at the appointed time." (Daniel 11:35)

This passage seems to refer to the refining and purifying taking place before the start of the GT. So you should not be quick to question God about the hardships you are suffering. The wicked prosper but will end up in hell; true Christians suffer but are being perfected so they can go in the Rapture. The remainder of Daniel 12, verses 11-12 were explained in chapter 5 on the 70 weeks.

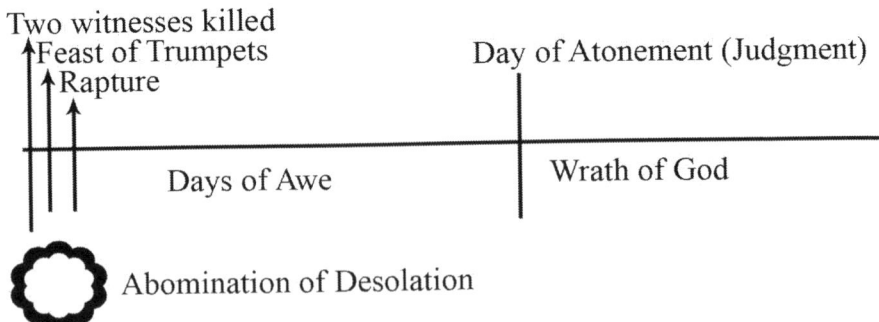

You may question why I have the Rapture taking place near the same time as the Abomination of Desolation. The AoD will take place 1,290 days after the beginning of the last half of Daniel's 70th week. You may ask, *wouldn't it be better to have the*

Rapture at the 1,260th day? That would seem to make sense, but it does not fit the Fall Feasts and even the timeline seen in Daniel 12. The Day of Atonement (Judgment) begins 10 days after the Feast of Trumpets, so if the Rapture were to take place 3 days after the 1,260-day point, then the period of God's judgment upon the world would be completed before the 1,290th day, which would mean the Wrath of God would be completed before the Abomination of Desolation takes place. The time of God's Wrath will only last a few weeks; 1,290 + 10 (Days of Awe) leaves 35 days to the 1,335 day point.

(5) Catholic Prophecies

Catholic prophecies say that in a future affliction of the Church, the enemies of Christ will enter the Vatican, kill the priests, and the pope will have to flee to another country where he will be killed. Pope Pius X in the early 20th century, had a vision:

> "I saw one of my successors taking to flight over the bodies of his brethren. He will take refuge in disguise somewhere and after a short retirement he will die a cruel death. The present wickedness of the world is only the beginning of the sorrows which must take place before the end of the world." (Yves Dupont, *Catholic Prophecy*, Tan Books and Publishers, 1973, page 22)

The pope is located in Italy which will be involved in WW3, so this prophecy could be fulfilled before the final global attack, but is probably part of it. Pope Pius IX (19th century) said:

> "There will be a great prodigy [sign or wonder in the sky] which will fill the world with awe. But this prodigy will be preceded by the triumph of a revolution during which the Church will go through ordeals that are beyond description." (Ibid, page 13)

This prophecy says Christianity will ultimately triumph after suffering great persecution during the GT. After the triumph, which is the Rapture, a great sign or wonder will be in the sky for all the world to see. It is a sign that global destruction is not far away. It will likely be planetary in nature. More about the signs of the Day of Judgment is in the next book.

1: The spread of the Gospel

2: Persecution of Christians

3: Destruction of Jerusalem & scattering of the Jews

4: The spread of Islam

5: Martyrs cry for justice

6: Birth pains and signs of the end

7: The seven Trumpets

1: Weather extremes, drought

2: Volcanic mt. slides into the ocean

3: Asteroid impact

4: Dark clouds from asteroid impact

5: The beast rises from the Abyss

6: World War 3 begins

7: Full Wrath of God

Seven Bowls of Wrath

Chapter 14
Matthew 24

(1) Events of The Gospel Age

The main focus of Matthew 24 is the Day of Judgment, but it also refers to events leading up to those days. This chapter applies to the whole planet, and certainly not merely the destruction of Jerusalem in 70 A.D.

The apostles asked Jesus about the signs of his return and the end of this age, but the answer Jesus gave included the entire period from the time of the apostles to his return. It is important to understand that the first one-third of Matthew 24 is in chronological order, and the remainder concerns the end. The first block of verses refer to the main period of the Gospel Age from Christ to the Great Tribulation:

> 4 Jesus answered: "Watch out that no one deceives you. 5 For many will come in my name, <u>claiming, 'I am the Christ,</u>' and will deceive many. 6 You will hear of wars and rumors of wars, but see to it that you are not alarmed. Such things must happen, <u>but the end is still to come</u>. 7 Nation will rise against nation, and kingdom against kingdom. There will be famines and earthquakes in various places. 8 <u>All these are the beginning of birth pains</u>. (24:4-8)

These verses describe many years of history, "*Nation will rise against nation.*" Such wars do not mean that we are near the end, "*but the end is still to come.*" This statement alone destroys the imminent Rapture/return theory, because this shows that there is a specific end to the Gospel Age, and that it is some time in the future. Even though we are not in the Great Tribulation yet, there are many false prophets publishing many false visions and dreams.

The birth pains were discussed in a previous chapter, and lead us into the GT. There will *not* be great weather then suddenly nature gone wild at the start of the GT, things will grow progressively worse up to the GT, like the gradual increase in birth pains. Earthquakes are increasing, and even hurricanes, tornadoes, and other natural events are increasing in numbers and severity. The next block of verses describe events during the GT.

(2) Events of the Great Tribulation

9 "Then you will be handed over to be persecuted and put to death, and you will be hated by all nations because of me. 10 At that time many will turn away from the faith and will betray and hate each other, 11 and many false prophets will appear and deceive many people. 12 Because of the increase of wickedness, the love of most will grow cold, 13 but whoever stands firm to the end will be saved. (24:9-13)

Jesus is not repeating himself. When he previously said false Christs will come, he was describing the period between the first century and the GT. The false prophets of verse 11 will arise during the GT. The GT will be difficult, but whoever stands firm will make it through and will see the Kingdom of God on Earth.

Jesus next describes the very end of the age, which is not the start of the GT but the last few months and weeks of it:

"And this gospel of the kingdom will be preached in the whole world as a testimony to all nations, and then the end will come." (24:14)

The preaching of the Gospel into all the world will *not cause* the end of the Gospel Age, but the Gospel Age will not end until that mission is accomplished; God's timing is perfect. After the task is finished, then the end will come. This idea that there is a difference between the Gospel of the Kingdom and the Gospel of Grace is total nonsense.

The reason the Gospel Age ends before the Great Tribulation ends, is because the beast and false prophet are not yet dead, and the full Wrath of God follows the Rapture, during which the beast and false prophet are killed. The coming of Christ technically begins with the Rapture and continues until the completion of the Wrath of God.

(3) The End of the Age

We have now reached the end of the Gospel Age in Matt. 24:

> 15 "So when you see standing in the holy place 'the abomination that causes desolation,' spoken of through the prophet Daniel-- let the reader understand-- 16 then let those who are in Judea flee to the mountains." (24:15-16)

This passage was discussed in the last chapter. Matthew 24 continues:

> 17 Let no one on the housetop go down to take anything out of the house. 18 Let no one in the field go back to get their cloak. 19 How dreadful it will be in those days for pregnant women and nursing mothers! 20 Pray that your flight will not take place in winter or on the Sabbath. 21 For then there will be great distress, unequaled from the beginning of the world until now—and never to be equaled again. 22 "If those days had not been cut short, no one would survive, but for the sake of the elect those days will be shortened. (24:17, 21-22)

When the abomination of desolation takes place, the Christians who did not go in the Rapture should flee to a place of shelter where they will remain until the Wrath of God is finished. They actually should flee large cities before the start of the tribulation so they will not suffer as much from the tribulation events such as rioting and looting and bombings. But at this time, just before the Wrath of God is poured out in full strength, those who have not done so already should most definitely flee large cities and coastal areas to escape the final Wrath of God. This is the time of greatest distress.

The "elect" are not Jews but the Christians who will not be in the Rapture, and includes Christian Jews. Those days being cut short refers to God's Wrath lasting only a few weeks, the worst of it only days. It does not refer to shortening the day from 24 hours to anything less than 24 hours, which some people have actually claimed will happen.

The next block of verses begins with *"At that time,"* which means Jesus is about to describe events that will take place during the final days, which is the time of greatest distress, just before the full Wrath of God is poured out:

> 23 At that time if anyone says to you, 'Look, here is the Christ!' or, 'There he is!' do not believe it. 24 For false Christs and false prophets will appear and perform great signs and miracles to deceive even the elect--if that were possible. 25 See, I have told you ahead of time. 26 "So if anyone tells you, 'There he is, out in the desert,' do not go out; or, 'Here he is, in the inner rooms,' do not believe it. (Matt. 24:23-26)

Again, Jesus is not repeating himself, he previously said that false Christs and false prophets will come, but that was to the earlier times from the start of Christianity to the GT and then during the GT. Here, Jesus is referring to the period after the Rapture at the end of the GT; people will come claiming to be the returned Christ or a returned prophet. Many people will be looking for the bodily return of Christ during this time, *"'Look, here is the Christ!'"* People will point to one of many false Christs that will appear at this time and say, *"There he is!"* But Jesus has gone into great detail to inform us that he will not be seen on Earth at this time; not indoors, not outdoors, because his coming will be in the clouds during the time of the Day of the Lord. He will not return bodily until the completion of the Wrath of God.

Many prophecy teachers use the above verses as they speak about the great deception that is supposed to come upon the world by the so-called worldwide dictator and his one-world religion, but nothing of the kind is referred to here. The *"great signs and wonders to deceive, if possible, even the elect"* are *not* performed by one man, but *many* false Christs and false prophets who appear at the time when the world is expecting the return of Christ. Many people will be tricked into believing they are seeing the returned Christ or a returned prophet, but true believers will know that it is not yet time for His bodily return, *"See, I have told you ahead of time."*

(4) The Wrath of God

As we would expect, Jesus now describes his coming in judgment upon the world. Jesus just told us that he will not be seen indoors or outdoors, now he continues:

> "27 For as lightning that comes from the east is visible even in the west, so will be the coming of the Son of Man. 28 Wherever there is a carcass, there the vultures will gather." (Matthew 24:27-28)

This tells us that he will come in the sky, and be very visible, like lightning. Then Jesus said, *"Wherever there is a carcass, there the vultures will gather."* In other words, following his appearing in the sky, the world will be covered with dead bodies. Jeremiah spoke of this:

> "At that time those slain by the Lord will be everywhere-- from one end of the earth to the other. They will not be gathered up or buried, but will be like refuse lying on the ground. (Jeremiah 25:33)

The reason they will not be gathered up or buried is because there will be too many carcasses for the people who are left alive; it would take decades to bury several billion people.

Many Biblical prophecies speak of the Day of Judgment in connection with clouds and darkness, including here in Mat. 24:

> "Immediately after the distress [tribulation] of those days 'the sun will be darkened, and the moon will not give its light; the stars will fall from the sky, and the heavenly bodies will be shaken.'" (24:29)

How is it that the stars fall from the sky "after" the time of great tribulation? The tribulation here is caused by the knowledge of the approaching nuclear war and Wrath of God, while people are fleeing to shelters. So by this time the Christians are already in shelters as they await approaching destruction.

Matthew 24 is mostly chronological, but it is here with verse 29 that it ceases to be chronological. We were told in verses 27-28 that at the coming of Christ the world will be covered with dead bodies, then in verse 29 it gives us more details on what will take place during the time when people are going to die. The same events that will cause the world to be covered with dead people, will also cause the stars to fall and the planets to shake; they are very much connected.

When explaining something, sometimes it is necessary to provide a few details then stop and go back and provide more details about what you have just mentioned. That is what Jesus does here.

(5) The Sign of the Son of Man

Matthew 24 continues:

> 30 "At that time the sign of the Son of Man will appear in the sky, and all the nations of the earth will mourn. They will see the Son of Man coming on the clouds of the sky, with power and great glory. 31 And he will send his angels with a loud trumpet call, and they will gather his elect from the four winds, from one end of the heavens to the other." (Matthew 24:30-31)

This passage seems to refer to after the previously mentioned events of lightning and dead bodies, and darkness, but the words "*At that time*" puts it at the same time, not after. Jesus just said he was coming in the sky, and here he gives us more details about his appearance in the sky, which includes the Rapture, just before the dead bodies will cover the world.

This passage tells us that during the time when Jesus is in the sky and the planets are about to fall and people are waiting for the Day of Judgment that will cover the world with dead bodies, the sign of the Son of Man can be seen in the sky, which will probably be a large cross-shaped light in the sky. This passage refers to the Rapture at the very beginning of the Days of Awe.

Several prophecies over the centuries, by both Catholics and Protestants, say that everyone on Earth will see a great sign in the sky, and will be shown their sins and whether they are, at that moment, headed toward heaven or hell. Some people will fall upon their faces in anguish for seeing the condition of their souls at this judgment, and will repent on that day, but many will not. In Matt. 24 it says the nations will mourn (v.30). So this could be the same event because it fits very well. It makes sense that an inward spiritual judgment will take place at the Rapture for those who remain on Earth. The sign of the cross signals the end of the age of grace and the start of the time of global judgment.

This passage in Matthew 24 does not refer to the gathering of people to Israel at the bodily return of Christ, because without airplanes, cars, or trains, it will be very difficult to make such a journey. They would have to be transported by angels, which I doubt would happen. The reason there won't be any planes, trains, or automobiles after the Wrath of God is because all those things will have been destroyed by or broken up by earthquakes and asteroids.

We know that 99% of the survivors will be Christians, so, for this to refer to a gathering at the bodily return of Christ, it would mean that the whole world is going to be gathered to Israel, and that is just not the case. There will be millions of survivors of all races and most nations; the whole world is not going to live in the Middle East. Chinese Christians who survive will rule China, Brazilian Christians will rule Brazil, etc. So the gathering of the elect must be the Rapture.

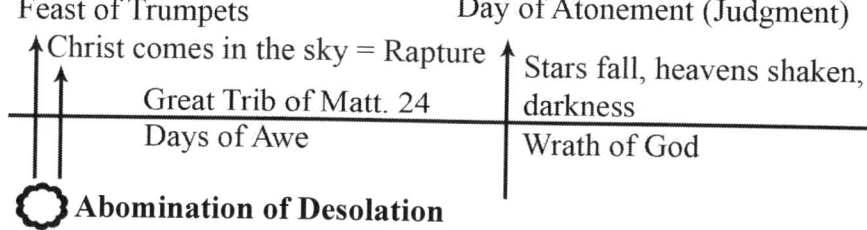

Feast of Trumpets	Day of Atonement (Judgment)
↑Christ comes in the sky = Rapture ↑	Stars fall, heavens shaken,
Great Trib of Matt. 24	darkness
Days of Awe	Wrath of God

Abomination of Desolation

Concerning the Sabbath mentioned in Matthew 24:20, Robert H. Gundry, in *The Church and The Tribulation*, says Jesus himself violated traditional Sabbath travel restrictions, and Jesus merely refers to fewer services available that *"might hamper the flight of Judean Christians"* fleeing on that day (page 133). In Israel today, everyone must keep the Sabbath, even the nonreligious, because it is a national law.

(6) One Will Be Taken, the Other Left

This is a good place to put a discussion about the passages that some people wrongly say refer to the Rapture, such as where Jesus said one will be taken but the other left:

> 41 Two men will be in the field; one will be taken and the other left. Two women will be grinding with a hand mill; one will be taken and the other left. 42 "Therefore keep watch, because you do not know on what day your Lord will come. (Matthew 24:41-42)

The context of this passage requires that it refer to people dying in the Wrath of God, because the previous verses connected above it speak of Noah's Flood. It says:

> . . . they knew nothing about what would happen until <u>the flood came and took them all away</u>. <u>That is how it will be</u> at the coming of the Son of Man.
> 40 Two men will be in the field; <u>one will be taken</u> and the other left. (Matthew 24:39-40)

Clearly, those taken are killed and not Raptured. It takes a lot of blindness caused by doctrine to see the Rapture here. The reason they are taken by complete surprise is that they have no knowledge of the signs pointing to the global destruction, or they choose to ignore the prophets who will proclaim the warning.

The posttribulation viewpoint has a problem with this passage, because if all the Christians go in the Rapture and all the wicked are killed in the Wrath of God, then no one is left to repopulate the Kingdom of God. In response, a posttrib theologian said:

> . . . suppose the destruction of the entire unsaved population of the

earth. . . . By no means does the text authorize the supposition. On the other hand, a partial destruction would leave the remaining unsaved to populate the millennial earth. (Gundry, *The Church and The Tribulation*, page 137)

At no place in the Bible is there ever a hit that people who are judged to be wicked, or "goats," will survive the judgment. Though there could be a few isolated individuals, it is totally contrary to everything the Bible teaches in both the Old and New Testaments. So, it appears that the posttrib theory has the wicked who are *not* the most wicked, surviving the Wrath of God and inheriting the Kingdom of God. But the Bible says the *righteous* will inherit the Kingdom, not the least wicked!

This passage is not a problem with my posttrib/prewrath view, because only those saved before the GT begins will go in the Rapture, those saved during the GT will inherit the Kingdom. But even they won't all survive, because the world will still have too high a population. In order to get the population down to where humans are *"more rare than fine gold,"* (Is. 13:12) (LIT), many of the newly saved will die in the global earthquake and fire of the Wrath of God. Many prophecies say as much (see a future book).

In the corresponding passage in Luke 17, where it mentions two people in one bed and one is taken and the other left, the disciples asked Jesus about where the people will go:

"Where, Lord?" they asked. He replied, "Where there is a dead body, there the vultures will gather." (Luke 17:37)

So Jesus said the people that are "taken" will be killed and will be scattered on the ground for the vultures to eat. That certainly does not sound like the Rapture to me.

The passage just before the one about being taken told us to keep watch, likewise, the next passage also tells us to keep watch, because Christ will come like a thief, which means with destruction. It was explained in chapter 3 section 3.

Chapter 15
A Brief History of Christianity

Up to now, in the book of Revelation, we have seen the beginning of Christianity, the spread of the Gospel, the coming of the GT, and the start of the Wrath of God upon the world with the 7th Trumpet; in this chapter we begin the history of Christianity over again with different information being presented to us.

(1) Christianity Begins

This chapter gives us many of the details of 2000 years of Christian history:

> A great and wondrous sign appeared in heaven: a woman clothed with the sun, with the moon under her feet and a crown of twelve stars on her head. 2 She was pregnant and cried out in pain as she was about to give birth. (Rev. 12:1-2)

According to Genesis 37, the twelve stars are the twelve tribes of Israel, the sun is Jacob, and the moon is Rachel. Therefore, the woman here represents true Israel, but not all of Israel, just the righteous remnant. Likewise, the Church is seen as a woman in 2 Cor. 11:2, Ephesians. 5:25-27. t

In Rev. 12:17 we are told that the offspring of the woman *"hold to the testimony of Jesus."* Therefore, the woman must be spiritual Israel. It cannot refer to the physical unbelieving Jews who were cut off the tree of promise when they rejected their Messiah; so it does not refer to literal Israel but to spiritual Israel. The Jews who converted to Christianity in the first century remained part of true spiritual Israel along with the Gentiles who converted, so we see that her offspring are Christians later in this chapter. Rev. 12 continues:

> 3 Then another sign appeared in heaven: an enormous red dragon with seven heads and ten horns and seven crowns on his heads. 4 His tail swept a third of the stars out of the sky and flung them to the earth. The dragon stood in front of the woman who was about to give birth, so that he might devour her child the moment it was born. (Rev. 12:3-4)

The dragon is later identified as Satan. Satan took one-third of the angels with him when he was cast out of heaven. Right after Jesus was born, Satan tried to kill him through King Herod who ruled under the authority of Rome, which was one of the seven heads of the beast. (The word "dragon" is often translated "serpent.") Rev. 12 continues:

> 5 She gave birth to a son, a male child, who will rule all the nations with an iron scepter. And her child was snatched up to God and to his throne. 6 The woman fled into the desert to a place prepared for her by God, where she might be taken care of for 1,260 days. (Rev. 12:5-6)

Jesus, of course, is the one who will rule with an iron scepter at his return (Psalm 2:9). And Jesus ascended to heaven after his resurrection.

One important point to learn from these verses is that the events shown took place 2,000 years ago, and are not events yet to take place after the Rapture. You will never arrive at the correct interpretation of Revelation if you ignore 2,000 years of incredible Christian history. Revelation 12, gives us many of the details of that history, starting at the beginning.

The woman fleeing into the desert is a picture of the Gospel spreading into Europe, which was a spiritual desert, and being taken outside of the domains of the Roman Empire. The *Smith's Bible Dictionary* defines desert as, "*Not a stretch of sand, an utterly bar-*

ren waste, but a wild, uninhabited region" (p. 149). The *Westminster Dictionary of The Bible* says, "*an unenclosed, uncultivated plain, where wild beasts roam at will... often terrible in its solitude and desolateness... yet also capable of affording pasturage*" (p. 137). It is translated "wilderness" in the KJV, NKJV, and ESV.

The literal translation says the reason she goes into the wilderness is, "*that they might nourish her*" (LIT). The NKJV says, "*Then the woman fled into the wilderness, where she has a place prepared by God, that they should feed her there*" (12:6). The Greek for "nourish" and "feed" is *threpso* (5142), and means "*To nourish, feed, nurture . . . . bring up*" (CWD). Luke 4:16 uses the word this way, "*He went to Nazareth, where he had been brought up.*"

This tells us that true Christianity was to grow physically and spiritually in a place prepared for that purpose, which was mostly in Britain and Europe. The historical record in Britain shows clearly that Christianity was taken to the British Isles within 20 years of the death of Jesus. There are historical accounts that claim Joseph of Arimathea took the Gospel to Britain, but it is not the purpose of this chapter to prove this point; it has been written about by others, and is considered an established fact to British Christians. There is even evidence that the Apostle Paul visited Britain, (*St. Paul in Britain*, by R. W. Morgan). The point is that Britain and Europe are the earliest locations for the spread of the Gospel outside the Roman Empire. Eventually all of Europe became solidly Christian.

What about the fact that the Roman Empire was gradually converted to Christianity? Yes, that happened, most of the Middle Eastern nations were 90-95% Christian for several centuries. But Christianity was still very young at that time, and before it could grow to adulthood, figuratively speaking, it was all but wiped out by hoards invading of Muslims. Though it spread widely in the Middle East, it was not the place where it grew to full maturity, but the place where it was devoured and almost died.

Perhaps the Apostles took the Gospel north beyond the Roman Empire because they knew that a new religion would rise in Arabia and send armies throughout the Middle East, North Africa, and Asia Minor to kill Christians and force them to convert, and that it would become the dominate religion throughout the region.

But it was in Britain and Europe where Christianity was able to grow up. All of Europe eventually became Christian, but it did so through the missionary outreach of the monks of Ireland and Britain that evangelized northern Europe. The most famous was Boniface who was responsible for evangelizing Germany:

> Because of his British background and connections, he was able to bring a steady stream of Irish and British monks over to Germany. The latter were instrumental in founding many centers of evangelism and learning throughout Europe. (Wells, *History Through The Eyes of Faith*, p. 57)

Though Christianity has almost ceased to exist in its original locations because of Islam, Christianity grew in size and knowledge in Britain, Ireland, and Europe. Martin Luther was a German, which means the Protestant Reformation likely can be traced back to the missionary efforts of Britain and Ireland.

As the facts of history show, Christianity slowly developed in Europe as the Christians there grew in the knowledge of the Bible. Martin Luther was not the first reformer; he was merely the first who was successful, because of the printing press. Never mind that the Protestants were divided and warred with each other and with the Catholics, they were still growing in spiritual maturity. You have to look at the big picture. Even the Roman Catholic Church matured because of the reforms it underwent over the centuries.

The 1,260 days the woman is nourished represent the final 1,260 days of the Gospel Age, not the length of the Great Tribulation or even one half of it, just the last 3.5 years of the Gospel Age. So this tells us that true Christianity will be found in Europe right up to the conclusion of the Gospel Age. It does not say it will be the dominate belief system in Europe at the time, but merely that it will be there.

(2) The Defeat of Paganism

At this point in Rev. 12, you might suppose that we would have progressed to the end of the Gospel Age, but we have not gotten there yet. This is one of the reasons that Rev. 12 is so difficult to understand; it partly repeats. But instead of beginning at the start of Christianity, this next section of verses begins with the defeat of paganism.

The battle between darkness and light first takes place in the spiritual realm, and then it is played out on Earth. So next we see a battle in the heavens which resulted in a major victory here on Earth, and Satan being cast down from his place to the earth:

> 7 And there was war in heaven. Michael and his angels fought against the dragon, and the dragon and his angels fought back. 8 But he was not strong enough, and they lost their place in heaven. 9 The great dragon was hurled down--that ancient serpent called the devil, or Satan, who leads the whole world astray. He was hurled to the earth, and his angels with him.
>
> 10 Then I heard a loud voice in heaven say: "Now have come the salvation and the power and the kingdom of our God, and the authority of his Christ. For the accuser of our brothers, who accuses them before our God day and night, has been hurled down." (Rev. 12:7-10)

The first and biggest victory of Christianity was the defeat of paganism within the Roman Empire, "*Now have come salvation ... and the authority of his Christ.*" This represents pagan Rome being converted to Christianity in 325 A.D. Never mind that Christianity had become infected with some pagan beliefs, it was still a major victory.

Pagans were frequently persecuting and killing Christians. They were also known to accuse Christians of horrible crimes such as cannibalism and incest. But here we see paganism defeated. Though it still exists in other countries, it was defeated in a vast area; the area where the Gospel first spread, which is within the Roman Empire.

Do we not have the authority of Christ in the world now? Yes, we do. Why would that wait until the coming of the Great Tribulation? Salvation becoming openly and freely available does not wait for the Great Tribulation. Though Christ gave us victory and authority with his death and resurrection, the blood of many martyrs bought our freedom to worship God. Rev. 12 continues:

> 11 They overcame him by the blood of the Lamb and by the word of their testimony; they did not love their lives so much as to shrink from death. 12 Therefore rejoice, you heavens and you who dwell in them! ...

The Greek for "testimony" is *marturia* (3141) and means, "*A witness . . . It is a declaration by a witness who speaks with the authority of one who knows*" (CWD). It is the same word used in Rev. 11, where it said the two witnesses, "*have finished their testimony.*" It refers to the proclamation of the Gospel. Many people were tortured to death or burned at the stake because they refused to worship pagan gods. The above passage describes how paganism was defeated, not by an army but by Christians dying for Christ, while preaching and speaking the truth. Many thousands of Christians died during the periods of Roman persecution, which only resulted in more people converting to Christianity until finally Christianity was legalized; then paganism was outlawed. This made Satan angry. Rev. 12 continues:

> 12 Therefore rejoice, you heavens and you who dwell in them! But woe to the earth and the sea, because the devil has gone down to you! He is filled with fury, because he knows that his time is short." (Rev. 12:12)

Notice that the events described in this second section contain both good news and bad news. Satan is cast down, which depicts the defeat of paganism, yet there is a woe to the earth and the sea. In the next chapter of Revelation it shows a beast coming out of the sea and one out of the earth.

Satan was filled with fury because of the defeat of pagan Rome, so he raised up another way to attack Christianity, which was Islam that began in the early 600s in Arabia. Rev. 12:

> When the dragon saw that he had been hurled to the earth, he pursued the woman who had given birth to the male child. (Rev. 12:13)

The Greek for "pursue" also means "persecute." It took 300 years, but Satan raised up Islam to again wage war against Christianity. Islam truly did purse Christianity as the armies swept through region after region like a raging flood. The Christians who lived in the Middle East and North Africa were soon attacked, imprisoned, killed, or sold into slavery by the next head of the beast that came out of the sands of Arabia.

Notice the wording, *"woe to the earth and the sea, because the devil has gone down to you!"* In the very next chapter a beast comes out of the sea and another comes out of the earth, which represent Satanic empires. The seven empires represented by the seven heads of beast continued to attack Christians and Jews. After the Roman Empire, came the Arabic empire, then the Ottoman Empire. The final head is soon to come.

(3) The Woman Flees Again

The last half of Rev. 12 appears to be a partial restatement of the first half that I just explained, but it is not; it is actually a continuation of Christian history. We saw the woman, true Christianity, flee into England and Europe where she was allowed to mature, but the Church in the Middle East was badly attacked by Islam. Islam conquered the Middle East, North Africa and even Spain, but the French stopped Islam's progress, otherwise it would have conquered Europe. During the time of the Crusades, Islam was weakened and was not able to make any progress into Europe. This caused Satan to raise up some Turks who began growing in power beginning about 1300 A.D. and eventually created the Ottoman Empire. The Turks became strong and tried to conquer Europe but were stopped at the gates of Vienna in 1529 and 1683. Now we continue in Rev. 12:

The woman was given the two wings of a great eagle, so that she might fly to the place prepared for her in the desert, where she would be taken care of for a time, times and half a time, out of the serpent's reach. (Rev. 12:14)

The woman first fled into the wilderness of Britain, Ireland, and Europe, but she was still within the serpent's reach. This passage in Revelation 12 tells us that Christianity will flee once more, this time to a place that is out of the serpent's reach, to a land that became the United States.

The woman is not given a ride on an eagle or an airplane, she is *"given the two wings of a great eagle."* The word "great" probably refers to both the large size of the United States and to America's importance as a great nation. There has never been any significant religious persecution in America. There will always be an isolated case here and there but nothing compared to the history of Europe, the Roman Empire, or the Islamic empires.

The United States of America was the first government in the history of humanity to offer political and religious freedom on a permanent basis. As our one-dollar bill says, "NOVUS ORDO SE-CLORUM," or NEW ORDER OF THE AGES. America's founding was truly a new order; a new kind of government. Many other nations have since followed America's lead, but America was the first to offer religious and political freedom in the form of a successful democratic government.

The Puritans who came to Massachusetts in 1628 literally said they were making a journey or *"errand into the wilderness."* They were separating themselves from the wicked world and saw themselves as a light in the darkness, as an example to others. Although the original group believed they failed in their mission, if they could have seen the final result, the United States of America, they would have seen their mission as a success.

The woman first fled into the wilderness of England and Europe to be nourished; she grew up spiritually with the coming of Protestantism and its development, as well as reforms within Catholicism. Then she fled to what became the United States. In both places she continues to be nourished. Originally intolerant of other groups, superstitious, and accepting of slaves, Christians grew and matured so that they eventually played a major role in the abolition of slavery in England and the United States. Christians also played a major role in the civil rights movement and many other reform movements during the past two hundred years that have helped make America and the world a better place.

But we have not advanced that far yet in Rev. 12. England itself became one of the heads of the beast when it became an empire, invading and exploiting other nations. The American colonists even saw the British government as the beast of Revelation. According to a *PBS Frontline* special called *Apocalypse!*, the colonists viewed the book of Revelation as you would expect at the time. Historian James West Davidson said:

> King George could be seen as the Antichrist. The Stamp Act was not just some piece of bureaucratic legislation. This was the mark of the beast being put upon all those who followed it and accepted it. . . .
>
> And when the Stamp Act came and mobilized the colonies, [Paul] Revere did a wonderful engraving, trying to convince people not to use stamped paper. And there he used for his imagery a beast -like dragon, very much like the beast of Revelation, with wings of a dragon, a fierce tail, talons clutching the Magna Carta and ripping it to shreds, and the colonists being ground underfoot. . . .
>
> For preachers, the Revolution was something they firmly grounded in the prophecies, [of] scripture. (PBS.org)

In the woodcut Paul Revere did, the dragon is trying to tear up the Magna Charta. The beast represents powerful empires that oppress Christians and Jews, so the British Empire could certainly have been one of the seven heads, and in fact was one of them, as will be seen in the next book. Rev. 12 continues:

> 15 Then from his mouth the serpent spewed water like a river, to overtake the woman and sweep her away with the torrent. 16 But the earth helped the woman by opening its mouth and swallowing the river that the dragon had spewed out of his mouth. (12:15-16)

Even though Britain (England) ruled the American colonies, the colonists enjoyed more religious freedom than their brothers in England. Satan was not happy about the religious freedom of the colonists and sent the British army against them; but against all odds the Americans won their freedom from Britain. Later in 1812 the British sent another army in an attempt to overtake America that set fire to the White House, but this army was destroyed by a 2-hour storm with tornado-force winds. The British then left the U.S. forever. But this made Satan angry. Rev. 12 continues:

> Then the dragon was enraged at the woman and went off to make war against the rest of her offspring--those who obey God's commandments and hold to the testimony of Jesus. (Rev. 12:17)

Satan was angry at the religious and political freedom of America, which put America out of the reach of religious and political persecution. But Europe was still within the serpent's reach, the result was war on top of war in Europe, the Middle East, and North Africa, that was almost continuous for the next 150 years. Napoleon's armies marched all the way to Moscow, bringing much death and suffering. The European nations fought many wars with each other, there were also several civil wars, and then World War 1, civil war in Spain, and World War 2.

The Ottoman Empire, based in present-day Turkey, committed several massacres of Christians during the 1800s, and a horrible massacre during World War 1 that is still causing strife today as Turkey denies it ever happened, but France and other nations insist that it did. The Ottoman Empire also waged several wars with Europe in North Africa and the Middle East in the 1800s, and also warred with Russia on several occasions; the war list is very long.

All this warfare was one of the reasons millions of immigrants came to America throughout the 1800s and early 1900s. The religious and civil wars in Europe also helped to turn people away from religion; many of the people are now secular, without any religion, or are religious in name only. Some governments in Europe are now actually against Christianity. During this time, Europe also became the birthplace of many of the harmful ideas in the world today, like Communism, atheism, evolution, and the higher and lower criticisms of the Bible.

Satan is still making *"war against the rest of her offspring"* as Christians are still dying for Christ in many areas of the world, but Rev. is mainly concerned with the countries around the Middle East and North Africa, followed by Europe and America. There is much more to this story, but there is a limit to the amount of information that can be presented in a symbolic prophecy like Revelation.

Notice that the woman who gave birth to Christ remains in Europe during the 1,260 days, which is 3.5 years, and then later she is given the wings of a great eagle where she will be protected for *"a time, times and half a time,"* which is the same period of time. It uses different language to refer to the same period of time, which is a clue that it refers to a different location on Earth. This tells us that true Christianity will exist in Europe and the U.S. during the final 3.5 years of the Gospel Age.

So the woman gave birth to Christ, grew up in Europe and the United States, and will remain in those areas to the end of the 3.5 years. This shows that the righteous, which is the woman, will not be Raptured before the end of the 1,260 days. *This is the smoking gun that kills the pretribulation Rapture*!

Chapter 16
Final Thoughts

As we have learned, the coming hardships of the Great Tribulation are designed to get the world to repent, and to get lukewarm Christians to repent, because many of them are not ready for the Rapture or the Day of Judgment. Christians will be judged before everyone else. Are you ready for the judgment?

There was a fellow online who said Christians will not go through the GT because God would have given us lots of warning in the Scriptures if we were going to. I replied that every day there are Christians who are told to convert or die! But we are not going to go through the GT? What nonsense! This twisted thinking is what happens when Christians are allowed to live comfortable, easy lives in America, but this will soon change. Americans are going to suffer greatly during the Great Tribulation and WW3. There will be much more about WW3 in the next book.

The evidence just keeps piling up against a European Antichrist, or Roman Catholic pope Antichrist. Many of the new interpretations presented in this book have much more powerful evidence that hold more Scriptural weight than the entrenched doctrines being taught today about Bible prophecy, especially in connection with Daniel 9:27. Even so, many people will reject this new information because it conflicts with what they have always believed about the Great Tribulation and return of Christ.

But those doctrines were thought up by fallible humans who did not have the benefit of the increase in knowledge that we have today. Most of the doctrines of eschatology being taught today are more than 100 years old. The teachers back then simply could not put all the pieces together.

The letters to the seven churches of Asia contain lots of end time references. Therefore, most commentators believe that the letters refer not only to the churches that received the letters but also to many churches that will see the GT and the return of Christ, which is now upon us. Not all the seven churches will go in the Rapture. For example, of all the Christians in the world today, which Christians do you think are most like the Laodiceans? I think most Christians around the world would agree that many American Christians are like the Laodiceans. The Laodiceans are NOT going in the Rapture. This means American Christians need to be prepared to go through the Wrath of God (more about this in Book Two).

The GT could be years away, but because of all the birth pains and signs that are happening now, including the war in Syria, I would not be surprised if the 2nd Trumpet were to happen in 2015 or 2016. It could be as early as 2014, but I would be surprised if it were to begin that soon. Regardless, it is not too soon to begin moving away from the east coast, and the west coast; also Las Vegas, Chicago, New York, and many other places that will have civil unrest and finally nuclear missiles during WW3.

There is more information that points to 2015 than the four Blood Moons, such as a book called The Harbinger, by Jonathan Cahn. He said the stock market crash in 2001 and 2008 both occurred on the same day on the Jewish calendar that occurs only once every seven years. That day is called Shemitah, which is a day for wiping out debits. It is the last day of the Shemitah (Sabbatical) year. The next one is Sept. 25, 2014 thru Sept. 13, 2015; (9/13/15) is the day to watch.

Also, R. Loren Sandford, pastor of New Song Church in Denver, said he and a person in his church both had the same dream in 2010, which he said means there will probably be five years before a judgment from God hits America. (Visions of the Coming Days, by R. Loren Sandford, 2012)

President Obama and his administration are trying to make it illegal to criticize Islam or to offend Muslims, which would be a great violation of free speech and create a lot of Christian persecution in the United States. Persecution has already begun because of homosexuals who are demanding that Christians accept them, and if we don't, then we get fired, fined, or prosecuted. Even fired from the military. The federal government has put evangelical Christians onto a list with terrorists because Obama is afraid we will rise up against what he is doing. Christians are even being told they cannot hold public office in many cities because they do not approve of homosexuality.

If you are unaware of this, you need to get your news from sources other than ABC, CBS, and NBC evening news programs that have liberal bias. Most newspapers also have liberal bias. Some of the places to get factual news is Fox News channel, talk radio, and online, but watch out for the invented news. There are sites that claim to be reporting true news, but the events reported never happened, it is fake news, so be careful.

So we are seeing the arrival of an antichristian federal government. I remember hearing and reading prophecies made decades ago, that said Christians in the America will face persecution before the Rapture. We are seeing it happen now.

Just as shocking, the U.S. government is becoming totalitarian which could result in a civil war. Many people are having dreams and visions of civil war in the U.S. Some people report seeing a split going across the nation from east to west, others from north to south, but those images could simply mean that there will be division, not necessarily that it will be between the north and the south or the east and the west. The split could also be within states. Perhaps there will be states that withdraw from the union.

The first person to predict a civil war was Demitru Duduman, a former pastor from Romania who came to the U.S. in the 1980s. He said that Russia and China, (and certainly the beast of Revelation as well), will take advantage of the civil war and nuke America. But Revelation tells us that the nuking will not take place until after the 7th Trumpet, which is after the Rapture and is part of the Wrath of God upon the world, which is explained in the next book.

I hope you have learned a lot in this book, but chances are you have read it too fast and should read it again to get the most out of it. I have gotten many emails from people commenting on the contents of a book or an article, but they clearly did not read the book or article very well because they missed what I actually said on a particular point. So I recommend reading this book a second time.

The next book will cover the remainder of Revelation not covered here, as well as Daniel 11. And it will contain even more information on America in Bible prophecy. *Yes, even more!* You were probably surprised to learn in this book that America is in Bible prophecy several times, so don't believe anyone who tells you that America will be destroyed before the start of the GT, or that America is not found in Bible prophecy.

The information in this book has raised a lot of questions among people who have studied Bible prophecy, and they may ask, *what about this passage,* or *what about that passage?* It is not possible to answer all questions in a book such as this. Nor is it ever possible to answer all the questions people raise.

Many people will attack me and this book because it disagrees with the pretribulation Rapture. This does not bother me as I am used to being attacked. Satan has been trying to destroy me for twenty years, but the fact that you are reading this book proves that he failed.

If you want to be notified when the next book comes out, just visit my website and sign up for website updates that will only be sent out when there is an update on the website.

Also, there is additional information and pictures on my website that are related to the contents of this book, including some of the pictures in this book so that you can use them in articles on your own website or in a video. Just be sure you credit this book or my website, www.usbibleprophecy.com.

The website also contains news articles related to Bible prophecy, so it will keep the information in this book up-to-date. This book only has a small advertising budget, so tell everyone you know about it. Post on Facebook, Twitter, blogs, and Youtube.

God be with you in the coming tribulation, and God save America.

Scripture Index

Genesis .... Chapter: Section
41:57 .... 1:2

Exodus
16:4b 6:2

1 Kings
10:24 .... 1:2
12:11 .... 8:1

Esther
3:13 .... 11:4

Psalm
2:1-2 .... 11:3

Jeremiah
4:11-13, 20 .... 8:6

Isaiah
3:5 .... 8:4
13:9-12 .... 1:7
19:2 .... 8:4
29:5-6 .... 8:6
34:9-10 ....
53:5 .... 5:2
53:11-12 .... 5:2

Ezekiel
30:3 .... 1:7
38:21 .... 8:4

Daniel
2:41-43 .... 9:1
2:34, 44-45 .... 9:1
2:42-43 .... 9:1
2:43 .... 9:1
2:34-35 .... 9:3

4:17 .... 2:5
7:3 .... 10:1
7:4 .... 10:2
7:5 .... 10:3
7:6 .... 10:4
7:7, 24 .... 10:5
7:8 .... 10:5
7:8, 23-26 .... 10:6
7:9-18 .... 10:7
7:11-12 .... 10:1; 10:5
7:21-22 .... 10:6
7:24 .... 10:6
8:5 .... 1:2
9:24-25 .... 5:1
9:24 .... 5:2
9:26 .... 5:1
9:27 .... 5:2; 13:2;
11:35 .... 13:4; 12:2
12:1-2 .... 13:4
12:3 .... 13:4
12:5-7 .... 13:4
12:9-10 .... 13:4
12:11-12 .... 5:3; 13:4

Hosea
5:15 .... 5:2

Joel
2:1-3 .... 8:6
2:3-9 .... 8:6
2:10 .... 8:6
2:11, 31 .... 8:6
2:30-31 .... 3:1

Obadiah 1:15 .... 1:7

Zephaniah .... Chapter: Section
1:14-16,18 .... 1:2

Zechariah
12:2-3 .... 1:2
12:4 .... 8:4
5:5-11 .... 7:1
5:10-11 .... 7:1
14:13 .... 8:4

Malachi 3:2-3 .... 1:7

Matthew
10:34, 36 .... 2:4
12:40 .... 1:2
23:39 .... 5:2
24:4-8 .... 14:1
24:6-7 .... 1:4
24:9-13 .... 6:2; 14:2
24:13 .... 6:2
24:14 .... 14:2
24:15-16 .... 13:3; 14:3
24:15-22 .... 13:2
24:17, 21-22 .... 14:3
24:23-26 .... 14:3
24:27-28 .... 14:4
24:29 .... 3:1; 14:4
24:30-31 .... 14:4
24:39-40 .... 14:6
24:41-42 .... 14:6
24:48-49 .... 1:4
25:31-32 .... 1:7
26:28 .... 5:2
27:51 .... 13:1

Mark
4:17 .... 6:1

Luke
2:1 .... 1:2
8:11, 13 .... 6:2
17:29-30 .... 3:1
17:37 .... 14:6
20:35-36 .... 4:4
21:11 .... 3:1
21:24 .... 11:2
21:25-26 .... 3:1
21:27-28 .... 3:1
21:29-32 .... 3:1
21:33-36 .... 3:1
24:42 .... 3:3
24:42-44 .... 3:3
24:44 .... 3:4
24:7-8 .... 3:7

John
1:29 .... 2:2
12:19 .... 1:2
16:33 .... 6:1
19:30 .... 11:3

Acts
1:8 .... 11:3
3:19-20 ... 1:4; 5:2

Romans
5:19 .... 5:2
11:15 .... 5:2
11:20 .... 4:1
11:25 .... 5:2
13:1-2 .... 2:5

1 Corinthians
3:12 .... 6:2
10:33 .... 5:2

1 Thessalonians .... Chapter: Section
5:1-3 .... 12:3; 12:4
5:4-6, 9-10 .... 12:4
4:16 .... 12:4

2 Thessalonians
1:6-9 .... 12:4
2:1-12 .... 12:1
2:2 .... 1:4
2:3-4 .... 13:2
2:4 .... 12:2; 12:3

Colossians
3:11-12 .... 4:1

Ephesians
1:9-10 .... 11:1
3:6 .... 4:1

James
1:27 .... 6:1

Hebrews
8:13 .... 13:1
9:28 .... 5:2

1 Peter
2:5 .... 11:2
4:17 .... 11:2

2 Peter
1:20-21 .... 1:3

Revelation
2:9 .... 4:1
3:1 .... 4:7
3:3 .... 4:7
3:4 .... 2:3; 4:7
3:10 .... 6:2
4:1-7 .... 2:1
4:8-11 .... 2:1
5:1-4 .... 2:2
5:5-10 .... 2:2
5:11-14 .... 2:2
6:1-2 .... 2:3
6:3-4 .... 2:4
6:5-6 .... 2:5
6:7-8 .... 2:6
6:9-11 .... 2:7
6:12-17 .... 3:1
7:1-8 .... 4:1
7:3 .... 4:4
7:9-17 .... 4:5
8:1-6 .... 6:3
8:7 .... 6:4
8:8-9 .... 6:5
8:10-11 .... 6:7
8:12 .... 6:8
8:13 .... 6:9
11:7 .... 8:1
12:17 .... 4:1
14:3-4 .... 4:4
14:4 .... 4:4
17:8 .... 8:1
9:1-2 .... 8:1
9:3-6 .... 8:1
9:4 .... 2:6
9:6 .... 8:1
9:7-12 .... 8:1
9:7 .... 8:1
9:11-12 .... 8:2
9:13-16 .... 8:5
9:17-19 .... 8:5

10:1-7 .... 11:1
10:8-11 .... 11:1
11:1-2 .... 11:2
11:1 .... 11:2
11:3-9 .... 11:3
11:10 .... 11:4
11:10-12 .... 11:6
11:13-14 .... 11:6
11:15-19 .... 11;7
12:1-2 .... 15:1
12:3-4 .... 15:1
12:5-6 .... 15:1
12:7-10 .... 15:2
12:11-12 .... 15:2
12:12 .... 15:2
12:13 .... 15:2
12:14 .... 15:3
12:15-16 .... 15:3
12:17 .... 15:3
16:17-18, 21 .... 11:7
16:18 .... 8:6
17:12 .... 1:2
21:9-21 .... 4:2

2 Ezra
13:29-31 .... 8:4
15:28-29 .... 2:6
16:70-73 .... 11:5
16:4-78 .... 6:10

Selected Bibliography

Air Force ROTC Air University. Fundamentals of Aerospace Weapon Systems. Washington D.C.: U.S. Government Printing Office, 1961.

Al-Khairiyyah, Mussasat Al-Haramain. Saad bin Abi Waqqas. Riyadh, Saudi Abrabia: Alharamain Islamic Foundation, 1999.

Ali, Maulana Muhammad. The Religion of Islam. Ahmadiyyah Anjuman Ishaat Islam Lahore: Columbus, OH, 1990.

Armerding, Carl E. and W. Ward Gasque, Editors. A Guide To Biblical Prophecy. Peabody, MA: Hendrickson Publishers, 1989.

Barclay, William. The Revelation of John, Vol. 2, revised edition. Philadelphia: Westminster Press, 1976.

Bellock, Hilaire. The Battle Ground: Syria and Palestine: The Seedplot of Religion. San Francisco: Ignatius Press , 2008.

Birch, Desmond A. Trial, Tribulation & Triumph: Before, During, and After Antichrist. Goleta, CA: Queenship Publishing Company, 1997.

Bolt, Bruce A. Nuclear Explosions and Earthquakes, The Parted Veil. San Francisco: W. H. Freeman and Company, 1976.

Booker, Bruce R. The Feasts of the Lord, and Their Fulfillment in Messiah Yeshua. (self published thesis, 2008)

Butler, Alfred. The Arab Invasion of Egypt, and the Last 30 Years of the Roman Dominion, 1902. Republished by A & B Publishing Group, Brooklyn, New York: 1992.

Croutier, Alev Lytle. Harem: The World Behind the Veil. Abbeville Press: New York, 1989.

Dinet, Etienne and Sliman Ben Ibrahim. The Life of Mohammad: The Prophet of Allah. Secacus, NJ: Chartwell Books, 1990.

Dupont, Yves. Catholic Prophecy: The Coming Chastisement. Rockford, IL: Tan Books and Publishers, 1973.

Earle, Ralph. Word Meanings in the New Testament. Grand Rapids: Baker Book House, 1986.

Farrer, Austin. A Rebirth of Images: The Making of St. John's Apocalypse. Gloucester: Peter Smith, 1970.

Funk & Wagnells New Encyclopedia. New York: Funk & Wagnells, Inc., 1975.

Gibbon, Edward. The Decline And Fall Of The Roman Empire.

Green, Jay P. General Editor and translator. The Interlinear Greek-English New Testament. Peabody, MA: Hendrickson Publishers, 1985.

Gundry, Robert H. The Church and The Tribulation: A Biblical Examination of Posttribulationism. Grand Rapids: Zondervan, 1973.

Hailey, Homer. Revelation: An Introduction and Commentary. Grand Rapids: Baker Book House, 1979.

Halley, Henry H. Halley's Bible Handbook. 24th ed. Grand Rapids: Zondervan, 1965.

Hendrikson, W. More Than Conquerors. Grand Rapids: Baker Book House, 1940.

Hoekema, Anthony A. The Bible and The Future. Grand Rapids: Eerdmans Publishing Co., 1979.

Kaiser, Walter C. Jr. Back Toward the Future: Hints for Interpreting Biblical Prophecy. Grand Rapids: Baker Book House, 1989.

Leiner, Frederick C. The End of Barbary Terror: America's 1815 War Against the Pirates of North Africa. Oxford U. Press, 2007.

NIV Study Bible. Grand Rapids: Zondervan Corp., 1985.

Peters, F.E. The Hajj: The Muslim Pilgrimage to Mecca and The Holy Places. Princeton: Princeton University Press, 1994.

Powell, Bill. "A Religious War?" Newsweek, 14 October 1996.

Pyke,Royston. Encyclopedia of Religion and Ethics. George Allen and Unwin Ltd., London, 1951.

Riordan, Michael, ed. The Day After Midnight-- The Effects of Nuclear War. Based on a report by the Congressional Office of Technological Assessment. Palo Alto, CA: Cheshire Books, 1982.

Sabini, John. Islam: A Primer. Washington, D.C.: Middle East Editorial Associates, 1983.

Sagan, Carl. "The Nuclear Winter." Parade Magazine, 30 October 1983.

Stone, Jr., Perry. Unleashing the Beast. Cleveland: Voice of Evangelism, 2003.

Twitchell, Karl Saben, and Eward Jaabra Jurji. Saudi Arabia: With an Account of The Development of Its Natural Resources. Princton: Princton Univ. Press, 1947.

Vester, Bertha Spafford. Our Jerusalem: An American Family in the Holy City, 1881-1949. Garden City, NY: Doubleday, 1950.

Vine, W. E. Vine's Expository Dictionary of Old and New Testament Words. Old Tappen: Fleming H. Revell, 1981.

Woldben, A. After Nostradamus, translated from the Italian by Gavin Gibbons. New York: Granda Publishing, 1973.

Zodhiates, Spiros. The Complete Word Study Dictionary: New Testament. Chattanooga, TN: AMG Publishers, 1992.

Zondervan NIV Bible Commentary. Vol. 1 & 2. Grand Rapids: Zondervan Publishing House, 1994.

Made in the USA
Lexington, KY
13 October 2014